The Kelvin Timeline of *Star Trek*

The Kelvin Timeline of *Star Trek*
Essays on J.J. Abrams' Final Frontier

Edited by
MATTHEW WILHELM KAPELL and
ACE G. PILKINGTON

McFarland & Company, Inc., Publishers
Jefferson, North Carolina

ALSO OF INTEREST AND FROM MCFARLAND

Science Fiction and Futurism: Their Terms and Ideas
by Ace G. Pilkington (2017)

The Play Versus Story Divide in Game Studies: Critical Essays,
edited by Matthew Wilhelm Kapell (2016)

*The Fantastic Made Visible: Essays on the Adaptation
of Science Fiction and Fantasy from Page to Screen,*
edited by Matthew Wilhelm Kapell *and* Ace G. Pilkington (2015)

The Films of James Cameron: Critical Essays, edited by Matthew
Wilhelm Kapell *and* Stephen McVeigh (2011)

Star Trek *as Myth: Essays on Symbol and Archetype at the Final
Frontier,* edited by Matthew Wilhelm Kapell (2010)

LIBRARY OF CONGRESS CATALOGUING-IN-PUBLICATION DATA

Names: Kapell, Matthew, editor. | Pilkington, Ace G., editor.
Title: The Kelvin timeline of Star Trek : essays on J.J. Abrams' final frontier / edited by Matthew Wilhelm Kapell and Ace G. Pilkington.
Description: Jefferson, North Carolina : McFarland & Company, Inc., Publishers, 2019 | Includes bibliographical references and index.
Identifiers: LCCN 2019004714 | ISBN 9781476669663 (paperback : acid free paper) ∞
Subjects: LCSH: Star Trek films—History and criticism. | Star trek (Motion picture : 2009) | Star trek into darkness (Motion picture) | Star Trek beyond (Motion picture)
Classification: LCC PN1995.9.S694 K45 2019 | DDC 791.43/75—dc23
LC record available at https://lccn.loc.gov/2019004714

BRITISH LIBRARY CATALOGUING DATA ARE AVAILABLE

ISBN (print) 978-1-4766-6966-3
ISBN (ebook) 978-1-4766-3623-8

© 2019 Matthew William Kapell and the estate of Ace G. Pilkington. All rights reserved

*No part of this book may be reproduced or transmitted in any form
or by any means, electronic or mechanical, including photocopying
or recording, or by any information storage and retrieval system,
without permission in writing from the publisher.*

Front cover images © 2019 Shutterstock

Printed in the United States of America

*McFarland & Company, Inc., Publishers
Box 611, Jefferson, North Carolina 28640
www.mcfarlandpub.com*

Table of Contents

Acknowledgments   vii

Introduction: Toward a "Many Texts" Theory of the Star Trek Multiverse
    MATTHEW WILHELM KAPELL *and* ACE G. PILKINGTON   1

A Switch in Time: Nero's Disruptive Trickster Force in J.J. Abrams' *Star Trek*
    SARAH BETH KILIMAN   13

Khanned: Whitewashing Khan in *Star Trek into Darkness*
    LYNNETTE PORTER   25

Race, the Final Frontier: *Star Trek*, Trump and Hollywood's Diversity Problem
    PENELOPE INGRAM   39

Star Trek into Colonialism
    BART BISHOP   58

Uhura and Linguistics of *Star Trek*
    OLGA A. PILKINGTON   72

All Talk and No Action: What's a Girl Gotta Do to Get Noticed Around Here?
    TERESA CUTLER-BROYLES   84

"Throw a punch and kiss a girl": Gender and Sexualization in the Kelvin Timeline
    ANDREA WHITACRE   99

Science Fiction and the New *Trek* Timeline
    ACE G. PILKINGTON   115

Priming the Multiverse: Contextualizing the Kelvin Timeline Through Gene Roddenberry's Original Narrative
　JESSICA SELLIN-BLANC　　135

Illegible and Unacceptable Representation: The Liminality of Spock in *Star Trek* (2009)
　NATASHIA LINDSEY　　151

James T. Kirk, Ideal Citizen: Shifting Rhetoric for a New Timeline
　CAIT COKER　　166

Conclusion: Is There a Future for *Star Trek*?
　ACE G. PILKINGTON *and* MATTHEW WILHELM KAPELL　　177

About the Contributors　　185

Index　　187

Acknowledgments

I would like to thank all the contributors who waited far too long for this book to be finished. At McFarland I finally get to thank an entire team that, over the years, has made many books possible for me. This especially includes Tyler Cloherty and Layla Milholen. At San Jose State University, Jennifer Hoyman, Shannon Rose Riley, Scot Guenter, and many others helped with moral, professional and emotional support during a particular trying time in my life but also just offered encouragement. I also offer thanks to Zoe Sluka-Kapell, a gloriously, wonderfully, amazingly, fantastically transcendent young adult who was on the cover of my second book a full twelve years ago, as well as Amy Kapell. I would especially like to acknowledge the important contributions of the late Ace G. Pilkington in helping to finish this book. He died in the final stages of this project. He was a good scholar, teacher and poet but more importantly a great friend and wonderful husband. He will be missed.

Matthew Wilhelm Kapell

Introduction

Toward a "Many Texts" Theory of the Star Trek Multiverse

MATTHEW WILHELM KAPELL
and ACE G. PILKINGTON

In January of 2008, Paramount Pictures released an "Under Construction" teaser trailer for their new *Star Trek* film. With historical quotes like "Godspeed John Glenn" and "The Eagle has landed," the teaser showed construction workers welding together the USS *Enterprise* as the words "The Future Begins" flashed across the screen and ended with Leonard Nimoy proclaiming "Space, the Final Frontier." Trekmovie.com, a relatively well-known webpage that was founded initially (in 2006) as the "Trek XI Report" put it bluntly: "It shows that *Star Trek* is not a fantasy, not from a galaxy far[,] far away ... it is real and it is us" (Pascale).

Directed by J.J. Abrams, the film that would eventually be released in 2009 was not quite a reboot, not quite a prequel, and not quite a voyage to the "final frontier." It was instead a rewriting and re-imagining of texts that had long ago entered the mainstream of American culture. Perhaps because of that, perhaps in spite of that, it grossed $385 million globally, making it the highest grossing *Trek* film by hundreds of millions of dollars as well as the highest grossing *Trek* film when adjusted for inflation. Well-reviewed as well, the film seemed to live by the phrase "this is not your father's *Star Trek*" and, surprising or not, seemed to help save a franchise that looked to be floundering since the cancellation of the television show *Star Trek: Enterprise* in 2005 and the horrific reviews and box office of the *Trek* film that preceded it, *Star Trek: Nemesis* (2002). Indeed, it made over $300 million more than *Nemesis* globally ("Star Trek").

Manohla Dargis of the *New York Times*, a reviewer that occasionally misses the point of genre films, doesn't miss the point this time. In a review with the headline "A Franchise Goes Boldly Backward," she notes that the film exists in part as "a testament to television's power as mythmaker" but also doesn't seem to like its "chicks in minis" and "heroically clenched male jaws" very much. While the film received generally positive reviews, a good portion of those reviews, in fact, agree with Dargis' opinion that the film is a little too much about "muscled boys who can act and leggy girls who aren't required to" and not enough about *Star Trek*'s traditional topics of politically liberal styles of equality on the final frontier. We point out here the obvious conclusion that both males and females in the new *Trek* films are sex objects, part of the box office appeal, which is, good and bad, one of the time-honored functions of actors and one of the less admirable actions of producers.

Writing about the new film before its two sequels had been released, Stephen McVeigh put the issue front-and-center, noting that Kirk's path "from rebellious youth to starship captain comes into focus as a version of [President George W.] Bush's own journey" (McVeigh 199). From such a perspective this new *Star Trek* is anything but a version of Kennedy's New Frontier in interstellar space. Kirk's journey is largely derived from having the right parentage, as McVeigh notes. This is a plot device that has more in common with *Star Wars* than it does *Trek*. While diversity remains part of the central cast, it does so only because they are new versions of old characters. New additions are, with the exception of Sofia Boutella in *Star Trek Beyond*, mostly white, and usually male.

There are literally hundreds of academic works on *Star Trek*, and it has been a tradition in the introductions of those books to reference Kennedy's New Frontier, to reference the American Frontier Ideology of the original series in the 1960s (*TOS*), and to reference *Trek*'s ongoing attempt at diversity and inclusion. The above quote from Stephen McVeigh is in Matthew's 2010 book, *Star Trek as Myth*, and the introduction to that book is full of references to the American frontier historian Frederick Jackson Turner and frontier character Buffalo Bill Cody. Few of these references are necessary in an edited volume on this new version of *Star Trek*.

In the first film, the *Enterprise* journeys to the planet Vulcan and back to Earth spending most of its time in Earth's solar system. In the second film the ship goes to the Klingon homeworld and, again, returns to Earth—this time ending on Earth, itself. It is only in the final film of the new trilogy of films that the *Enterprise* goes anywhere new—and when it does it encounters a villain from, of all places, Earth. It's a far cry from "the human adventure is just beginning," blazoned on the screen at the end of *Star Trek: The Motion Picture*. Or from Gene Roddenberry's son, Eugene "Rod" Roddenberry helping to fund X Prizes and other scientific research.

The Kelvin Timeline films are new texts, but they are superimposed on old texts which are somewhere between iconic and mythical, with other critics labeling them instead dated and dangerous. "Many passages from Marcel Proust's *Swann's Way* are by now so well known that they have turned into clichés and reference points and occupy a permanent place in contemporary Western culture. Scenes and episodes are familiar even to many who have not actually read the book." (Davis 2). It may sound excessive to make the same claim for *Star Trek*, but allowing for certain variables in the respective audiences, it seems largely true. Both Proust and *Star Trek* are cultural icons, though of rather different types. Both are ubiquitous and transformative with distinctive visions that many people feel attached to, protective of, and even (though more in the case of *Trek*) militant or even highly critical about.

In addition, *Star Trek* exists as many different texts, not only because its viewers see different versions of it from their different perspectives, but also because there have been many people who created movies and television series in the more than fifty years the franchise has existed. Getting a group of fans or a group of scholars, come to that, to agree about a specific element in those texts is difficult, especially when, for various reasons, one of the texts that is superimposed is some version of reality itself so that *Star Trek* becomes a pattern to achieve, an old imprinting we must free ourselves from, or strangely, some paradoxical combination of the two.

This book has not accomplished the feat of reconciliation and unification. While the two editors are largely in agreement, there are, as you would expect of a scholarly work with multiple authors, many different viewpoints expressed in the essays, some of them directly contradictory. In part this is an advantage because it means that many more texts were examined, in part it is a disadvantage because essays sometimes ignore important additional perspectives in their commitment to their own, and in part it is unavoidable in a world where *Star Trek* looms as large as it does. For example, one of the essays we did not get for this book (alas) would have been about other science fiction series and their interactions with *Star Trek*. It would probably not have provided enough direct information about the Kelvin Timeline films and so would not have been suitable, but here is an example of that struggle to see *Trek* from one perspective that fails so often and so interestingly. In *Stargate Atlantis* Season 1, Episode 14, "Sanctuary," Major Sheppard, Doctor McKay, and two others in a jumper encounter a strange woman of great power on a world that is mysteriously protected from the Wraith (powerful, vampiric aliens, the main villains for the series). (We apologize for not providing more background information on *Stargate*, but it is, after all, a different franchise.)

When Sheppard invites her to come back to Atlantis to get to know them better, she agrees. Her name is Chaya, and eventually they discover she is an Ancient and an ascended one at that. (Note: "Ancients" are the first coming of the human race, very old, very powerful, nearly immortal. Ascended Ancients have become energy beings, though they can resume human form.) McKay finds the romance between Sheppard and the woman troubling, perhaps because he is jealous, but he says, "A word of caution—the whole Captain Kirk routine is problematic, to say the least, let alone morally dubious." When Sheppard asks what routine, McKay continues, "The romancing the alien priestess. It's very 1967 of you. Actually, I'm surprised." In Sheppard's defense, Chaya has done most of the romancing in what has been a very brief and low-key relationship, but McKay has pretty much summarized the negative reaction to Captain Kirk's affairs. And then Chaya is asked why she came to Atlantis. Her response is, "You, John.... I have lived in solitude for so long that when you asked me to come to Atlantis, I..." And McKay sits down suddenly with the words, "Oh, my God, he is Kirk." Suddenly, Captain Kirk is a mythic figure who lives a life impossible to mere mortals. Inside McKay's head and the heads of some critics similar conflicting texts shift and impose themselves on each other. Kirk is a symbol of the past while he is also the shining example of how we get to the future. Here, as we said before, *Star Trek* becomes a pattern to achieve, an old imprinting we must free ourselves from, and strangely, some paradoxical combination of the two.

A large part of the criticism of the new movies has more to do with this textual transposition and overwriting than it does with the movies themselves. Plus, there is a general reluctance to confront the television shows and movies as films even when the discussion is ostensibly about films. McKay does not condemn Kirk directly as an imaginary character, though perhaps that would be a little too metacinematic in a situation where one character in a television show is commenting on another. Take Andrea Whitacre's cogent and well-supported essay in this volume—she objects to a situation where Uhura has to work for what she gets while Kirk is "destined to command." We agree with her that that is an unfair (and unrealistic) situation, but it applies only to the text she is examining. *TOS* gave us a captain and first officer who had worked very hard for their positions and won them against much competition. Ace shows in his essay that it is this very element in Kirk and Spock that alienated J.J. Abrams and caused him to recast them in the mold of Luke Skywalker. The fact that Kirk was "brilliant" was one of the qualities about him that bothered Abrams. Skywalker, on the other hand, "was this kid who didn't know where he was going to go, didn't know what his life was going to be. He was an average farm boy" (Altman and Gross 756). Leaving aside the fact that Luke Skywalker is a secret prince with strange, occult powers (which Abrams seems to have missed), he is a farm boy destined for greatness with little effort on his part, a male fantasy familiar to watchers of Tom Cruz movies. Perhaps the motorcycle motif that has been imposed on Kirk in the new timeline (in *TOS* episode "A Piece of the Action," his inept attempts to drive a 1920s automobile terrify Spock) is an homage to such films, but all of this is about films and film directors; none of it is about *Star Trek* or gender inequality, though, admittedly, there's a strong element of unsophisticated male fantasy running through it.

Here is another example of the willingness to treat *Star Trek* as a realistic (and even reality-based) structure or, to put it another way, a reluctance to look behind the curtain. In her essay in this volume, Teresa Cutler-Broyles says about Captain Kirk's middle name in what is admittedly a tossed-off parenthetical note, "Tiberius ... how much more militant and imperial could you get?" Well, first of all, Tiberius was an infamous Roman emperor associated with torture, among other things. But more importantly, Captain Kirk didn't always have that middle name, and the way he got it was not an attempt to emphasize his military and imperial heritage. Of course, this is the kind of history that's not written for Memory Prime descriptions of the character as though he actually exists.

David Gerrold, who has been involved with *Star Trek* since *TOS* and who has won SF's two biggest awards, the Nebula and the Hugo, was asked if he had given Kirk his middle name. He answered, "Yes, I did. I think it happened at a *Star Trek* convention, where we all started speculating about what the T stood for. *I, Claudius* had just aired on PBS, so I said 'Tiberius' as a joke. Later on, others picked up on it. So when *TAS* [the animated series] started, I wrote it in as a line of dialog. DC Fontana passed it by Gene [Roddenberry] at some point, and it stuck" ("The David Gerrold *TAS* Interview"). "BEM" by David Gerrold in *TAS* is the first time the middle name appears. *I, Claudius* was a Masterpiece series based on two novels by Robert Graves, *I Claudius* and *Claudius the God*. Claudius is presented as a good emperor and Tiberius as something of a monster, so perhaps it's unwise to vest too much meaning in Kirk's name beyond an expression of David Gerrold's sense of humor and his viewing habits.

Teresa Cutler-Broyles also inadvertently gives us a chance to look at another question of "authorial intent" in *Star Trek*. In her essay she labels (as part of her logical argument) all the major characters except Uhura as either white male or coded white (including Spock and Sulu). We are not disagreeing with her, and discussions of how *TOS* characters have been perceived over the years are part of several essays in this book. However, it's worth noting that Gene Roddenberry seems to have sent a subversive message in his casting, whether entirely intentionally or not. And, of course, whatever he did, it was not done independently of the practical issue of putting a show together.

Nevertheless, *TOS* has a captain (William Shatner) who has described himself as "a little Jewish kid from Montreal (Shatner)." The second in command (Leonard Nimoy) was also Jewish, and some of what made Spock Spock came from Jewish culture. Uhura (Nichelle Nichols) is African American,

6   Introduction

and Sulu (George Takei) is Japanese American. Montgomery Scott (James Montgomery Doohan, speaking of middle names) was Canadian, though both of his parents emigrated from Northern Ireland. Doctor McCoy (De Forest Kelley) was born in Georgia, and his name is Irish. And finally, Pavel Chekov (Walter Koenig) was born in Chicago, but his parents were Russian-Jewish immigrants from the Soviet Union. Admittedly, there is only one woman. However, whether by chance or design (and it's hard to believe there's not some design involved), there is not one Anglo-Saxon male in this list, not one clear example of the then-existing and since much-maligned power structure. One is Asian (and homosexual), three are Jewish, and two are Celtic. And, oh yes, two, including the primary representative of American might and power, are Canadian. Even if Roddenberry's casting wasn't meant to be subversive, it certainly turned out that way. It is people who have been persecuted in this country—the Jews, the Slavs, the Asians, and the Celts—who are on that list. Of course, Uhura is on the list of persecuted peoples as well as on the cast list, but she is never described as coded white or suggested to be part of the power structure.

There is another value to the multi-texts world of *Star Trek* that we have not explicitly mentioned. It makes possible an amazing range of approaches to the films, whole disciplines applied to the process, and clashing worldviews generating their wildly different outcomes. For instance, this volume contains interpretations that focus on such wide ranging issues as mythology and colonialism, linguistics and sexuality, plus race and citizenship.

Sarah Beth Kiliman examines the Romulan Captain Nero as "a malevolent trickster whose consequential chaos reaches far beyond both his immediate target and the scope of most of his trickster forbearers." However, Nero, just like many other tricksters before him, serves as a plot-driving character. Kiliman writes, "He fractures the original timeline, inadvertently pushing the universe and its occupants to alternative lives within the inverted Kelvin timeline." Kiliman's essay continues to explore the implications of Nero's actions and firmly positions the character, and by extension the new films, in the realm of mythology.

Ace G. Pilkington looks at the Kelvin Timeline from the point of view of science fiction and finds the new iteration of the franchise lacking where *TOS* excelled. The new films, according to Pilkington's essay, show the virtual elimination of any technology that might inspire today's engineers to usher in tomorrow—"the Abramsverse is a smaller and less interesting place," as a result. Gone are the attributes and values of Hard SF, which have been replaced with such blockbuster attractions as mass death scenes and action sequences. "Clearly, inside the Abramsverse, genocide and its parallels are entertainment," Pilkington observes. He does, however, have kinder words for *Star Trek Beyond*, the third film in the sequence and the first one not directed by Abrams, "Finally, the message *Star Trek Beyond* sends from in front of the camera and behind it is one Roddenberry might have approved. Indeed, it is clearly one that Roddenberry inspired." Ace even points out some tech that this *Trek* might itself inspire.

Cait Coker also notes the more violent nature of the Kelvin Timeline films. Her essay shows them as more militaristic compared to *TOS*. She explains that "the Federation and Starfleet evolved from a primarily exploratory and diplomatic entity to one that is highly militarized: examples include Sulu's hobby of fencing from The Original Series (*TOS*) became, in Abrams's vision, a martial skill suitably useful for special ops missions, to the massive technological shifts that transformed the *TOS Enterprise* with its crew complement of 400 to a ship of over 1,100."

The theme of violence and militarism finds further exploration in Bart Bishop's essay, where he looks at colonialism and imperialism asserting that, "J.J. Abrams and Roberto Orci insert their perspective into what they view as the racism and colonialism inherent in the original *Star Trek*."

At the same time, Jessica Sellin-Blanc cautions about drawing overly tight connections with *TOS*, proposing that the new films involve a "unique mode" of adaptation and "referring to the Kelvin Timeline films as mere reboots, or even preboots, does not do their narrative temporalities justice." The central idea of her essay is that "the new films take on a 'Jack of All Trades,' persona, where they are simultaneously conveying a multitude of perspectives, constantly negotiating their position within the existing universe, without ever invalidating any previous iterations." Or in our words, texts imposed on texts, shifting and readjusting.

Jessica Sellin-Blanc's essay also touches on the questions of gender and sexuality; however, it is in Andrea Whitacre's contribution where these issues manifest more prominently. "Competent professionalism tied to sexual objectification" is how her essay sees interpretations of female characters in the Kelvin Timeline. Whitacre goes further to propose that marginalization of women in *Star Trek* (both *TOS* and new films) is "a symptom of its [the franchise's] larger ideological commitments, which consistently center male characters."

As a whole, this collection is dominated by the interpretations focusing on social issues currently occupying American viewers of the films. For example, Penelope Ingram writes, "Released in 2013 and 2016, respectively, these science fiction films provide a sort of road map for understanding that particular brand of white resentment and rage expressed by many who voted for Donald Trump in the 2016 election." Lynnette Porter echoes this sentiment with, "Perhaps as a reflection of post–2016 U.S. election politics, which has often underscored a lack of unity among U.S. citizens and, unfortunately, has encouraged an increase in online hate speech against non-whites, as well as people who do not share the same gender, sexual orientation, religion, or political party as the people posting messages, the CBS All Access *Star Trek Discovery* series has faced backlash *because* of its diversity in casting."

Penelope Ingram, Lynnette Porter, Natashia Lindsey, and Teresa Cutler-Broyles focus on race and diversity. Each of these essays is devoted to an analysis of a different character in the franchise, and thus each approaches the discussion from a new perspective. Lynnette Porter's main concern is Khan Noonien Singh and his incarnation in the Kelvin Timeline. Teresa Cutler-Broyles examines Uhura. Natashia Lindsey looks at Spock. And while other essays in this collection discuss these characters as well, they do not offer the same level of intimacy. For instance, Olga A. Pilkington's exploration of Uhura as a representative of the linguistics scholarly community and a popularizer of language study is very different from Cutler-Broyles' analysis. For Pilkington, "Uhura allows for an examination of the *Trek* universe from the point of view of linguistics in many of its manifestations, be it historical or gender linguistics, technology assisted translation or foreign language acquisition." While for Cutler-Broyles, discussing the *TOS* character, "Uhura's meaning depended in large part on … broader contextual issues for its power, and viewers understood her based on their own beliefs, understandings, and expectations." The new films, according to Cutler-Broyles miss the opportunity to create certain contextual issues, being more concerned with "viewers' comfort" than with developing their characters in new and unexpected ways. She writes, "If indeed the fact that seeing a black Nyota with a Scottish Montgomery Scott would have been less familiar or less acceptable to viewers, then that is exactly what Abrams should have done."

Natashia Lindsey's discussion of Spock illuminates some important events in the character's life through the look at racial mixedness and the stereotypes that come with it. For example, she suggests that "the discursive power of race works to heap punishment upon him. These punishments, the destruction of Vulcan and the murder of his mother, act, but ultimately fail, to reinstate him into one of the legible stereotypes." According to Lindsay's essay, "Spock … occupies … [a place] that exists between the stereotypes of the tragic mulatto and hybrid vigor."

Lynnette Porter's arguments against the whitewashing of Khan Noonien Singh also go along the lines of emotion and physicality. She argues that with the casting of Benedict Cumberbatch as Khan, in the new films "the original character's Indian heritage is not emphasized." Moreover, the storyline involving Khan is structured in such a way as to promote his "action-movie villain's physicality far more than his intellect or emotions." We note that the actor's box office (and sex) appeal was one of the reasons for his casting.

Issues of race and diversity are inevitably sensitive, and scholarly analyses that deal with them cannot avoid the sensitivity of the subjects. But that is what makes these approaches relatable and humanistic. Some readers, no doubt, will be able to recognize their personal circumstances reflected in these discussions.

The value of this volume is, therefore, in its multitude of approaches. If the new films made it possible to see the world of *Star Trek* as a multiverse, with various timelines and destinies existing alongside each other, this volume positions *Star Trek* studies in a similar vein, with a variety of opinions, interpretations, and arguments expected from the many-texts theory of *Star Trek*.

Finally we point out that the many texts of *Star Trek* have produced an ethnic diversity and even a range of power structures that are not always acknowledged even in (or perhaps especially in) the most pointed arguments. From the current *Star Trek Discovery* with its rearranging of traditional roles to *Star Trek: Voyager* with its creation of what amounted to a female *Enterprise*. We present Ace's words from Matthew's book *Star Trek as Myth* at some length to make the point:

> *Voyager* was one place in Federation space where women truly had equal rights. The captain (Janeway), the chief engineer (B'Elanna Torres), the de-facto science officer (Seven of Nine), the crewmember who evolves into a higher life form (Kes), the precocious child who will grow up to be a Starfleet officer (Naomi Wildman), the main villain (Borg Queen), and the most important traitor (Seska) were female. It would take all the other *Trek* series combined to equal that number of major female roles. And Janeway more than holds her own among *Trek* captains. She operates on a farther frontier than the others faced, and on this seven-year odyssey, she becomes Odysseus, wily and violent but bound by her own rules.
>
> If Picard is cautious and Kirk is dangerous, Janeway, who sometimes seems to be an authentic maniac, has left such conservative strategies far behind. In "Scientific Method," after plunging her ship between the suns of a binary pulsar, Janeway says to her blindly loyal Vulcan security officer, "I never realized you thought of me as reckless, Tuvok." He responds, "It was clearly an understatement." In the two-part episode "Year of Hell," Janeway struggles with Annorax, captain of a time ship. Tom Paris, *Voyager*'s irreverent helmsman, labels him "Captain Nemo" and says of his behavior, "That's called paranoia ... with a hint of megalomania." But Janeway is equally unyielding. She states, "We're going through their space whether they like it or not." She fights her ship for the year of the title until it is not much more than wreckage, and then, alone on *Voyager*, she destroys Annorax, kills herself, and restores the timeline by ramming the time ship.
>
> In the long arc of *Star Trek*'s storylines, the partly mechanical, partly biological Borg are the Federation's most terrifying enemies. Only Janeway regards their powerful ships as good places from which to take technology by force. She makes deals with the Borg, steals Seven of Nine from them, and comes back from the future as Admiral Janeway to crush the Borg Queen one last time. In *The Farther Shore*, a *Voyager* novel set after the end of the series, Christie Golden has Janeway say, "The Borg are so familiar to us, they're like old friends" (31).
>
> But *Star Trek* is never about one gender or one person, however indomitable. *Voyager*'s journey is, as all *Trek* journeys are (and Odysseus's was), a quest for human-

ness. Seven of Nine, a human assimilated by the Borg when she was six and forcibly rescued by *Voyager* eighteen years later, reluctantly abandons her Borg nature and struggles to rediscover and reinvent her humanity. Or as the title of *Star Trek Scriptbooks Book Two* puts it, *Becoming Human: The Seven of Nine Saga*. In "The Gift" Janeway says of the appeal of the Borg, "You were part of a vast consciousness, billions of minds working together, a harmony of purpose and thought, no indecision, no doubts, the security and strength of a unified will." In this description the Borg seem to be more than unity; they are approaching divinity. Seven complains, "This drone is small now, alone, one voice, one mind, the silence is unacceptable." But she fights her way from nonentity to identity, from despair to hope. In the process of finding herself she questions the assumptions and values of her crewmates. Though Janeway is her mentor, Seven finds the strength to question and even defy her, no mean feat where Janeway is concerned. In "Prey," Seven, who has just disobeyed the Captain's orders and saved the ship, complains, "You made me into an individual.... You encouraged … my independence and my humanity, but when I try to assert that independence, I am punished."

Janeway responds, "Individuality has its limits. Especially on a starship where there's a command structure." But Seven is not easily silenced, "I believe that you are punishing me because I do not think the way that you do, because I am not becoming more like you." It is a continuing argument, an engagement with the self who is also the other, that leads to enlightenment for them both, just as Seven's journey to humanness and hope illuminates the transformations of the other crewmembers and their joint struggle to get home [Pilkington 63–65].

We think this is a core message for *Star Trek* in all its intertextual manifestations and one of the reasons why so many people can't help reading a utopian text behind the many other facets of *Trek*. We think this is one of the reasons why people fight so hard for their own interpretations of this massive cultural icon and why they seem, at times, so disappointed when it does not live up to their expectations. This accounts for both the enthusiasm and bitterness in all those *Star Trek* essays including the ones in this book, and hovering over it all is that utopian dream and McKay's involuntary exclamation, "He is Kirk."

Works Cited

Altman, Mark A., and Edward Gross. *The Fifty-Year Mission: The Complete, Uncensored, Unauthorized Oral History of Star Trek: The Next 25 Years: From the Next Generation to J.J. Abrams*. St. Martin's Press, 2016.

Dargis, Manohla. "A Franchise Goes Boldly Backward." *New York Times*, 7 May 2009. https://www.nytimes.com/2009/05/08/movies/08trek.html.

"The David Gerrold TAS Interview." *Star Trek Animated*, http://www.startrekanimated.com/tas_david_gerrold.html. Accessed 19 Sep. 2018.

Davis, Lydia. Introduction. *Swann's Way: In Search of Lost Time, Volume 1*, by Marcel Proust, Penguin, 2004. Amazon Kindle.

Golden, Christie. *The Farther Shore*. Pocket Books, 2003.

McVeigh, Stephen. "The Kirk Doctrine: The Care and Repair of Archetypal Heroic Leadership in J.J. Abrams' *Star Trek*." *Star Trek as Myth*, edited by Matthew Wilhelm Kapell, McFarland, 2010, pp. 197–212.

Introduction (Kapell & A.G. Pilkington) 11

Pascale, Anthony. "*Star Trek* Teaser Trailer Review & Video." TrekMovie.com. 18 Jan. 2008. https://trekmovie.com/2008/01/18/review-star-trek-teaser-trailer/.

Pilkington, Ace G. "2009 Postscript: *Star Trek*'s Myths to Live By." *Star Trek as Myth*, edited by Matthew Wilhelm Kapell, McFarland, 2010, pp. 63–66.

"Sanctuary." *Stargate: Atlantis*, season 1, episode 14, written by Brad Wright, directed by James Head, 11 Feb. 2005.

Shatner, William. *Up Till Now: The Autobiography*. St. Martin's Press, 2008.

"Star Trek." *Box Office Mojo*. https://www.boxofficemojo.com/franchises/chart/?id=startrek.htm. Accessed 20 Sep. 2018.

STAR TREK MEDIA CITED

"Prey." *Star Trek: Voyager*, season 4, episode 14, written by Brannon Braga, directed by Allan Eastman, 18 Feb. 1998.

"Scientific Method." *Star Trek: Voyager*, season 4, episode 7, written by Sherry Klein, Harry Kloor, and Lisa Klink, directed by David Livingston, 29 Oct. 1997.

The Star Trek Scriptbooks: Book Two: Becoming Human: The Seven of Nine Saga. New York: Pocket Books, 1998.

"Year of Hell, Part I." *Star Trek: Voyager*, season 4, episode 8, written by Brannon Braga and Joe Menosky, directed by Allan Kroeker, 5 Nov. 1997.

"Year of Hell, Part II." *Star Trek: Voyager*, season 4, episode 9, written by Brannon Braga and Joe Menosky, directed by Mike Vejar, 12 Nov. 1997.

A Switch in Time

Nero's Disruptive Trickster Force in J.J. Abrams' Star Trek

Sarah Beth Kiliman

Gene Roddenberry's *Star Trek* universe is abundantly populated with tricksters eager to interfere with the United Federation of Planets. From *The Next Generation*'s impish Q to *The Original Series*' Harry Mudd and the tyrannical Khan Noonien Singh, these tricksters vary in personality, role, and purpose, but the chaos each enacts spotlights the Federation and the moral and legal codes it privileges. J.J. Abrams' 2009 reboot follows this mythic tradition. Nero, *Star Trek*'s Romulan villain, questions the Federation's inaction in the events leading to his home planet's destruction, and he directs his vengeful wrath toward finding, capturing, and punishing the Federation's representative, Ambassador Spock. Crossing boundaries of space and time, Nero transforms himself into a malevolent trickster whose consequential chaos reaches far beyond both his immediate target and the scope of most of his trickster forbearers. He fractures the original timeline, inadvertently pushing the universe and its occupants to alternative lives within the inverted Kelvin timeline.

The Kelvin's *Enterprise* and its crew show this disorder. James T. Kirk begins his cinematic journey not as a cadet inspired by his father to join Starfleet but instead, as Captain Pike accuses him in *Star Trek*, as "the only genius level repeat-offender in the Midwest." Having never known his father, Kirk joins Starfleet only after being dared to do so by Pike, and his roguish nature continually leads to detention and demotion. Thus, the man who captained the *Enterprise* in *The Original Series* (*TOS*) finds himself subordinate to Spock, his former second-in-command. By interfering with the original timeline, Nero reverses Kirk and Spock's positions within the Federation order. Similarly, *Enterprise* mainstay and third-in-command Montgomery Scott is, instead, in the Kelvin timeline, denied his high-ranking position and marooned on a remote Federation outpost as punishment for his scientific curiosity. Nero's trickster disruption of ordered time instigates this reversal of hierarchy on the *Enterprise*, and the *Enterprise*'s carnivalesque inversion then acts as a microcosmic agent through which the Federation's resolve is tested.

The Nebulous Trickster

Nero's malicious personality stands in stark contrast to Q's playful pestering or Khan's manipulative cunning, and this diversity in each trickster's disposition reflects the struggle to describe the trickster trope in a single, universal way. Helena Bassil-Morozow discusses this difficulty in her book, *The Trickster in Contemporary Film*. An "enemy of boundaries" (5), the trickster "resists the narrow framing of definition" (5). Because the trickster inherently disregards and pushes against boundaries, the trickster repels attempts to delineate exactly what his role entails. Bassil-Morozow uses Paul Radin's *The Trickster: A Study in American Indian Mythology* as a lens through which she describes the trickster's slippery nature. According to Radin, the "trickster is at one and the same time creator and destroyer, giver and negator, he who dupes others and is always duped himself" (xxiii). For every role the trickster embodies, he becomes equally tied to its opposite and can express any character trait on the spectrum between the two ends. Tricksters are then as diverse as the situations they spawn.

William J. Hynes and William G. Doty agree with the complex definition of Bassil-Morozow's trickster figure in their *Mythical Trickster Figures: Contours, Contexts, and Criticisms*, but the pair take Bassil-Morozow's approach one step further by claiming that the trickster's indefinability is an integral part of his existence. For Hynes and Doty, the trickster's "plurality, plurivocity, and ambiguity are essential to the trickster Gestalt" (9). The trickster's indeterminate nature acts as a marker against which he is labeled and fulfills a specific cultural purpose. The reason the trickster remains ambiguous is not merely because he resists social boundaries, but also because he "encompasses many different social positions" (9). Within this prescribed role, he "is utilized … to inculcate various types of behavior" (9). Because each trickster is tied to the culture that creates him and because that culture uses the trickster for any number of didactic ends, elasticity is key in the trickster's makeup. Hynes and Doty and Bassil-Morozow's findings are not in conflict, however. Instead, Hynes and Doty offer a perspective which focuses on cultural creation of the mythic figure while Bassil-Morozow emphasizes the trickster's role within a cinematic narrative. Regardless of the lens used to view the trickster, each analysis hopes to narrow the scope of the trickster to better understand his purpose.

Both approaches favor diverse representations of trickster figures over rigid delineations, and, therefore, Bassil-Morozow and Hynes and Doty offer a variety of traits common to tricksters across mediums and cultures. By focusing on how personality patterns in trickster figures arise across a range of narratives, each perspective gives the trickster room to move freely within and between his multiple personas. Again, neither approach attempts homogenization in its findings. As Hynes and Doty explain, they instead hope to "identif[y] … an initial guide or typology … [a]t the heart of [the] cluster of manifest trickster traits" (34). Though *Star Trek*'s Nero embodies each characteristic on the Hynes and Doty list, three stand out as particularly useful. Similarly, Bassil-Morozow outlines five major trickster attributes—each of which readily applies to Nero. However, due to some overlap with Hynes and Doty and to fully showcase the most appropriate traits, three are highlighted below.

Stormy Starts, Mythic Births

Nero's malevolent personality sets him apart from other tricksters within Roddenberry's universe, and he is similarly positioned as an outsider when he enters *Star Trek*'s narrative arc. From the moment his mining ship, the *Narada*, makes its bold entrance into the Kelvin Timeline, Nero embodies the primary category through which Hynes and Doty filter all trickster characteristics—anomaly. "Ambiguous, a-nomos, [and] without normativity" (34), Nero storms—quite literally—into the film's opening scene from "the edge" of another universe "just beyond existing borders, classifications, and categories" (34). Materializing from what a *Kelvin* crewman calls "a lightning storm in space" (*Star Trek*), Nero's god-like entrance acts as a visual transition and clearly marks the trickster's movement out from his universe of origin and into a new, foreign playground. He exists as Hynes and Doty's "'out' person … [whose] activities are often outlawish, outlandish, outrageous, out of bounds, and out of order" (34). For the *Kelvin* crew—as well as the audience watching the scene unfold—Nero is an outsider bringing chaos to the natural flow of events.

This narrative birth cements Nero as a trickster, but it fails to illuminate his true origins. Nero's transformation is twofold, containing both his narrative trickster birth which begins with his entrance into the Kelvin timeline and his mythic trickster birth which begins the moment Romulus falls. During his narrative birth, Nero's ship does not merely appear near the *Kelvin* from another point in space but is rather pushed through all that remains of his obliterated home planet—a black hole. Only later does Nero reveal the catalytic role this destruction played in his development. He shares this exposition with the imprisoned Captain Pike. Though Nero formerly "live[d] a normal life," a "life filled with honest labor," the trauma of "watch[ing his] planet br[eak] in half" from an unchecked supernova's explosion changes him. Before he is introduced as an outsider in the Kelvin universe, Nero is first relegated to an outside position in his own culture and universe of origin. He stands, in his own words, as the "last of the Romulan empire," a forced outlaw with no home to which he can return. Nero's transformation unfolds through this trauma, isolation, and rage, and his harsh mythic birth informs the malevolent trickster personality he adopts.

Nero further separates himself from his now obliviated Romulan culture when he undergoes a physical transformation to match his psychological shift. While Nero displays his facial tattoos throughout the film, Mike Johnson and Tim Jones's graphic novel prequel, *Star Trek: Countdown*, proves Nero's tattoos to be both a new development and a direct response to the destruction of his home world. In a speech to his crew which spans several pages and sits atop panels of Nero's inkwork emerging, Nero says:

> There was a tradition on Romulus that when a loved one died ... you would *paint* your grief upon your skin. Ancient symbols of love and loss. In time the paint would fade and with it the period of mourning. Life would go on. We paint those symbols on our skin now. But we *burn them deep*. So they will *never* fade. Because life does not go on. We died with our friends. We died with our families. *We died with Romulus*. And all that is left is *revenge* [Johnson and Jones, *Star Trek: Countdown*].

Nero changes his form after his mythic trickster birth in order to suit his new emotional state. Hynes and Doty find "shape-shifting" to be another key component throughout various trickster figures (34). Because of his inherently slippery nature, the trickster is easily able to "alter his shape or bodily appearance" (36). Nero's physical change is neither a complete alteration nor an extensive one, but Hynes and Doty find that "[r]elatively minor ... disguise[s]" still meet the criteria of shape-shifting—even if they "involve nothing more than changing clothes with another" (36). The reason for a particular trickster's shape-shifting can be as diverse as the tricksters themselves, but Nero's purposeful transformation honors the moment of his mythic birth while mourning the Romulans lost during it.

That Nero uses a Romulan ritual as the inspiration for his marker does not necessarily work to bring Nero closer to his lost Romulan society, however. He perverts the tradition for his own ends, refusing to use paint for his mournful design. Hynes and Doty's assessment of common trickster characteristics aligns with Nero's behavior. According to the pair, "The trickster is often the official ritual profaner of belief" (37). The trickster disregards sacred ideologies in order to "bring[ ] into sharp relief just how much a society values these beliefs" (37), and "[t]hese profanations seem to exhibit a clear pattern of proportionality" wherein the level of disrespect matches the "sacred[ness of] a belief" (37). By ignoring the cultural constraints of the tradition, Nero invalidates the cultural authority assigned to the custom. Thus, he pushes himself further away from traditional Romulan culture and further into his new mythic role. The permanence of the tattoos reflects Nero's permanence as outsider in Romulan society. He has become something other than before, something new and separate from his Romulan identity. Because he survived Romulus's cataclysmic end, he exists forevermore in this outsider state, and that he marks his surviving crew with similar designs implicates all of them as outsider-survivors acting both beyond Romulan authority and Federation control.

Once he completes his physical and emotional transformation, Nero has one final hurdle to cross before finalizing his trickster identity, thus freeing him to cross the temporal and spatial boundary into the Kelvin timeline; he must choose his trickster name. For Bassil-Morozow, names act as one of the most substantial and powerful signifiers for the trickster figure. In a bold proclamation, she states that "[t]he trickster's name (or names) is his passport into the world" (31). Without one, he is trapped, unable to break the barriers against which tricksters longingly press. A trickster's "acquisition of a name is psychologically equal in importance to the metaphorical moment of emergence from a restrictive space" (31). In Nero's case, his name is the signifying equivalent of his movement away from his life as an everyday Romulan miner and toward his new role as a mythic trickster.

Nero's renaming—like his physical transformation—takes place in the film's supplementary materials. Alan Dean Foster's novelization of the *Star Trek* film gives Nero more space to develop, and Foster's written scene between Nero and the captive Captain Pike reveals the trickster's original Romulan name: "Ȯrên" (172). Nero then has two names—another phenomenon Bassil-Morozow addresses. According to her, while "[a] trickster without a name is the one who has not yet had his breakthrough" (31), a trickster like Nero who has "several names is [either] unsure of his identity ... or ... does not have a stable identity yet" (31). Nero's name change therefore has a larger role than Nero first admits. In the novelization he claims that the reason he allows humans to "address [him] as Nero" is because his "formal distinction contains "an accent and syllabic stress that is difficult for ... human larynx[es] to deal with" (172).

However, more than just human and humanoid acquaintances address Nero by his chosen name. His Romulan crew refer to him as Nero throughout both the film and its novelization. Nero's new identity is so prominent that the word Őŗên only appears in this single scene and is omitted from the novelization's cinematic counterpart. Here, Nero's identity stabilizes. When Nero changes his name from Romulan to a human-accessible counterpart, he finalizes his break away from his former self. He bids farewell to Őŗên, the Romulan miner and family man, and he fully becomes Nero, the trickster obsessed with chaotically dismantling the Federation.

Nero's transition into the trickster figure begins with his planet's destruction, and this moment acts as his mythic birth. Before he is ready to enter the Kelvin universe and enact the narrative shift which puts him on a collision course with his target, the Federation, Nero first goes through a series of changes which prepare him for his new role. His new, malevolent personality stems from the trauma of his personal and social loss. He alters his face with tattoos which mark him as distinctly Romulan while they, at the same time, distance him from the social authority represented in the markings. Finally, he embodies this struggle between identities when he adopts a new name, but only when he commits to his single identity as a trickster by surrendering to his name does Nero complete his development. Nero then enters the Kelvin universe as this new mythic figure and commences the disruptions which test the Federation's strength against his vengeful fury.

Broken Boundaries, Inverted Identities

Once Nero experiences his narrative birth in the film's Kelvin timeline, his purpose is clear: to funnel his full malevolent trickster energy toward his new enemy, the Federation. As a representative for the Federation, the Spock from Nero's Prime timeline (distinguished in this chapter from his younger, Kelvin-timeline alternative through his title, Ambassador), is tasked with diverting the supernova's collision with Romulus. Ambassador Spock arrives at Romulus only to find his mission has failed, and he meets Nero who is in vengeful pursuit. Nero accuses Spock of "betray[ing]" the Romulans' trust. However, because Ambassador Spock is a representative for the Federation, Nero's blame extends to it as well. Once his trickster quest puts him in the Kelvin timeline, he obsesses over not only "avoid[ing] the destruction" of Romulus in the alternate universe but also "creat[ing] a Romulus ... free of the Federation" since only through breaking the Federation's order can Romulus "be truly saved" (*Star Trek*). In order to break the chain of events leading to his planet's death, Nero believes he must break the Federation which governs much of the galaxy. Nero then directs the malevolent energy garnered through his trickster spirit at Spock, the *Enterprise*, and the very Federation the two represent.

Bassil-Morozow discusses how the trickster finds his purpose by "challenging the social order" throughout her analysis of the trickster in film (6). The trickster's favorite method for this task is "introducing destabilization and imbalance into" the system he wishes to disrupt. Anarchical chaos is a useful tool in this process, but the trickster's purpose is calculated and well-defined even if the exact effects of his interference are less certain. Karl Kerenyi put this another way in "The Trickster in Relation to Greek Mythology." For Kerenyi, the trickster's social role is "to add disorder to order and so make a whole, to render possible, within the fixed bounds of what is permitted, an experience of what is not permitted" (185). Bassil-Morozow builds upon Kerenyi's assertion, noting that "civilization is associated with stability, rationality, and order, whereas the trickster is always the one 'outside'" (20), and because he sits outside of the social order, the trickster invests in "goading, challenging, destroying, and urging it to move on" (20). Here, "civilization" is a stand-in for the Federation and the worlds represented within its bureaucracy. The "stability [and] rationality" the Federation values lies in both its regimented, military-inspired hierarchy which orders beings by their social function and the natural flow of uninterrupted chronological time in which it exists. Nero, the trickster on the "outside," interacts with this order by forcibly colliding with the Federation and, once inserted into its system, destabilizing the foundational hierarchy upon which it stands.

While Nero tests the universe's permissible bounds—a transgression which fits with his trickster disinterest in restrictions—he brings Kerenyi's "disorder" and Bassil-Morozow's "destabilization" into the new Kelvin timeline, and by destroying the *Kelvin*, he assures that the chaos stretches far beyond the immediate interaction. This destruction begins a widespread inversion of the Prime Federation's hierarchy—an inversion seen on microcosmic proportions through the *Enterprise* and its crew years later. First, George Kirk's early death aboard the *Kelvin* leaves his son, the future Captain James T. Kirk, in a less-than-encouraging childhood. Rather than idolizing his father's role in Starfleet and using George Kirk's career as inspiration upon which he models his own driven, successful career, the James Kirk from the Kelvin timeline grows up resenting Starfleet's role in his father's death.

Even though his "aptitude tests were off the charts" (*Star Trek*), he finds himself on the desolate path Pike ominously lays out in the film's novelization. Though Kirk has what it takes to succeed as a leader, Pike explains he is likely to "mak[e] the acquaintance of every jail between Chicago and St. Louis" if he doesn't accept a future with Starfleet (52). Kirk relents, but he never shakes off his rebellious attitude nor his unease with Starfleet's rigid system, and he thus finds himself on a trajectory subordinate to the rest of his Prime-timeline crew. Spock, then, takes command of the *Enterprise* when Pike is taken hostage by Nero. Kirk spends the majority of the film fighting his way from shipless cadet to his rightful place as the *Enterprise*'s captain. Nero boasts about his role in this shift: "James T. Kirk was considered to be a great man ... [who] went on to captain the USS *Enterprise*, but that was another life" (*Star Trek*). He concludes by threatening to "deprive" Kirk of his "life ... just like [he did for Kirk's] father." Nero accepts responsibility for the changes in the Kelvin universe, and he takes pride in his ability to disrupt a key component of Kelvin's Federation: the USS *Enterprise*.

This hierarchical inversion of the *Enterprise* crew further proves Hynes and Doty's classification system as it reflects Nero's role as a "situation-inverter" (34). Tied to his "ability to overturn any person, place, or belief, no matter how prestigious" (37), the trickster's situation-inversion creates confusion in all directions—"[b]ad becomes good, good becomes worse, worse becomes better, ... [t]ranquility ... become[s] disaster and vice versa" (37). The effect is "an unending concatenation of contingency" (37). Bonded friends Kirk and Spock become enemies, Spock becomes Captain, Kirk loses his ship and crew, and poor Scotty doesn't even make the cut to begin with. Uhura, Sulu, and Bones only come into their traditional positions due to the inability, illness, or death of the crewmembers who inhabit their expected roles—further reflecting the "contingency" of Nero's inversive disruption. As long as Nero continues to intervene in the Federation's path, the crewmembers' places on the *Enterprise* remains in a state of fragile transition, and as long as this state of transition exists, Nero's authority as a trickster strengthens.

Liminal Transition, Ambiguous Return

Although Nero transgresses the Prime/Kelvin boundary to enact this social inversion, the *Enterprise* crewmembers' movement in and out of their Prime universe roles remains safely within the confines of their independent timeline. Bassil-Morozow explores this phenomenon by looking to Victor Turner's work on the trickster figure and its purposes. An anthropologist, Turner focuses on "a structural solution to the ... trickster" (16). Turner finds that the "essence of the trickster principle—[the] movement and progress" discussed in depth above—sits neatly against the general cultural tendency for "change and transition" (16–17). This "liminality" works as a "mechanism for letting off steam" amongst populations, with "societies allocat[ing] special temporal pockets for the release" of nonstandard practices (17). By creating a safe space separate from the traditional order, societies test ideas and practices which have no immediate bearing on their organization and values. However, before reincorporating the partitioned and experimental group back into the population, the society considers the test's results and decides whether to integrate the new ideas discovered during the separation or to return unchanged to the traditions central to its existence before the temporal shift.

The trickster thrives in this realm because of its "uncertainty, turbulence, and chanciness" (17). Both before the shift away from the natural order and after the separated group reincorporates into the regular population, the trickster holds little power because of the power these normative social, political, and economic regimes hold within the culture. Turner's alignment of trickster and cultural rituals is "useful for the reconstruction of the otherwise erratic, evasive, and patchy trickster principle" because it explains the tricksters' "explosive, aggressive, [and] marginal" interactions with the societies into which they insert themselves (18).

Nero's role as "situation-inverter" finds greater purpose and explanation in Turner's theories. The alternate universe he creates "becomes a revolutionary force ... that appears during transitional periods and drives society out of stagnation" (18). By pushing the *Enterprise* crew outside of their normal trajectories, Nero creates a universe separate from the original in which both the strength of the crew's relationships and the ideal Prime hierarchy of Kirk as Captain/Spock as First Officer are scrutinized. The Kelvin timeline then acts as one of Turner's "special temporal pockets" within which the crewmembers are forced to test new identities while the Federation is challenged to hold up against these notable changes.

The first step in Turner's trickster-induced ritual involves "the end of the old state of things and the beginning of a new 'order'" (Bassil-Morozow 17), and it begins the moment Nero enters and splinters the Kelvin timeline. Both Nero's role as instigator of this shift and the changes he effects on the *Enterprise*'s crew are pertinent to Nero's *Star Trek* role, but the physical shift between the two timelines expands beyond the immediate story, touching on issues central to the *Star Trek* universe as a whole. The most important connection between Turner's theory of separation and the newly-established Kelvin timeline is that the entirety of J.J. Abrams' re-imagined *Star Trek* narrative exists within Turner's "special temporal pocket." Regardless if the narrative eventually rejoins the Prime timeline or remains on its unique course, it always exists as a fragmentary moment which stands away and separate from *TOS*'s narrative and is canonically established as a splintered arc beyond the Prime universe. On the flip-side of this theory exists the opposite perspective, however: the Prime universe still exists on the other side of the Romulus-devouring black hole through which Nero's inversion occurs. The role of the temporal pocket is highlighted here as it accurately represents the two paths as existing parallel- to-yet-distinct-from each other, and any reunifications between the two paths in no way flatten the two timelines into a single chronological entity.

After pushing the Prime timeline into its liminal bubble, Nero and the

Kelvin universe's occupants transition into Turner's second step, which Bassil-Morozow calls "the playground of the trickster" (17). This is an important phase in understanding Nero's purpose. Within the relative safety of the Kelvin timeline—this bold statement merely referring to the security of the *Enterprise*'s crew within the Prime timeline which moves forward beyond the Kelvin timeline and not the dangers inherent to the Kelvin's own universe—the newly reorganized *Enterprise* crew can play at being captain, at being prisoner, or even, as is the case with Scotty, at being absent altogether from their unrealized expectations in the Prime timeline. The Federation gets to experiment with its Starfleet organization and whether or not its decorated Captains hold-up in subordinate situations or if their second-in commands have equal leadership talent. The freedom within the narrative cycle then opens the characters to new experiences and potential.

However, just as the crew experiences this freedom, so, too, is the audience granted the opportunity to doubt its favorite characters and the hierarchy forced onto them by *TOS*'s traditional narrative. As Anne Doueihi notes in "Inhabiting the Space Between Discourse and Story in Trickster Narratives," looking beyond the story to the larger implications of trickster play helps "participants and spectators"—in this case, audiences who watch *Star Trek* and its companion media—"realize how far they have fallen short of or transgressed their own ideal standards, or even, in some kinds of ritual, to call those very ideals into question under conditions of sharp social change" (487).

A more specific way of thinking about Doueihi's claim is that the temporal bubble Nero enacts as part of his trickster plot gives the real-world audience a chance to both question whether the *Star Trek* universe's role stands up against renewal, rebirth, and reimagining and to consider if the story they've followed closely over multiple iterations truly offers the ideal story arc or if the new world order holds more potential. That these fans can experience the inversive scenarios along with the characters they follow makes the experience of *Star Trek* compellingly interactive, and it gives Nero's trickster energy power beyond the fictional realms he inhabits. Thus, Nero crosses another boundary—the boundary between fiction and reality, and he exists as a trickster figure in the real world for actual audiences. With this in mind, Nero becomes not just a malicious force equivalent in stature to other infamous villains but also a character who shakes the *Star Trek* universe with such malevolent trickster energy that it forces the show's characters, writers, and audiences to reevaluate their understandings of the narrative which had, before 2009, existed in relative normality along a sometimes-fractured but ever-unified chronology created by Gene Roddenberry in 1966.

Finally, neither *Star Trek into Darkness* nor *Star Trek Beyond* offers a complete return to the Prime timeline which would signify the completion of Turner's full trickster cycle, but with each step forward in the alternate universe, the narrative moves closer to equilibrium with its parallel story. In each film, Kirk regains the Captain's chair, and Spock settles comfortably into the Second-in-Command role. Scotty, thankfully, finds his way to Engineering, and the *Enterprise* eventually leaves for its original five-year mission. Ambassador Spock foretells the possibility of a complete refolding of the Kelvin pocket into the Prime timeline in Alan Dean Foster's *Star Trek* novelization. After running into the Kelvin-timeline Kirk on Delta-Vega, the marooned Ambassador Spock takes heart in their chance encounter:

> Doctor McCoy would assert our meeting here is not a matter of coincidence, but rather indication of a higher purpose.... It may represent the time stream's way of attempting to mend itself. We know far too little about the physics of such deviations to determine actualities and can only speculate on how they function in the greater continuum. In both our histories, the same crew found its way onto the same ship in a time of ultimate crisis. Therein lies our advantage [191].

Whether by chance, coincidence, or fate, the *Enterprise* crew find each other and their appropriate roles, and with little help from outside sources like Spock, the social order slowly regains balance.

Indeed, the *Enterprise* crew does return to its equilibrium at the end of each movie, and it begins subsequent tales with its Prime-normative hierarchy firmly in place. When that established equilibrium is threatened in *Star Trek into Darkness* and *Star Trek Beyond*, the crew responds with greater confidence to maintain its social order, and with each subsequent film the time spent away from their original roles decreases exponentially. Whether or not the two timelines will ever bridge remains unclear. All the audience can do is take Ambassador Spock's words to heart: "We must hope that events bear this out. Indeed, we can only proceed on that assumption" (191). Only time and future incarnations of Captain Kirk, Mr. Spock, and the rest of the crew will reveal if the splinter created by Nero ever heals itself, and if and when the starship *Enterprise* again sets out on a voyage, the most anticipated details will surely deal with the ripples left over from Nero's malevolent trickster energy.

Works Cited

Bassil-Morozow, Helena. *The Trickster in Contemporary Film*. Routledge, 2012.
Doueihi, Anne. "Inhabiting the Space Between Discourse and Story in Trickster Narratives." *Mythical Trickster Figures: Contours, Contexts, and Criticisms*, edited by William J. Hynes and William G. Doty. Tuscaloosa, University of Alabama Press, 1993.
Hynes, William J., and William G. Doty, editors. *Mythical Trickster Figures: Contours, Contexts, and Criticisms*. University of Alabama Press, 1993.
Kerényi, Karl. "The Trickster in Relation to Greek Mythology." *The Trickster: A Study in American Indian Mythology*, edited by Paul Radin, Schocken Books, 1998.
Radin, Paul. *The Trickster: A Study in American Indian Mythology*. Schoken Books, 1988.

Turner, Victor. *Process, Performance, and Pilgrimage: A Study in Comparative Symbology.* Concept, 1979.

STAR TREK MEDIA CITED

Foster, Alan Dean. *Star Trek* [Film novelization]. New York: Pocket Books, 2010.
Johnson, Mike, and Tim Jones. *Star Trek Countdown.* IDW Publishing, 2016.
Star Trek (2009). Directed by J.J. Abrams, Paramount Pictures, 2009.
Star Trek Beyond. Directed by Justin Lin, Paramount Pictures, 2016.
Star Trek into Darkness. Directed by J.J. Abrams, Paramount Pictures, 2013.

Khanned

Whitewashing Khan in Star Trek *into Darkness*

LYNNETTE PORTER

Before *Star Trek into Darkness* opened in 2013, fans already suspected that the new film might be a reboot of *Star Trek II: Wrath of Khan* (1973). The first trailer released months earlier featured the deep, mesmerizing voice of Benedict Cumberbatch before his appearance on screen. Even when his unnamed character offers healing to another man's daughter, Cumberbatch's demeanor indicates that his character has something other than an altruistic agenda in mind, as the rest of the trailer indicates (Pascale).[1] Fans online debated whether Cumberbatch's character, whose name was listed as John Harrison in interviews (a reference to an innocuous red shirt in the original *Star Trek* television series), might really be Khan. Cumberbatch, sworn to secrecy before the film debuted, later explained that he, like director J.J. Abrams, wanted audiences to be surprised at the revelation that the actor is indeed Khan (Shah-Williams). As one critic noted, "it would have been near impossible to convince fans that the *Star Trek into Darkness* villain wasn't Khan, had an Indian actor been cast in the role" (Shah-Williams). At least to Cumberbatch, the secrecy was not based on whitewashing and the potential for backlash. Nevertheless, the rebooted Khan became much more controversial than the original character portrayed by Ricardo Montalbán in the *Star Trek* television episode "Space Seed" (1967) and the film *Star Trek II: Wrath of Khan* (1973), and many fans felt Khanned by the way that director Abrams handled the character's big reveal on screen.

As a result of the Eugenics Wars on Earth, the original Khan Noonien Singh has both a superior intellect and genetics when compared with other humans. Montalban was made up darker skinned to indicate his Indian heritage, but the actor, like Cumberbatch, was not Indian—yet the casting was not subject to backlash from fans at the time. In fact, Montalbán's casting can be considered significant in that a non–Anglo actor was signed to a prominent role not only in one television episode but in what turned out to be a fan-favorite film (Bird) in a time when diversity in casting was even worse than it was pointed out to be in the 2014–2015 #OscarsSoWhite campaign, when all Oscar-nominated actors were white. Television series creator/writer Gene Roddenberry and *Star Trek* invited controversy during the series' three-year run.

Television in the 1960s

A key example of controversial *Star Trek* episodes illustrates the climate in television in the mid–1960s, when Roddenberry's show seemed determined to break racial barriers (or at least stretch them on television) and create a diverse leading cast. The groundbreaking episode "Plato's Stepchildren" (1968) includes a scene in which a black woman (Lieutenant Uhura, played by Nichelle Nichols) kisses a white man (Captain Kirk, played by William Shatner). Although aliens made them do it, which somewhat dilutes the impact, a few NBC affiliates did not carry the episode, and an edit was planned for Southern NBC affiliates. The kiss "was anticipated to be contentious. In fact, the scene was not intended for the entire country to see. NBC executives were concerned the kiss would anger viewers in the South. According to reports, they planned to censor the kiss from Southern viewers entirely, showing only an embrace" (Buck). However, when several takes were unusable when the dailies were screened, the kiss scene remained for broadcast.

In 2016, *Digital Spy* included the kiss in an article debunking television's urban legends and misconceptions about specific series' episodes. The argument the critic made is that "no kiss is actually seen as both actors turned their heads away from the camera at the last moment. However, Nichols has asserted that the kiss was real" (Eames). She has also discussed the kiss as real at various fan conventions, despite what was not explicitly shown to ward off as much backlash as possible and make it more likely that affiliates would air the episode. Most fans, if not *Digital Spy*, consider the kiss real and a landmark U.S. television moment. The designation "first interracial kiss on television," however, only applies to the U.S. by 1968, when the episode was first broadcast. In the U.K., the first interracial kiss on television took place in 1962 during the Granada-broadcast play *You in Your Small Corner* ("First Interracial Kiss").

Furthermore, including in the *Enterprise* crew green-blooded, pointy-eared Vulcan Spock was even considered going too far by some viewers; after all, Spock's ears could be considered Satanic. Thus, Montalbán's casting and becoming a fan-favorite villain is significant by 1960s' television standards. "[C]onsidering the studio pressure on Roddenberry to cast only white actors, it was an important statement just to have Khan played by a person of color" (White). Furthermore, "[b]y making the 'ideal' Indian, Roddenberry was pointing out that genetic composite of all humans wouldn't end up white" (White). The fact that Khan is a villain who vexes Kirk more than any other in the original series and spinoff movies starring the original cast is not considered as important as the fact that Montalbán was cast. Whereas U.S. television may have lagged in depicting diversity and interracial relationships, they, along with the U.K., were gradually, sometimes grudgingly responding to the changing societal values during a time, especially in the U.S., of Civil Rights demonstrations and legal challenges.

Some fans, however, do not consider Montalbán to be a person of color (POC), despite Montalbán considering himself a non-white minority. Agreeing with Montalbán, *io9* writer Charlie Jane Anders, like other fans, considers the actor to be a POC. She explains that Khan is "a POC character who was played by a POC actor" and is "one of the most iconic people of color in space." Fans who see him as a POC, even if dark makeup was applied for the television episode and not nearly so much for the film, have less trouble with the original casting.

This casting was personal to *Star Trek*'s Roddenberry on several levels. He named Khan after a friend made during World War II who disappeared after the war. Roddenberry hoped that Kim Noonien Singh would see Khan, recognize his namesake, and get in touch ("Has Star Trek's Khan Noonien Singh Been 'Whitewashed'"). That never happened, however, but the legacy of Khan survives beyond the lifetime of these World War II veterans.

More important to the issue of whitewashing, Roddenberry promoted the *Star Trek* ideal of Infinite Diversity in Infinite Combinations (IDIC). The original cast includes Jewish Leonard Nimoy and William Shatner, African American Nichelle Nichols, and Japanese-American George Takei. Although only the character Pavel Chekov, played by Walter Koenig, is a Russian, the actor's parents were Russian Jewish immigrants. Roddenberry tried to illustrate that, in the future, the Federation includes non–Earth officers as well as humans of every religious belief, nationality, race, or ethnicity.

Anders notes that "[m]aking the ultimate representation of eugenics into a vaguely Asian villain played by a Latino was an oddly clever choice—it divorces his claims of genetic superiority from the real-life advocates of eugenics and forces [viewers] to see the issue in a new light" and not as a Hitleresque or Ku Klux Klan type of white supremacy. Roddenberry believed and tried to illustrate in his television series and series-based movies that the "very notion of one group of humans being innately better than another devalues us all" (Anders). Despite such aspirations evident in his casting choices and scripts, Roddenberry's decision to subvert whitewashing did not always make it into finished episodes or films, and rebooted *Star Trek* film director/producer Abrams' vision for a new, revised *Star Trek* timeline with re-imagined characters has resulted in more critics and fans taking a closer look at the whitewashing of Khan. As previously indicated in the description of "Plato's Stepchildren," the "suits" who monitor filming and try to make films or television series as lucrative as possible often consider the bankability of an actor instead of aiming for diversity in casting. That fact has not changed in the more than fifty years since *Star Trek* debuted.

Arguments For and Against Hollywood Whitewashing

The argument that POC should be cast in roles representing POC reached a peak in 2014 with the Oscars So White campaign, with its own Twitter hashtag and commentary by the media before, during, and after the Oscars television broadcast. Despite more nominations and higher profiles for some mainstream films featuring POC (e.g., in 2016–2017 including films like *Fences*, *Moonlight*, and *Hidden Figures*, which received Oscar nominations in 2017; "Nominees"), the industry still has faced backlash for casting some roles. For example, in 2016, *Doctor Strange*'s Ancient One was once an Asian man who, for the film, became a white Celtic woman—ostensibly to avoid Asian stereotypes but raising the issue of why a role for an Asian man could not simply have been updated to avoid stereotyping. Similarly, Matt Damon's role in *The Great Wall* (2017) received backlash because, at least to some critics and viewers, he plays a white savior figure to save the Chinese (Shepherd). These more recent examples of whitewashing do not minimize the fact that *Star Trek into Darkness*' Khan is usually included in the continuing discussion of twenty-first century examples of Hollywood's casting preferences and whitewashed characters.

A different casting issue, but also one that provoked some backlash, involves sexual orientation instead of race. In the *Star Trek* film following *Into Darkness*, for example, Sulu is reunited with his male partner and their daughter during shore leave on a space station (*Star Trek Beyond*). When the revelation that Sulu is gay hit the media, actor/activist George Takei, who originated the role of Sulu in the classic television series, asked why a new, gay character could not have been introduced, instead of making Sulu, in honor of and like Takei, gay. The question also arose why a gay actor could not have been cast in a new role instead of a straight actor playing Sulu (whose homosexuality was revealed long after John Cho had been cast and played the role in two previous films). Casting an actor to match the character—in race, gender, or sexual orientation, for example—matters a great deal to many fans, critics, and actors, if, apparently, not so much to many producers and casting agents. Should matching an actor by specific characteristics to a character be necessary? The answer is divisive, as the following media examples in light of Cumberbatch's casting in *Star Trek into Darkness* indicate.

Yo Zushi, writing for *New Statesman*, suggests that whitewashing may not be the problem its critics say it is. The crux of the argument that casting a white actor to play a character of color may not be a big deal depends on the original source and the additional backstory created through follow-up sources, such as novelizations, or what is canon and what is added as professionally published fanon. Zushi notes that:

> [A]lthough Khan may have been "one of the most iconic people of colour in space opera" [to quote *io9* writer Anders, cited earlier] he was a villain, and his villainy had been needlessly racialised in earlier appearances. In the 1967 *Star Trek* episode *Space Seed* and in the 1982 film *Star Trek II: the Wrath of Khan*, he was played by the Mexican actor Ricardo Montalbán. Khan's heritage went unmentioned until later spin-off novels expanded his biography, yet his name and the use of an ethnic-minority actor to portray him seemed intended to present him as an untrustworthy, foreign "other."

Demonizing villains, when they are played by POC representing characters of color, according to Zushi, is worse than casting a white actor to play a role that, through years of additional texts, emphasizes Khan's backstory and race. Zushi adds that *Star Trek into Darkness* screenwriter Roberto Orci has stated that he did not want to demonize a POC, which may be one reason why Cumberbatch was cast [in addition to his talent and the failure to keep originally cast Benecio del Toro, who left the production in its early stages ("Benecio del Toro Has No Regrets")]. Most important, however, is Zushi's claim that "By choosing a white actor, the film-makers decoupled Khan's villainy from his brownness—which was significant, especially in the light of Khan's terrorist attack on a skyscraper in the film." After the 9/11 attacks on New York City and elsewhere, the filmmakers may have decided that choosing a POC to be associated with terrorism would be more harmful than whitewashing the character. Cumberbatch's Khan asserts that white men can be terrorists, too.

An interesting, if somewhat convoluted discussion took place on the *Trek BBS* forum thread about Cumberbatch's casting and whitewashing. Some posts complained that the casting of Khan had been off from the first. After all, Hispanic actors, such as Montalbán and Del Toro, are not Indian, so originally casting a Mexican actor to play an Indian character already was problematic, even if Montalbán was cast as the best actor to play the role. In response, one poster admitted that "I can see what you're saying about casting Cumberbatch as the Asian Khan is no better than casting Montalbán as the guy in 1967.... Also in that context, casting Del Toro would've been no better, either. The only thing I can say is it seems with Khan, the *STID* folks were stuck dealing with the 'sins of the fathers'" (Franklin). Another person posting in this forum had no problem with another Mexican actor being cast as Khan, as that casting would be consistent with the original portrayal. However, Khan's appearance as a white actor (although some fans consider Hispanic actors white instead of POC) seemed disturbing simply because brown makeup was used in "Space Seed" but not in *Wrath of Khan* (trekster). Throughout this forum, fans commented on what bothers them about the non–Indian casting of Khan, but the reasons diverge widely.

A final argument, made in fan forums and online articles, is that black-washing [e.g., casting African American actors in *Annie* (2014), based on a comic strip about rich white characters and the white orphan they save] is the same thing, only viewed by some as a fresh instead of troubling interpretation—although more Internet and Twitter commenters were angry about *Annie*'s casting than about *Star Trek into Darkness*'. The same holds true for casting Lucy Liu as Watson in *Elementary*, for example (e.g., Elyse, among other writers providing this and similar examples). Some fans and critics wonder why whitewashing is singled out as bad, although the argument against this sentiment is that whitewashing is more prevalent than the casting of POC actors as originally white characters.

Perhaps *Racebending* provides the clearest discussion of why *Into Darkness*' casting of Khan is problematic to many people. First, the issue of demonizing POC as villains is debunked:

> [T]here's one thing that most fans of *Star Trek* will agree on, it's the fact that Gene Roddenberry's vision for the show—and, more optimistically, for human society—was predicated on the idea that all life is valuable, and that the worth of a person should not be judged by their appearance. Much of this was done through the old sci-fi trope of using aliens to stand in for oppressed groups, but *Star Trek* didn't rely on the metaphor.... [In addition to crew regulars and extras of color,] ... here and there, it had anti-heroes and villains who were people of colour ... one of whom, Khan Noonien Singh, became well-nigh iconic ["Star Trek into Whiteness"].

According to this argument, as long as POC are well distributed throughout a film, it is realistic to assume that some will be heroes and some villains, some leading characters and some extras. The distribution, not tokenism, is what is important. Choosing box office potential as a prime reason for casting an actor should not be the major consideration (ideally, but probably not pragmatically for Hollywood businesspeople). Although *Racebending* acknowledges that the original casting also had its problems, "having a brown-skinned man play a brown character was a hard-won victory." What is the much bigger disappointment, according to *Racebending*, is that "Abrams chose not to honour the original spirit of the show, or the symbolic heft of the Khan character, but to wield the whitewash brush for ... [what? the] hopes that casting Benedict Cumberbatch would draw in a few more box office returns?" The assumption is that any talented actor would have been as good as Cumberbatch, but his rising star power might bring in more ticket buyers.

The secrecy surrounding Khan's identity is also presented in a more sinister way by *Racebending*. The article adds that, because the "surprise" of Khan was revealed only when the film premiered, critics and fans could not adequately mount a protest. Because many fans had waited a long time for a new *Star Trek* film, those who might have protested already had seen the film on its opening day, thus preventing an effective boycott by people who might not have wanted to see a whitewashed character. The secrecy, according to this argument, indicates that *Star Trek*'s producers and promoters did not want anything to hinder their film's box office, especially on the first crucial few days of its wide release.

U.K. Mag Live did not mention *Star Trek* specifically in its article about whitewashing and Hollywood. However, it included an important comment about the problems of whitewashing in films:

> In 2012, a study [by the Media Diversity & Social Change Initiative, University of Southern California] found that three-quarters of characters with speaking roles in top-grossing films were white. Ironically, the same study found that 44% of movie tickets purchased that year were by people of colour. David White, Director of the Screen Actors Guild, stated that Hollywood: "Is driven by a group of risk-averse decision-makers who continually make inaccurate assumptions about the abilities of people of colour" [Legarda-Alcantara].

Although the study was focused on black or Hispanic characters, actors, and directors, the point still applies to the casting of POC. Whether screenwriter Orci or director Abrams was being risk averse is unclear from their interviews. What is clear is the support for Cumberbatch in the role by, in particular, the director, fellow castmates, and Cumberbatch fans, who had only praise for the actor's performance and a role that furthered his Hollywood career. The number of online articles discussing whether the whitewashing of Khan is bad or harmful is outnumbered by the plethora of (mostly fan-site) articles, blogs, or discussion boards praising the performance of or posting comments about Cumberbatch's/Khan's sex appeal. If a less capable white actor had been cast, the criticism specifically about Cumberbatch's casting may have been more vocal.

Khan in Star Trek into Darkness

Both the Abrams film and Alan Dean Foster's novelization fail to mention Khan's Indian heritage. Instead, the connecting link between Montalbán's and Cumberbatch's Khan is his mental and physical superiority over other humans. However, the plot undermines Khan's superiority in several ways. Reviewer Julian Darius picks apart perhaps the greatest flaw in the rebooted story of Khan and his crew being discovered adrift in space, only Khan being awakened, and—without any failsafes and with the assumption that Admiral Marcus (Peter Weller) knows who Khan is—Khan being turned loose to help the Admiral but left unsupervised enough that he can blow up Starfleet in London and San Francisco. Furthermore, as Darius explains, relying on Khan's superior intelligence is also relying on a relic to adapt quickly to a couple of centuries' technological advancements, which makes no sense, even in an action movie where events, not analysis of them, is encouraged:

> [W]ho responds to the discovery of genetically advanced humans by deciding *to only revive their leader and use his brain as part of a secret scheme* [original emphasis]? Khan might be smart and a ruthless warrior, but it's not like he's *so* smart and ruthless that anyone would naturally respond to him by thinking, "Man, I gotta tap that guy's ideas!" Admiral Marcus probably has scores of Albert Einsteins available to him, as head of Starfleet, and he's already got people employed on secret plans. Moreover, why would Khan be working on *weapons* [original emphasis]—which use technology 300 years more advanced than what he's familiar with?

For all the implausibility of this scenario, Khan seems to adapt to the twenty-third century extremely quickly, as well as retaining his ability to put his powers of persuasion to work in order to convince Starfleet personnel (at one point, Kirk included) to follow his instructions. However, the ruthless Khan also seems to have a legitimate soft spot for his still-asleep crew "family," even shedding a tear when he thinks of them being held captive by Starfleet. Nevertheless, by the end of the film, Khan is truly a vicious megalomaniac who takes over the Admiral's ship and wreaks havoc on the *Enterprise* and Earth. Fortunately for Khan's survival, he has a saving grace—the life-giving power of his blood (a new development for the rebooted franchise). When Spock chases Khan through the rubble of San Francisco, he primarily does so not because Khan is a terrorist bent on destroying Starfleet in order to retrieve his crew or because he has killed not only Starfleet personnel but innocents within the range of his destruction but because Spock's good friend and captain, Kirk, can only be plucked from death by an infusion of Khan's blood. After Khan's blood has been secured, he is returned to cryogenic sleep, leaving the possibility for his return at some point in a future film.

Although Cumberbatch convincingly plays Khan with a range of emotions larger than the audience may have expected, the lack of logic fueling many scenes encourages audiences to remember this action-movie villain's physicality far more than his intellect or emotions. In fact, Khan might just as well have been named John Harrison and given a similar backstory about being an enhanced human; the original character's Indian heritage is not emphasized in either the film or the book based on it.

Comics Khanned

Whether the IDW comic book series *Star Trek: Khan* was planned to address the reason why Indian Khan turned into Northern European Khan before the film received charges of whitewashing is unknown. However, the comic book series' plot focuses on the time in the film after Khan is captured by Spock and Khan's later return to the cryogenic freezer. The five-issue series, later combined into one graphic novel, takes place during Khan's trial for his crimes against Starfleet and humanity. However, the trial only provides a framework to allow Khan to present an elaborate backstory.

In many respects, Khan is a victim first of cruel scientists who experiment on a group of orphaned children and, after their genetic enhancement and mental reprogramming is completed years later, sell them to Earth's governments as super soldiers. Much later in his life, after conquering the world and becoming the lead tyrant of a global alliance of his genetically and physically superior peers, Noonien Singh renames himself Khan. When the majority of the ordinary population revolts worldwide, killing some of their genetically-enhanced overlords, Khan and his surviving peers escape Earth. He and his crew launch themselves into space aboard the *Botany Bay* and enter cryostasis. Starfleet's Admiral Marcus finds the vessel and thaws Khan. However, Marcus envisions using the super soldier for his own purposes and does not want Khan to recall his past. Marcus uses twenty-third century medicine to change Khan's appearance, including facial structure, skin color, and voice. He renames Khan as John Harrison and, for a time, convinces Khan that he has amnesia as a result of a brain injury and is struggling to remember his life as a devoted Starfleet officer. Thus, the explanation of Khan's changing race and physical characteristics attempts to make him a more sympathetic character, and the transformation left unexplained in the film is finally "logically" detailed as part of the rebooted Khan's backstory.

Within the one-volume collection, as well as on the individual issues' covers and in many artists' drawings of Khan, the transformed Khan looks exactly like Benedict Cumberbatch in the film role. On select covers of individual issues or photos inserted between the "chapters"—or formerly printed individual issues in the graphic novel—stills of Cumberbatch-as-Khan from the film reinforce the actor as the new face of Khan. This reinforcement paves the way for Cumberbatch to reprise the role of Khan in a future film. In fact, a Cumberbatchesque Khan is featured in the January 2017 comic book *Star*

Trek/Green Lantern #2. In announcing the issue, *Nerdist* reinforced the actor's association with Khan, noting "the version of Khan Noonien Singh as played by Benedict Cumberbatch ... making his first return to Trek lore since being put on ice at the end of *Star Trek into Darkness*" (Diaz).

The reboot's revisionist history also attempts to erase the former backstory of Montalbán's Khan with a new backstory taking place within a different time frame than that of the classic television series. According to the *Star Trek: Khan* comic books, the orphan child begins his incarceration and indoctrination in a scientific testing facility in 1971 and leads a revolt of the genetically-enhanced inmates in 1985, for example. The discovery of the *Botany Bay* and re-emergence of Khan also take place earlier in Kirk's tenure as captain and by Admiral Marcus rather than the *Enterprise* crew.

Like new Spock, who is sexier and more emotional—as well as romantically involved in a long-term relationship with Uhura—new Khan has been drastically altered from his original incarnation. He is more easily identified as a modern terrorist and now has regenerative powers that can heal himself or, through a transfusion of his blood, others. He is an attractive villain with potential box office appeal for additional films compatible with the image of the *Enterprise* main cast as attractive, sexy young officers.

According to the *Star Trek: Khan* comic book series, Khan has not been whitewashed for the film; he simply has undergone a remarkable racial and physical metamorphosis to change him so completely that he might not recall his true past. As Admiral Marcus explains, "We opted for a Northern European look. Figured the further away we got from India, the better" (Johnson Chapter 5).

Khan's racial transformation also suggests that Roddenberry's vision of a future where white men are not the primary illustration of genetic superiority, for good or evil purposes, has been supplanted by pragmatic, "traditional" Hollywood casting. Perhaps, at least to some people, whitewashing an Indian character is less important than the diversity in casting the familiar characters on the *Enterprise*—gay actor Zachary Quinto (Spock); Zoe Saldana (Uhura), whose ethnic heritage includes parents from Puerto Rico and the Dominican Republic; Anton Yelchin (Chekov), whose parents immigrated from Russia; and South Korean–born John Cho (Sulu), in addition to white American Chris Pine (Kirk) and white Englishman Simon Pegg (Scotty). The concept of IDIC in casting villains or background characters now seems less important as a theme to attract idealistic audiences.

A more important fact in casting Khan may have been the increasing popularity of then-star-in-the-making Cumberbatch, whose success as Sherlock Holmes in the BBC television series *Sherlock* may have been considered as possibly bringing a new, young, largely female audience to the rebooted *Star Trek*. At the time he was cast, the then-unmarried Cumberbatch was often called "the Internet's boyfriend," which could also potentially attract ticket buyers who had not previously been *Star Trek* fans.

After all, the muscular, velvety voiced character in the form-fitting uniform could be considered even sexier than silver haired, chest-baring Khan of the 1982 film. The comic book series show Khan as a powerful man, and the photos display Cumberbatch-as-Khan in body-hugging attire to emphasize his buff body. Facial close ups emphasize Cumberbatch's interestingly shaped light eyes and sharp cheekbones, both features described in detail on some fan sites. The stills reinforce the image of Khan's physical strength and attractiveness promoted shortly after the film's release.

One illustration of Cumberbatch's and Khan's sex appeal used to promote the film is the ten-second clip, not used in the film, of Khan in the shower. The camera lovingly caresses Khan's naked, glistening torso. The clip was first broadcast during an interview with Abrams on Conan O'Brien's U.S. talk show *Conan* (Team Coco, "Benedict Cumberbatch Deleted Shower Scene"), and it soon became a fan-favorite Internet (especially Tumblr) meme or animated gif. When Cumberbatch later was a guest on *Conan*, O'Brien again played the clip, accompanied by brown cow (i.e., porn film-styled) music (Team Coco, "Benedict Cumberbatch on His Steamy Cut 'Star Trek' Scene"). The audience cheered and applauded while Cumberbatch looked more embarrassed than proud, which further endeared him to his fans. This sexualization of Khan helped promote the film and possibly deflect concerns about whitewashing or sexism against women, because Alice Eve's character disrobed in front of Kirk, and the camera's female gazing angered some viewers. Abrams, not Cumberbatch, reinforced the idea that this casting, in part because of the actor's sex appeal, is highly desirable and potentially lucrative. Whereas critics applauded Cumberbatch's ability to portray vengeance and menace, while also allowing the resolute Khan to shed a tear for his hijacked crew, many Cumberbatch fans simply enjoyed the sexier physical image of Khan being hyped on *Conan* and via online fan sites. The fact that Khan was played by Cumberbatch was emphasized in the media and especially on fan sites more than complaints about a whitewashed character.

Cumberbatch's positive reviews from film critics and his friendly but humble personality on U.S. talk shows to promote the film also led many to dismiss the film's whitewashing months before the comic book series published its first issue to legitimize Khan's new backstory. Cumberbatch's audience appeal, even as a movie villain, won over many viewers and muted the criticism about his character's changing face and race. Nevertheless, Khan continues to be cited as a whitewashed character, both on fan sites and in mainstream media articles reporting a history of whitewashing film characters (e.g., the *New York Times* 2016 article "Whitewashing, A Long History"). Whereas the film's actors, producers, director, and writers may not have considered Khan's casting as whitewashing a popular POC character, some fans and critics did and were troubled or outraged by this casting decision. For this portion of the potential audience, as *Geekquality* notes in the title of an article about whitewashing, "Yes, it really hurts" (Elyse).

Perhaps as a reflection of post–2016 U.S. election politics, which has often underscored a lack of unity among U.S. citizens and, unfortunately, has encouraged an increase in online hate speech against non-whites, as well as people who do not share the same gender, sexual orientation, religion, or political party as the people posting messages, the CBS All Access *Star Trek Discovery* series has faced backlash *because* of its diversity in casting. As *Entertainment Weekly*'s James Hibbard reports, "There's been a rather ugly strain of criticism of *Star Trek: Discovery* online and it goes like this: The upcoming CBS All Access show's cast is too diverse for some of the franchise's longtime fans. The term 'white genocide' has been bandied about." In her reply to those complaining about the level of diversity in the series' casting, the "first black woman to lead a *Trek* cast," Sonequa Martin-Green, encourages viewers to "key into the essence and spirit of *Star Trek* that has made it the legacy it is.... [W]e are all one.... That's something that *Star Trek* has always upheld." Furthermore, she suggests that viewers look beyond social conditioning and their opinions to see what *Discovery* is doing: "telling a story about humanity that will hopefully bring us all together" (Hibbard). In light of this later backlash to *Discovery*, *Star Trek into Darkness*' whitewashing would be unimportant to the online critics of *Discovery* because it reinforces a belief in white supremacy—the very concept that Roddenberry fought against with his vision for *Star Trek*. Whereas *Star Trek into Darkness* is perceived as a setback to diversity—at least for many vocal fans—perhaps the subsequent shift toward greater diversity in *Discovery* (albeit not by Abrams and not on film) is one indication that Roddenberry's interpretation of the future is not dead and is needed more than ever.

Note

1. The author viewed the nine-minute Paramount trailer at the AMC Theatres in Altamonte Springs, Florida, in December 2012. It is not available online, but a similar description of Cumberbatch's Khan in this IMAX "special event" trailer is provided by Anthony Pascale at TrekMovie.com.

Works Cited

Anders, Charlie Jane. "The Real Problem with Benedict Cumberbatch's Villain Role in Star Trek 12." *Io9*, 3 May 2013, www.io9.gizmodo.com/5907467/the-real-problem-with-benedict-cumberbatchs-villain-role-in-star-trek-12. Accessed 26 Jan. 2017.

"Benicio del Toro Has No Regrets About Being Replaced by Benedict Cumberbatch in Star Trek." *Radio Times*, 8 Oct. 2015, www.radiotimes.com/news/2015-10-08/benicio-del-toro-has-no-regrets-about-being-replaced-by-benedict-cumberbatch-in-star-trek. Accessed 26 Jan. 2017.

Bird, Jonathan. "The Top 6 Star Trek Movie [sic]—From the Wrath of Khan to the Search for Spock." *Movie Pilot*, 18 Jan. 2016, www.moviepilot.com/posts/3741330. Accessed 26 Jan. 2017.

Buck, Stephanie. "Star Trek's Interracial Kiss the South Almost Never Saw." *Business Insider*, 22 Jul. 2016, www.mobile.businessinsider.com/star-treks-interracial-kiss-deep-south-almost-2016-7. Accessed 26 Jan. 2017.

Darius, Julian. "*Star Trek into Darkness* Hostile to Star Trek, Intelligence." *Sequart*, 20 May 2013, www.sequart.org/magazine/21469/star-trek-into-darkness-hostile-to-star-trek-intelligence/star-trek-into-darkness-poster-excerpt. Accessed 26 Jan. 2017.

Diaz, Eric. "Benedict Cumberbatch's Khan Returns in Star Trek/Green Lantern #2." *Nerdist*, 25 Jan. 2017, www.nerdist.com/Benedict-Cumberbatchs-Khan-Returns-In-Star-Trek green-Lantern-2-Exclusive/. Accessed 26 Jan. 2017.

Eames, Tom. "9 Pieces of TV Trivia That Simply Aren't True." *Digital Spy*, 23 Sept. 2016, www.digitalspy.com/tv/feature/a808786/9-pieces-of-tv-trivia-that-arent-true/. Accessed 26 Jan. 2017.

Elyse. "Hollywood Whitewashing (Yes, It Really Hurts)." *Geekquality*, 22 Mar. 2012, www.geekquality.com/hollywood-whitewashing/. Accessed 26 Jan. 2017.

"First Interracial Kiss on British TV Rediscovered." *BBC News*, 30 Nov. 2015, www.bbc.com/news/entertainment-arts-34869452. Accessed 26 Jan. 2017.

For the Love of Spock. Directed by Adam Nimoy, FilmRise, 2016.

Franklin. *The Trek BBS* [Forum post], 7 Mar. 2015, www.trekbbs.com/threads/why-did-people-complain-about-khans-white-washing-in-stid.266905/page-2. Accessed 26 Jan. 2017.

"Has Star Trek's Khan Noonien Singh Been 'Whitewashed'?" *American Turban*, 16 May 2013, www.americanturban.com/2013/05/16/has-star-treks-khan-noonien-singh-been-white washed/. Accessed 26 Jan. 2017.

Hibbard, James. "*Star Trek: Discovery* Star Replies to Show's Racist Critics." *Entertainment Weekly*, 22 Jun. 2017, www.ew.com/tv/2017/06/22/star-trek-discovery-diversity/. Accessed 11 Aug. 2017.

Leganda-Alcantara, Melissa. "Whitewashing: The Dark Side of Hollywood." *Live Mag UK*, 15 Jan. 2015, www.livemaguk.com/why-is-whitewashing-bad/. Accessed 26 Jan. 2017.

"Nominees." *Oscars*, 24 Jan. 2017. www.oscar.go.com/nominees. Accessed 26 Jan. 2017.

Pascale, Anthony. "First Impressions of Star Trek into Darkness IMAX Preview + J.J. Abrams Talks 'Darkness.'" TrekMovie.com, 9 Dec. 2012, http://trekmovie.com/2012/12/09/first-impressions-of-star-trek-into-darkness-imax-preview-J.J.-abrams-talks-darkness/. Accessed 11 Aug. 2017.

Shah-Williams, Hannah. "'Star Trek into Darkness': Benedict Cumberbatch Discusses Villain Reveal." *ScreenRant*, 20 May 2013, www.screenrant.com/benedict-cumberbatch-star-trek-into-darkness-interview-spoilers/. Accessed 26 Jan. 2017.

Shepherd, Jack. "The Great Wall: Matt Damon Responds to 'Whitewashing' Controversy, Calls It a F**King Bummer." *The Independent*, 10 Oct. 2016, www.independent.co.uk/arts-entertainment/films/news/the-great-wall-matt-damon-whitewashing-controversy-backlash-response-a7353551.html. Accessed 26 Jan. 2017.

Smith, Stacy I., Chouciti, Marc, and Pieper, Katherine. "Race/Ethnicity in 500 Popular Films: Is the Key to Diversifying Cinematic Content Held in the Hand of the Black Director?" Media Diversity & Social Change Initiative, University of Southern California, 2012.

"Star Trek into Whiteness." *Racebending*, 8 May 2013, www.racebending.com/v4/featured/star-trek-whiteness/. Accessed 26 Jan. 2017.

Team Coco. "Benedict Cumberbatch Deleted Shower Scene from 'Star Trek into Darkness' Scene—Conan on TBS." *YouTube*, 22 May 2013, www.youtube.com/watch?v=7LXKJ.J.S-eZI. Accessed 26 Jan. 2017.

Team Coco. "Benedict Cumberbatch on His Steamy Cut 'Star Trek' Scene." *YouTube*, 12 Dec. 2013, www.youtube.com/watch?v=_ROaS4WAq4M. Accessed 26 Jan. 2017.

White, Hanna. "The Race of Khan: Whitewashing in the New Star Trek Film." *BitchMedia*, 21 May 2013, www.bitchmedia.org/post/the-race-of-khan-in-the-new-star-trek-into-darkness-movie-0. Accessed 26 Jan. 2017.

"Whitewashing: A Long History." *New York Times*, 22 Apr. 2016, www.nytimes.com/slideshow/

2016/04/22/opinion/whitewashing-a-long-history/s/chow-ss-slide-E871.html. Accessed 26 Jan. 2017.

Zushi, Yo. "Why Hollywood Whitewashing Isn't Always Racist." *New Statesman*, 18 May 2016, www.newstatesman.com/culture/observations/2016/05/why-hollywood-whitewashing-isn-t-always-racist. Accessed 26 Jan. 2017.

STAR TREK MEDIA CITED

Foster, Alan Dean. *Star Trek into Darkness* [Film novelization]. Pocket Books, 2013.

Johnson, Mike. *Star Trek: Khan*. IDW Publishing, 2014.

"Plato's Stepchildren." *Star Trek*, season 3, episode 10, written by Meyer Dolinsky, directed by David Alexander, 22 Nov. 1968.

"Space Seed." *Star Trek*, season 1, episode 22, written by Gene L. Coon and Carey Wilber, directed by Marc Daniels, 16 Feb. 1967.

Star Trek Beyond. Directed by Justin Lin, Paramount Pictures, 2016.

Star Trek into Darkness. Directed by J.J. Abrams, Paramount Pictures, 2013.

Star Trek II: Wrath of Khan. Directed by Nicholas Meyer, Paramount Pictures, 1973.

Race, the Final Frontier
Star Trek, *Trump and Hollywood's Diversity Problem*

PENELOPE INGRAM

In 2016, discrimination and diversity were the buzz words in Hollywood. For the second year in a row, The Academy of Motion Picture Arts and Sciences had failed to honor actors of color. Of the twenty Oscar nominations for acting, including Best Actor and Actresses in Lead and Supporting Roles, not one person of color was named. This had occurred in previous years when there were no viable contenders, but in 2016 there were several potential nominees, including Idris Elba for *Beasts of No Nation*, Benicio Del Toro for *Sicario*, Samuel L. Jackson for *The Hateful Eight*, Michael B. Jordan for *Creed*, and Will Smith for *Concussion*. Similarly, the nominees for Best Picture included white leads and predominantly white casts. Neither *Creed, Concussion*, nor *Straight Out of Compton* received recognition in the Best Picture category. While *Straight Out of Compton* did receive a nomination for Best Original Screenplay, the writers of the screenplay were all white. The hashtag #OscarsSoWhite (which first appeared in 2015 when the director and star of *Selma*, Ava DuVernay and David Oyelowo, were overlooked by the Academy even though the film itself was nominated for Best Picture) trended on Twitter and drew attention to the lack of diversity in Hollywood and in the Academy. Just a few days later, with rumors of a threatened boycott abounding, Cheryl Boone Isaacs, the Academy's first African American president, announced that it would double the membership of women and minorities in the academy by 2020 (Jagernauth).

A few weeks later, J.J. Abrams announced that his production company, Bad Robot, would institute a diversity policy with the aim of increasing the number of women and people of color involved in his productions. Citing the Oscars controversy as a "wake-up call," Abrams declared that Bad Robot would work with its agency partner CAA, as well as Warner and Paramount "to ensure women and minorities are submitted for writing, directing and acting jobs for the company in direct proportion to their representation among the US population" (Ford, Ryzik). It's tempting to view Abrams's policy as his response to the "whitewashing" controversy surrounding his 2013 reboot, *Star Trek into Darkness,* which cast white British actor Benedict Cumberbatch as Khan Noonien Singh, a South Asian, brown-skinned Sikh, played by Ricardo Montalbán in both *The Original Series* episode "Space Seed" (1967) and *Star Trek II: The Wrath of Khan* (1982). But it's also interesting in light of the progressive casting of John Boyega and Daisy Ridley as the leads in Abrams's *Star Wars: The Force Awakens,* the long-anticipated sequel to the *Star Wars* franchise. *The Force Awakens* (2015) might even be viewed as a corrective to the Khan debacle, generating its own racial backlash and hashtag—#BoycottStarWarsVII. Rather than being too white, *The Force Awakens* was considered by some diehard *Star Wars* fans as anti-white, some going so far as to say it promoted "white genocide" (Griggs).

In 2016, Abrams produced the third installment of the *Star Trek* reboot, directed by Asian-American director Justin Lin and featuring black British actor Idris Elba in a lead role as the evil Krall. On the surface, this film appears to be consistent with Abrams's stated commitment to diversity. *Star Trek Beyond* includes the most diverse cast of all the reboots, and actors of color are given extended story arcs. Idris Elba's character Krall, who plays the lead antagonist, is central to the film's exploration of questions of identity and belonging. However, far from the progressive film it seems to be, *Beyond* reproduces some troubling stereotypes and can be seen to reflect the growing racial divide evident in the U.S. towards the end of Barack Obama's presidency. Indeed, rather than standing as a corrective to *Into Darkness, Beyond* can be viewed as its natural successor, extending the disturbing racial politics of that film. The whitewashing controversy wasn't the only one that beset *Into Darkness*; it also received criticism for its irresponsible celebration of urban terrorism, depicting an aircraft destroying a building. Instead of departing from these themes, *Beyond* continues them. But here the terrorist is a black man whose body is a biological weapon with the capacity to destroy the purity and uncontested superiority of whiteness.

The representations of both Khan and Krall go far beyond the well-travelled sketch of the terrorist frequently populating our big and small screens; rather they betray a palpable ambivalence about whiteness and blackness, and us and them, which mirrors shared anxieties about race in so-called post-racial America. Released in 2013 and 2016, respectively, these science fiction films provide a sort of road map for understanding that particular brand of white resentment and rage expressed by many who voted for Donald

Trump in the 2016 election (Painter). Operating as a form of popular fantasy, science fiction both imagines and projects our current social and political realities into a future time. Most obviously, science fiction attempts to articulate the anxieties people feel in relation to scientific experimentation and weighs both the benefits and costs to our current world and life, as we know it. In short, it offers a productive space to express cultural concerns about science and technology. Adilifu Nama and Isaac Lavender have recently argued that science fiction has a history of using alien difference to comment upon issues of racial difference. "Science fiction often talks about race by not talking about race.... Even though it is a literature that talks a lot about underclasses or oppressed classes, it does so from a privileged if somewhat generic white space" (Lavender 7). What's different about these two recent *Star Trek* films is that racial difference is not transposed onto alien otherness; rather racial difference is clearly marked as human difference, even in the case of Cumberbatch's lily-white Khan. The whitewashing of Khan has implications for our current moment that go far beyond the Hollywood tendency to cast white actors in roles written for people of color. It betrays a significant unease about the power people of color possess in a time when the U.S. population is expected to be majority minority by 2050. As a journalist covering the early day of the Trump presidency revealed in a recent interview: "[T]here's a kind of deeper cultural discomfort with the growing population of people who are not white in this country, coming from a kind of traditional white sense of propriety of what America is about ... and it's part of what's driving the more extreme elements of this presidency" (Bazelon).

#OscarsSoWhite and #BlackLivesMatter

It seems evident that the hashtag movement #OscarsSoWhite was attempting to reckon with more than the problem of racial diversity in the academy. Its use and popularity sprang from ground tilled by explosive racial relations between members of the black community, police, and the justice system, and should be understood in the context of the activism of the Black Lives Matter movement. The hashtag #BlackLivesMatter first appeared in 2013, after the acquittal of George Zimmerman for the murder of unarmed black teenager Trayvon Martin. Black Lives Matter became increasingly visible and assumed a greater political and public role as violence against African Americans escalated in subsequent years. In 2014, communities of color were reeling from the fatal shooting of unarmed Michael Brown and the riots that followed the acquittal of Brown's killer, police officer Darren Wilson. In 2015, racial tensions between African Americans and police escalated further. Freddie Gray was killed while being transported to a police station after the officers failed to restrain him in the police van, causing extreme injuries to his spinal cord. A protest in Baltimore after Gray's death turned violent, and a state of emergency was declared by the Governor of Maryland with the National Guard being deployed. Charges against the officers were dropped. In May of 2015, *The New York Times* reported that "sixty-one percent of Americans now say race relations in this country are generally bad.... The negative sentiment is echoed by broad majorities of blacks and whites alike, a stark change from earlier this year, when 58 percent of blacks thought race relations were bad, but just 35 percent of whites agreed. In August, 48 percent of blacks and 41 percent of whites said they felt that way" (Sussman).

That race itself was the story at the 2016 Oscars reveals a number of things about the cultural politics of the second decade of the 21st century. Specifically, that "post-racial" or "colorblind" ideologies so prevalent after the election of Barack Obama in 2008, are not only myths, but covert exercises of white privilege. The attempt to sweep race under the rug, by liberals and conservatives alike, demonstrated in the subtly aggressive #AllLivesMatter, speaks to a greater fear about racial presence. Racial difference, it seems, is too visible, too threatening, and needs to be contained. As respected sociologists and theorists Michael Omi and Howard Winant make clear, "colorblindness" is not race neutral at all; rather it is a tactic utilized by the dominant racial hegemony for the purposes of containment and redirection. "As hegemonic racial ideology, colorblindness has to be enforced, not only in the state policies and court decisions, but in popular culture and everyday life as well" (Omi and Winant 263). Conservative anxiety about whiteness and its ability to stay dominant was heightened by Obama's presence in the White House and his popularity among diverse segments of the population. In his book, *A Black Man in the White House,* Cornel Belcher measured the degree of racial aversion among Democrats and Republicans during the two terms of Obama's administration and found that:

> Not only did overall attitudes change over time, demonstrating heightened levels of negative racial attitudes during the Obama presidency, but individual levels of racial antagonism and opinions of the president varied by party affiliation over time: Democrats became increasingly racially positive over the course of the Obama election and presidency, while independents and, primarily, Republicans became significantly more racially resentful ... partisan racial polarization of attitudes remains and, indeed, jumped astonishingly among Republicans going into 2016, helping to explain Donald Trump as the nominee for the GOP [Belcher 26].

Americans' anxiety about racial issues crystallized during Obama's presidency and was articulated in a variety of guises; while Republicans have historically sought to limit the power of minority voting blocs through voter id laws, redistricting, and dog whistles to the alt right, a more subtle assault on racial equality was being waged in film and television.

Hollywood is adept at exercising covert racism. In fact, Hollywood is a reliable barometer of race relations and prejudices within the larger populace. #OscarsSoWhite was effective in that it drew attention to the fact that Hollywood in its hydra-like involvement in business, politics, foreign markets, etc., is not quite the liberal mouthpiece the right so often accuses it of being.

> Of the 100 most popular movies released in 2014, only 12.5 percent of the movies' characters were black, according to a study done by the University of Southern California—and that statistic correlates to every year since 2007. It isn't just that the Academy—which was hugely revamped in June 2015 to become more diverse (a self-imposed change, by the way)—is largely uninterested in stories they consider "other".... The Academy picked a largely white slate of nominees this year (and last year), because that's mostly all they had to pick *from*. Yes, #OscarsSoWhite, but #HollywoodSoWhite is closer to the truth [Gruttadaro].

This disinterest towards, or active rejection of, otherness provides a context for the recent Sony Pictures email scandal. In December 2014, exactly one month before the first appearance of #OSW, Sony pictures made news when the emails of two of its key executives, Scott Rudin and Amy Pascal, were leaked to the press. The emails revealed a number of racist comments the two had made about President Obama, Denzel Washington, and Kevin Hart. They also speculated on Denzel Washington's lack of box office bankability in overseas markets (Stedman).

Far from liberal, these racially reactionary products coming out of Hollywood reflect a backlash against issues of race, or at least a degree of what some have called "racial fatigue."[1] But importantly these films don't just reflect, they also construct and shape those views about race at home and abroad. Furthermore, overtly racist representations often appear in movies which don't have specific racial storylines. Science fiction has a long history of obfuscating race, as Edward James notes in his seminal essay "Yellow, Black, Metal, and Tentacled: The Race Question in American Science Fiction." It's the sleight of hand, the overt allegorization of otherness in fantasy and science fiction where racial tension is evident. Nama agrees, "For the most part, black characters are absent from SF cinema, yet their omission does not eliminate blackness as a source of anxiety. Churning just below the narrative surface of many SF films, blackness is symbolically present" (Nama 11). Furthermore, as the #BoycottStarWarsVII "white genocide" claims reveal, when Hollywood remediates this absence, the white backlash is swift and decisive. Donald Trump's upset victory in the 2016 presidential election and the subsequent resurgence of neo–Nazi groups speaking on college campuses and openly demonstrating against the removal of Confederate statues in Charlottesville, VA[2] and elsewhere reveal that polarizing and vitriolic views about race have entered the mainstream. Trump, who ran on a racially divisive populist-nationalist platform, appealed, in part, to conservative, working class whites who felt invisible in the political landscape of Washington and ridiculed by what they perceived as a discourse of liberal elitism emanating from the East and West coasts. As #OscarsSoWhite and films like *Into Darkness* and *Beyond* articulate, the assumption of the right that Hollywood is part of some out-of-touch liberal elite needs further scrutiny. Social scientists have long recognized that various forms of media reflect and reproduce social inequalities. Indeed, "the production, content, and consumption of media may be used to justify and encourage racist, sexist, classist, and heterosexist understandings of the way the world is or should be" (Sumerau and Jirek 72).

The recent *Star Trek* reboots reflect America's changing views on race and bear the scars of the recent race wars. These films need to be understood as exemplary of the social discourse of our time and recognized for the part they play in responding to and shaping our racial landscape. Interpreting and analyzing films like these make visible the work that allegories of race in film perform and the ideologies that they veil. These ideologies seem particularly crucial to investigate in the new franchise because of Gene Roddenberry's desire for *Star Trek* to reflect his own liberal views. As he said of his series, "*Star Trek* is my statement to the world ... [it] is more than just my political philosophy. It is my social philosophy, my racial philosophy, my overview on life and the human condition (qtd. in O'Connor 185). *Star Trek* of the 1960s expressed the "utopian passions of countercultural relativism." "Refus[ing] to impose its values on alien races," it spent its time "spreading the gospel of liberal understanding" (Rothstein). By contrast, Abrams's reboots reinforce a neoconservative world order where whiteness trumps all.

Into Whiteness

Many Trekkers were outraged when it was revealed that Benedict Cumberbatch was to reprise the role of Khan Noonien Singh in the second *Star Trek* reboot. Fans immediately reacted with claims of "whitewashing," a disparaging term used when white actors are cast for non-white roles in film. Whitewashing was a common device in the early days of Hollywood film, when white actors would don blackface or yellowface, or adopt ethnically stereotyped accents or gestures. Some of the more egregious examples include Laurence Olivier as Othello in the 1965 film version of Shakespeare's play; John Wayne as Genghis Khan in the 1956 movie, *The Conqueror*; and Mickey Rooney's hideous caricature of the Japanese I.Y. Yunioshi in 1965's *Breakfast at Tiffany's*. Whitewashing is related to "racebending," where the ethnicity of the character is changed in a remake or alternative media version (video game, etc.) of the original production. The website racebending.com was swift to condemn the whitewashing of Khan in *Into Darkness*.

Racebending.com has always pointed out that villains are generally played by people with darker skin, and that's true ... unless the villain is one with intelligence, depth, complexity. One who garners sympathy from the audience, or if not sympathy, then—as from Kirk—grudging admiration. What this new *Trek* movie tells us, what J.J. Abrams is telling us, is that no brown-skinned man can accomplish all that. That only by having Khan played by a white actor can the audience engage with and feel for him, believe that he's smart and capable and a match for our *Enterprise* crew [Sammy.

Into Darkness manages to perform whitewashing and racebending at the same time. Benedict Cumberbatch is a white actor playing both a white character, John Harrison, and an Indian character, Khan Noonien Singh. *Into Darkness* doesn't attempt to explain the illogic of this, but I think that the film's two narrative strands of terrorism and superhumanness explain why Cumberbatch has to inhabit two entirely different ethnic identities simultaneously. In episode 24 of *TOS Space Seed* (1967), we learn that Ricardo Montalbán's Khan is a genetically bred superman from 20th century India who was part of the Eugenics Wars on earth. He and his crew were cryogenically frozen and drifted through space until 2267 when discovered by Kirk and his crew. Khan is literally the greatest man alive. (Although Khan's crew are similarly engineered, he still assumes a position of power over them.) When Cumberbatch's Khan explains his unique abilities to Kirk in *Into Darkness*, the facts of his "breeding" carry a different resonance: the threateningly superior brown man is completely erased by the British white man. After Khan explains to Kirk that his intellect and savagery were exploited by Admiral Marcus, Kirk asks: "Why would a Starfleet admiral ask a 300-year-old frozen man for help?" Khan responds: "Because I am better." Kirk: "At what?" Khan responds: "Everything" (*Into Darkness*). From the mouth of the crisply British Cumberbatch, offering an emotionally wrenching performance worthy of the Royal Shakespeare Company, superhumanness gets tied yet again to Imperial British whiteness.

The sanctity and entitlement of whiteness saturates the film, from the depiction in the opening scene of indigenous white "primitives" and Kirk's hubris in breaking the Prime Directive of non-interference, to futuristic London of 2259 where a black man devastated by the debilitating disease of his dying daughter performs a terrorist act for the white mastermind. In the Faustian pact, the child survives thanks to the restorative properties of Khan's white blood, while the father must pay the price with his life. In this film, as in others of the genre, "[W]hite blood [is] presented as a means to cure and repopulate a diseased and dying world ... [and] draws on the dual racial eugenic propositions that not only is black blood a contaminant to white bloodlines but white blood is also considered a neutralizing agent for biologically dictated mental deficiencies in blacks" (Nama 49). Not only does

Khan's recasting from brown to white enhance this meaning, it's also instructive to note that the blood of the brown Khan, in both "Space Seed" and *The Wrath of Khan*, has no such lifesaving properties. Further, in the *Wrath of Khan*, it is Spock, the perennial other, who heroically saves the ship by sacrificing his life by locking himself into a radiation chamber. In *Into Darkness*, the heroics are left to Kirk, who does the same thing as Spock in the previous film, but rather than dying, he is brought back to life by Khan's blood. Here the symbolism of the transfusion takes on a different quality as Khan passes on symbolic superman properties to Kirk, reinforcing Kirk's natural "fitness" to lead the *Enterprise*. Furthermore, white Khan's transfusion of blood to white Kirk prevents any suggestion of miscegenation. For the "racial convention" of the one drop rule "is an integral part of the cultural politics of race in American society in which 'black blood' is viewed as not only a potent pollutant but also a fundamental element in assembling an essentialized racial identity for both whites and blacks" (Nama 43). Although Khan is not black, "brown" blood has historically carried the same stigma.

While it is not directly addressed, the question of the ethical use of eugenics or genetic engineering informs the premise of *Into Darkness*. In 1967 and 1982, when we learned that Khan was a product of the Eugenics Wars, the kind of eugenics that could produce a super human "species" like Khan seemed far off. Not so today, when we are capable of genetically modifying food; have the capacity to screen for and correct genetic deficiencies through somatic gene therapy; can transplant embryonic stem cells to repair any diseased or injured organ; and thanks to the completion of the mapping of the Human Genome Project, can identify which genes potentially control intelligence and how they might be manipulated. The possibility that a man like Khan could exist seems inevitable, if not now, in the near future. Part of the ethical conversation around genetic engineering involves equity and access to the new technologies, but these concerns usually refer to the disproportionate benefits that the wealthy would obtain from human improvements, such as designer babies with exceptional IQs. Here, however, in replacing the brown man for the white one as the perfect specimen of humanness, *Into Darkness* introduces a latent fear expressed by some conservative commentators about bioengineering. Could genetic engineering level the racial playing field, or worse, make whites inferior? Far from the state-sponsored sterilization and lobotomization of years past, the "new eugenics" threaten to enhance those whom society deems weaker or less intelligent. As conservative commentators like Francis Fukuyama, a member of George Bush's Council on Bioethics from 2001 to 2004, have noted, "Under this scenario it is entirely plausible that an advanced, democratic welfare state would reenter the eugenics game, intervening this time not to prevent low–IQ people from breeding, but to help genetically disadvantaged people raise their IQs and the IQs of their offspring" (81). Lest there is any doubt that Fukuyama is making a connection between race and low IQ, elsewhere in his book he endorses Murray and Herrnstein's controversial findings in *The Bell Curve* that up to 70 percent (Fukuyama says the rate is closer to 40–50 percent) of IQ is heritable and that African Americans are genetically predisposed to have lower IQs. Further, he sees these new technologies as posing a danger to the political world order of the twenty-first century, cautioning that such technologies "will change our understanding of human personality and identity; they will *upend existing social hierarchies* and affect the rate of intellectual, material, and political progress; and they will affect the nature of global politics" (174, 82 my emphasis). In other words, they have the potential to push the white West off its perch.

By transforming superhuman Indian Khan Noonien Singh into the genetically gifted, white, British John Harrison, whose blood self-replicates and rejuvenates life, *Into Darkness* removes the possibility that non-whites could be stronger, smarter, and better than whites. This rewriting should be understood as a form of "racial rearticulation," which is employed by a dominant hegemony that "cannot explicitly name, utilize, or exploit the race concept; instead, it is forced to exercise racial rule covertly.... This is a contradictory and conflictual situation, in which the racial regime simultaneously *disavows* its raciality and *deploys* it as broadly and as deeply as ever" (Omi and Winant 263). Understood in these terms, the whitewashing of Khan not only reinforces the association between whiteness and superiority that the casting of Ricardo Montalban as Khan disrupted, it offers tacit support to the kind of white supremacist narratives that fueled support for Donald Trump in the 2016 election. When Khan reveals that he will undertake mass genocide of any species he finds inferior, the cautionary tale is complete. In a eugenic race war, whites will prevail.

White Terror

The casting of a white Khan has considerably different implications, however, when we examine the film's terrorist plot. Damon Lindelof, one of the film's screenwriters, has said of the emphasis on terror in the film: "All that stuff was in the air and I think we weren't trying to make a sociopolitical statement when we wrote the story, but we just started gravitating towards those ideals because that's what was on the news" (Sacks). Here it would seem a brown actor would be the perfect vehicle to feed Western hysteria about terrorism and to demonstrate the purported interconnectedness of race and violence. However, according to Roberto Orci, the filmmakers were conscious of that association and were "uncomfortable demonizing anyone" on the basis of race. In support of this position, one critic argues that "by choosing a white actor, the film-makers decoupled Khan's villainy from his brownness—which was significant, especially in the light of Khan's terrorist attack on a skyscraper in the film" (Zushi). It's certainly the case that a white Anglo terrorist is less of a political hot potato than a brown one.

But it's curious if the filmmakers wanted to "decouple" brownness and villainy why they borrowed so carefully and obviously from terror events perpetrated by Al Qaeda and its affiliates, and more recent attacks by ISIS. Precisely because the film depicts scenes of urban terrorism like 9/11 and more recent attacks in London and Paris, these representations are always already racialized. We don't need a narrative about John Harrison's radicalization by Islam to understand the film is pulling from the cultural zeitgeist of terrorism waged by Islamic militants, especially when the terrorist is a man named Khan.

Within the first twenty minutes of the film a bomb has destroyed a top-secret Starfleet research center in London. This, it turns out, is a mere prelude to his larger attack on Starfleet, where Khan uses a jump-ship (helicopter like vehicle) to target a skyscraper and kill a majority of Starship senior command. He then escapes to Kronos, the homeworld of the Federation's greatest enemy—the Klingons—where he is in hiding. Kirk and his crew are given orders to launch missiles on Kronos and destroy Khan. In pursuing this line of action, the film is clearly drawing from and commenting upon U.S. policy regarding Osama Bin Laden, the architect of the attacks of 9/11. Before Admiral Marcus knows that Khan has escaped off world to Kronos, he makes a speech reminiscent of George W. Bush's avowal to capture Bin Laden "dead or alive." Marcus says, "In the name of those we lost, you will run this bastard down. This is a manhunt, pure and simple so let's get to work" (*Into Darkness*). However, when he finds out that Khan is hiding on the remote Klingon homeworld, he orders Kirk to deploy missiles to kill, not capture, Khan.

That *Into Darkness* is both highlighting and commenting upon U.S. policy, and the ethics of kill or capture, becomes evident when Spock finds out the true nature of their mission. Spock makes clear that it is his duty to "strongly object to [the] mission parameters" because "there is no Starfleet regulation that condemns a man to die without a trial." And then if the case wasn't clear enough, he argues that "Regulations aside, this action is morally wrong." "Captain, our mission could start a war with the Klingons, and it is by its very definition immoral" (*Into Darkness*). It is telling that it's Spock, the representative of otherness, who voices the moral objection to such treatment. And because Spock is logical and can always intuit the correct path, even when not successful, the moral high ground is his, at least temporarily. Reluctantly, Kirk agrees to Spock's demands, but as the plot unfolds, Kirk's capitulation to Spock's ethical qualms is shown to be wrong. Sparing Khan's life results in significantly more lives lost. While Roddenberry's vision "both championed, and dissented from, [the counterculture's] peaceful, anti-militaristic vision" (Rothstein), Abrams's vision is jingoism at its finest. Ethical concerns about the taking of enemy life, whether Khan's or Bin Laden's, are shown to be soft and foolish, while the view of the military hardliners is shown as correct.[3] This overt support of military ops, regardless of their legal or ethical cost, is consonant with the politics of the right and the "war on terror." Although, it was Obama's administration that found and killed Bin Laden, his military operations were often criticized as not going far enough, as being "soft on terror," or, in the words of Donald Trump, being "sympathetic to Islamic Terrorism" (Blatter, Stein).

Beyond Racism? Not Quite

Themes of racial difference and terrorism are also on display in the third reboot in the new franchise: *Star Trek Beyond*. However, the terrorist narrative shifts in *Beyond*. Whereas *Into Darkness* uses whiteness to try to avoid making a political point about race and terrorism (even though, as I've explained above, it does so covertly), *Beyond* goes one step further by transposing fears of Islamic otherness to African American otherness. This is homegrown terrorism, but the cause of radicalization is different. Far from being created by an evil other, Krall/Edison is a product of the Federation. A former soldier turned captain, Balthazar Edison and his crew were abandoned by the Federation. As the defeated, resigned captain states in the last entry of his log: "All distress calls unanswered. Of the crew, only three remain.... I will do whatever it takes for me and my crew. The Federation do [sic] not care about us" (*Beyond*). This backstory of a soldier discarded and forgotten by the military finds an analog to contemporary stories about soldiers returning home from war with PTSD and inadequate veterans' benefits. On this interpretation, his anger at the Federation (the U.S. government) is justified. But instead of following this narrative, and allowing a sympathetic reading of Krall/Edison, the film demonizes and others him, and uses his race to underscore that demonization.

It's significant, of course, that we don't know that Krall is Edison until near the end of the film. Our first impression of him is as a reptilian humanoid alien creature who attacks the *Enterprise* and literally sucks the life out of his prisoners. But it's instructive to see the ways in which the narrative of the film builds and develops a theme of unity and disunity, of us and them, which resonates quite differently when we learn that Krall/Edison is not a them but an us. When questioning Uhura as to why she sacrificed herself to save Kirk, he taunts her: "You think you know what sacrifice really means. Federation has taught you that conflict should not exist. Ha! But without struggle, you would never know who you really are." When Sulu tells him that he has "no idea who we are." Krall reveals his plan to attack Yorktown, "Millions of souls from every Federation world holding hands. It's a perfect target." Uhura challenges him: "You're wrong; there is strength in unity." To which Krall counters, "The strength of others, Lieutenant is what has kept me alive" (*Beyond*). And to demonstrate this he transfers the life out of two *Enterprise* crewmembers—one white, one black—to himself through a biotechnological machine.

When voiced by someone/something who appears so completely other to the humanity that Uhura and Sulu represent, these words support the idea of Krall's monstrosity. For here, he is othered not just in his species difference, but by his philosophical view of the world. And this incapacity to recognize their philosophy can be explained by his difference, his otherness. Why would this murderous alien subscribe to the same theory of liberal humanism, of unity, as they do? *Of course,* he has no idea who they really are! But this easy philosophical binary is troubled by the fact that he does know who they are. He *is* who they are. Or is he?

In Krall/Edison we get an unflattering reflection of the Federation. It's Edison's story, the solider left behind who did what he was supposed to do, protect his crew, and wait for his rescue which never came, that forces us to question the shibboleths on which the Federation depends. Indeed, the mantra of not leaving anyone behind is reiterated several times in the film. Scotty, in trying to encourage Jaylah to join them on their rescue mission, pleads, "Look that's our friends out there, Lassie. We cannae just leave them behind." Bones refuses to beam back to the ship with the majority of the crew until Spock, Uhura, and Kirk are present, exclaiming, "Damn it, man, we're not leaving without them!" Scotty comments to Jaylah that "You're part of something bigger now … we'll sure as hell never give up on you. That is what being part of a crew is all about" (*Beyond*). And he's right. They don't give up on her; in fact, Kirk, who consistently goes out of his way to save his crew, risks his own safe passage to the ship in order to secure Jaylah's return and her ultimate admission to StarFleet. This stands in stark contrast to Edison's experience, who, though "one of the first heroes of Starfleet," is never rescued.

But the possibility of reading Krall's/Edison's story as a critique of the Federation is withheld by the film as Uhura and Sulu are proved right. They will all work together to secure their rescue; Yorktown will be saved; and Krall's evil counter philosophy will be destroyed. However, what this simple resolution covers over is that it's not Krall that gets destroyed, it's Edison. For by the end of the film, the monster has devolved back to his human form and, dressed in his Starfleet uniform, facing Kirk man to man, captain to captain. Though his body is in human form, Edison's face is not the same; it is marked by Krall, or the traces of Krall. Narratively, this suggests that the evil is still within Edison and helps explain his desire to destroy Yorktown and provides justification for Kirk's destruction of him. But as the film's disclosure of Krall as Edison demonstrates, Krall never occupied the place of other. Krall was a product of the Federation. And the scarred distorted face that he wears in the final battle with Kirk is the outward manifestation of this betrayal by his own.

However, *Beyond* holds fast to the unassimilable evil and otherness of Krall. The reason that Krall remains effectively othered in the film, and why the sympathetic abandoned soldier narrative and the pointed critique of Starfleet don't prevail is because Krall is doubly othered. He is monstrous *and* black—what monstrosity is to Krall, blackness is to Edison. Idris Elba's blackness, (almost) hidden for the majority of the movie, contributes in definitive ways to the film's reading of Krall as evil and treacherous, and takes on narrative emphasis similar to Cumberbatch's whiteness. Nama has astutely noted that in science fiction, "The black body is a representational canvas coated with signifiers of alien unsightliness, danger, fear, social inferiority, and even transgressive sexuality that evoke a wide range of racial anxieties and cultural politics circulating in American society" (72–73). Just as Edison bears the mark of Krall at the end, retroactively Krall, too, is marked by a black body, and his struggles as an outsider left behind allow for a different reading when his race is taken into account.

Fight the Power

It is telling that Krall speaks only to Uhura, the ship's black communication specialist, about strength and unity. When Syl gives up the Abronath to save Sulu, Krall turns to Uhura and says, "Lieutenant, unity is not your strength, it is your weakness." She is insistent that there is strength in unity, and he is insistent that there is not. Where Uhura speaks of unity, Krall champions sacrifice and struggle. In their first encounter, he practically spits at her: "You think you know what sacrifice really means. Federation has taught you that conflict should not exist. Ha! But without struggle, you would never know who you really are." And in a later scene he reinforces this idea: "The world I was born into was very different from yours, Lieutenant. We knew pain. We knew terror. Struggle made us strong. Not peace. Not unity. These are myths the Federation would have you believe" (*Beyond*). Again, from Krall's mouth, these words highlight his difference and secure him squarely in the box of other. But, when Krall is revealed to be Edison, a black man born a century prior, the words take on a different reading. If we understand, as Roddenberry always intended, that the Federation is a representation for the United States, it's hard not to read Krall's/Edison's words as a critique of Uhura's racial politics, of her naïve belief in inclusion and colorblindness. Krall repeatedly ties his actions against the Federation to an act of resistance, even using the language of colonized, oppressed peoples to justify his position. As he makes clear to Uhura, "The Federation has pushed the frontier for centuries. But no longer. This is where it begins, Lieutenant. This is where the Frontier pushes back" (*Beyond*).

This reading is further affirmed in the music that Jaylah finds on Edison's ship. Both Public Enemy's "Fight the Power" and Beastie Boys' "Sabotage" figure in prominent ways in the narrative action of the film. Both songs are protest hip hop anthems which challenge establishment views and positions. "Fight the Power" was written for Spike Lee's 1989 film *Do the Right Thing*, which explored racial and ethnic divisions in Brooklyn in the 80s, specifically the ways in which the interests of minorities are pitted against each other; in this case, those of Italians and African Americans. "Fight the Power" functioned as the film's anthem and reinforced the sense of simultaneous racial disenfranchisement of blacks and their strong history of resistance. *Do the Right Thing* culminates in the murder by police of a black character, Radio Raheem, who broadcast the song "Fight the Power" from his boom box wherever he went. In our current climate where black lives are routinely terrorized and taken by police, the choice of "Fight the Power" as one of the key songs in the film is significant. First, it works to "fill in" Edison, to give more weight to his backstory, to tell us something about his politics, not just his music. Public Enemy was known as a "hard-core" rap group, which used its music to comment politically about the treatment of African Americans in U.S. culture and media. That Edison as the captain of the ship brought this music with him "colors" his statements about struggle and resistance, and situates them firmly within a narrative of black power, which is anathema to Uhura's assimilationist philosophy of unity. Second, the song works to further other Edison from the crew of the Enterprise. For the only person who appreciates the song (she likes the "beats and shouting") and perhaps the sentiment, "Fight the Power," is the unconventional Jaylah, who has the audacity to ruffle Kirk by sitting in the USS *Franklin*'s captain's seat.[4] By tying Krall to Edison's black roots, the narrative provides a tacit justification for his betrayal of the Federation and conveniently explains the need for Kirk, the white savior to vanquish him. As Edison makes clear in his final Captain's log, "You'll probably never see me again. But if you do, be ready" (*Beyond*).

Beastie Boys' "Sabotage" is also a protest song, lending further support to Edison's political views. However, in the film Kirk and his crew use the song against Krall to disrupt the swarm pattern of his drones. Sabotage here, far from being an instrument of resistance, is appropriated by the power to quell the opposition. And because the song is already linked to Kirk and his stealing of his stepfather's car in the first reboot, Kirk's use of the song and the recoding of the nature of sabotage is endorsed by the film.

Superhuman Blackness

Beyond, like *Into Darkness*, links anxieties about biotechnology to race. As I've argued above, in its rewriting of the genetically enhanced brown skinned Sikh, Khan Noonien Singh, as white British John Harrison, *Into Darkness* does not simply eradicate the threat the posthuman/superhuman represents to the human, it links that threat to people of color and the fear that they, too, will take over the white race. Teeming hordes of black, brown and yellow skins are revealed to be as existential a threat as the "skin jobs" of science fiction. The representation of this fear is particularly interesting in *Beyond*, where Krall devolves from a techno monster capable of drawing energy from life forms to feed his power into a black human male. The black man, it seems, is even more monstrous than the monster, scarred as he is by his difference and his hatred of the Federation who abandoned him. Krall's biotechnological cannibalism is the epitome of white fear—a racial vampirism that strengthens the black man by weakening the rest. But both *Into Darkness* and *Beyond* eliminate the possibility that raced bodies could inhabit superhuman perfection. Unlike white Khan, whose life-prolonging power renders him beautiful and virile and recognizably human until the end, black Krall/Edison's analogous power makes him monstrous and repulsive, a deformed freakish human at the end. Indeed, "[j]ust beneath the special effects, monster makeup, and futuristic narratives churn and bubble repressed racial conflicts, mythologies, desires, sexual impulses, wishes, and fears" (Nama 72). Contemporary science fiction suggests that these historic fears of the black body take on a new urgency in the age of bioengineering. Rather than dying a forgotten death, Edison chose to fight back by adopting the life-prolonging technology of the indigenous peoples of his adopted planet. And in doing so, he demonstrated the threat that advanced biotechnology represents to whiteness when placed in the hands of people of color. One bioethicist has noted that "'Genetic engineering' is now a slogan used to rally conservative and neoconservative forces against a godless and soulless science.... [C]onservatives, pro-lifers, neoconservatives, and even an odd crew of neogreen thinkers ... see the genetic revolution as holding the seeds of the degradation and destruction of humanity" (Caplan 58). In today's science fiction, racialized biotechnology, whether in the form of AI, cloning, or genetic engineering, operates as a twenty-first century version of scientific racism.

Both *Beyond* and *Into Darkness* link fears of biotechnology to raced bodies and terrorism. As Spock realizes, "Armed with this bio weapon [Krall] could rid [Yorktown] of all life and use the base's advanced technology to attack an untold number of federation planets" (*Beyond*). Whereas *Into Darkness* consciously avoided associating terrorism with people of color, *Beyond* reaffirms the connection. Krall/Edison attacks Yorktown because he wants to destroy the Federation's way of life. The name "Yorktown" carries double significance, here: strength by evoking the battle of the successful repulsion of the British by the Americans during the Revolutionary War, and terror by evoking the assault on "American values" represented by the terrorist attack on New York on 9/11 (particularly as Krall's aircraft crashes into the city). Krall/Edison's attack on Yorktown secures his position as un–American, or rather it demonstrates that his kind of Americanness, the experience of the disenfranchised minority, is dangerous and must be defeated at all costs. This is apparent in the final battle scene between Krall/Edison and Kirk where the competing philosophies of the two men are fully exposed. Kirk, obviously shocked by the morphing of Krall to Edison, asks Edison what happened to him. On hearing his name again, Edison admits that he's "missed being me" but has found his purpose, "the means to bring the galaxy back to the struggle that made humanity strong." When Kirk suggests that he "underestimates humanity," Edison angrily reminds him that he "fought for humanity. Lost millions to the Xindi and Romulan wars. And for what? For the Federation to sit me in a captain's chair and break bread with the enemy." Like Uhura, Kirk embraces a politics of assimilation, "We change, we have to, or we spend the rest of our lives fighting the same battles" (*Beyond*). But it's clear that to Edison such a politics fails to acknowledge the specificity of his struggle and the fact that the same battles need to be fought. However, here as before, the film pulls back from a sympathetic reading of Edison and instead connects his struggle for justice to violence. Kirk and Edison engage in a battle of good vs. evil, represented as white vs. black. When Kirk tells Edison to give up, Edison makes a pointed comparison between the two men: "What, like you did? I read your ship's log. Captain James T. Kirk. At least I know what I am. I am a soldier." Kirk, employing reason to Edison's passion says "You won the war, Edison. You gave us peace." Edison responds, "Peace, is not what I was born into" (*Beyond*). And with that, he resumes his efforts to vaporize Yorktown. Rather than explain his defection as a result of his abandonment by the Federation, the film chooses to base it in his preference for fighting over peace—and by implication, in his inherent unfitness to captain a ship. As the Admiral regretfully makes clear to Kirk, "For decades the Federation taught that he was a hero." When Krall transitions from the reptilian alien form to a black human form in a Starfleet uniform, the battle between Kirk and Edison takes on a Manichean dimension. When the good and noble white man fights the hateful demonic black man and wins, white superiority is affirmed. Kirk has the last word: "Better to die saving lives than live with taking them. That is what I was born into" (*Beyond*). And so, the struggle and defeat of Edison has strengthened Kirk's wavering purpose, demonstrating his ability not just to save his crew, but all of humanity.

While there are moments in *Beyond* where alternatives to hegemonic whiteness can be seen, the film entertains such possibilities only to rearticulate them in the service of the dominant power structure. Although such blatant racial coding would seem anathema to the long-standing philosophy of the *Star Trek* franchise, when viewed in the context of the racial politics of the Obama/Trump era, we get a better understanding of the racism expressed here. By tying racial fears to advances in biotechnology and genetic engineering, *Into Darkness* and *Beyond* engage in a new form of social Darwinism or scientific racism. These films reflect the fact that current concerns about biotechnology intersect with anxieties about race and help explain the new brand of populist conservatism underwritten by race hatred that is the "Trump phenomenon." If bioengineering attempts to "solve biological problems through the application of technology, including engineering at the molecular and cellular level" ("What is Bioengineering"), these reboots appear to suggest that racial difference is the biological "problem" that bioengineering sets out to solve, and in exploring the ramifications of this, arrive at some frightening conclusions. Both *Into Darkness* and *Beyond* expose a conservative fear that if biotechnology is not controlled, white people will be dominated by racial "others."

Notes

1. Urban Dictionary defines racial fatigue as "Tired of hearing about racial this and racial that."
2. On August 12, 2017, neo–Nazis and alt-right groups converged on Charlottesville, Virginia, for a "Unite the Right" rally which ended in deadly violence, and prompted the Governor to call for a state of emergency.
3. The plot to kill Khan is complicated somewhat by Admiral Marcus's subplot to sacrifice Kirk and his crew to the mission so as to avoid detection of his involvement in "weaponizing" Khan.
4. Jaylah is played by the Algerian actress, Sofia Boutella. The alien whitewashing of Boutella's brown skin has interesting implications for the larger race issues traversing the film. Jaylah is marked as other, not by her skin, but by her identification with Edison's protest music. However, unlike Edison, she *is* rescued by the crew and finds a home with them, suggesting that her form of rebelliousness will be contained.

Works Cited

Bazelon, Emily. Interview with Terry Gross. *Fresh Air*, 9 Mar. 2017, http://www.npr.org/2017/03/09/519415023/what-is-steve-bannon-and-jeff-sessions-shared-vision-for-remaking-america.
Beastie Boys. "Sabotage." *Ill Communication*. Recorded 1994. Capital Records.
Belcher, Cornell. *A Black Man in the White House: Barack Obama and the Triggering of America's Racial-Aversion Crisis*. Uptown Professional Press, 2016.

Blatter, Emily. "Mark Levin: Obama Is 'Soft on Terrorism.'" *CNSNews*, 20 Jun. 2016, http://www.cnsnews.com/commentary/emily-blatter/mark-levin-obama-soft-terrorism.

Caplan, Arthur L. "Revulsion Is Not Enough." *American Journal of Bioethics*, vol. 2, no. 3, 2002, pp. 57–61.

Do the Right Thing. Directed by Spike Lee, 40 Acres & A Mule Filmworks, 1989.

Ford, Rebecca. "Hollywood's Casting Blitz: It's All About Diversity in the Wake of #Oscars sowhite." *Hollywood Reporter*, 2 Mar. 2016, http://www.hollywoodreporter.com/news/oscarssowhite-spurs-diversity-casting-boom-872005.

Fukuyama, Francis. *Our Posthuman Future: Consequences of the Biotechnology Revolution*. Picador, 2003.

Griggs, Brandon. "Internet Trolls Call New 'Star Wars' Movie 'Anti-White.'" *CNN*, http://www.cnn.com/2015/10/20/entertainment/star-wars-trailer-boycott-anti-white-feat/index.html.

Gruttadaro, Andrew. "No POC Deserved to Be Nominated for an Oscar This Year (But That's Not the Point)." *Complex*, 15 Jan. 2016, http://uk.complex.com/pop-culture/2016/01/oscars-so-white-2016.

Jagernauth, Kevin. "Academy Pledges to Double Women and Minority Members by 2020." Indiewire. *IndieWire*, 22 Jan. 2016, http://www.indiewire.com/2016/01/academy-pledges-to-double-women-and-minority-members-by-2020–88234/.

James, Edward. "Yellow, Black, Metal, and Tentacled." *Black and Brown Planets*, edited by Isiah Lavender, III, University Press of Mississippi, 2014, pp. 199–222.

Lavender, Isiah, III. *Race in American Science Fiction*. Indiana University Press, 2011.

Nama, Adilifu. *Black Space: Imagining Race in Science Fiction Film*. University of Texas Press, 2008.

O'Connor, Mike. "Liberals in Space: The 1960s Politics of *Star Trek*." *The sixties*, vol. 5, no. 2, 2012, pp. 185–203. Doi: 10.1080/17541328.2012.721584.

Omi, Michael, and Howard Winant. *Racial Formation in the United States*. 3rd ed. Routledge, 2014.

Painter, Nell Irvin. "What Whiteness Means in the Trump Era." *New York Times*, 13 Nov. 2016, http://www.nytimes.com/2016/11/13/opinion/what-whiteness-means-in-the-trump-era.html.

Public Enemy. "Fight the Power." *Fear of a Black Planet*. Recorded 1990. Def Jam Recordings.

Rothstein, Edward. "The U.S.S. Enterprise, in Strange New World of Museum." *New York Times*, 30 May 2009, http://www.nytimes.com/2009/05/30/arts/design/30star.html.

Ryzik, Melena. "J.J. Abrams Takes Steps to Lift Diversity in Filmmaking." *New York Times*, 3 Mar. 2016, http://www.nytimes.com/2016/03/03/movies/J.J.-abrams-takes-steps-to-lift-diversity-in-filmmaking.html.

Sacks, Ethan. "'Star Trek into Darkness' Political Themes Stir Up Controversy." *New York Daily News*, 22 May 2013, http://www.nydailynews.com/entertainment/tv-movies/star-trek-darkness-political-themes-stir-controversy-article-1.1351740.

Sammy, Marisa. "Star Trek: Into Whiteness." *Racebending*, 9 May 2013, http://www.racebending.com/v4/featured/star-trek-whiteness/.

Stedman, Alex. "Leaked Sony Emails Reveal Jokes About Obama and Race." *Variety*, 10 Dec. 2014, http://variety.com/2014/biz/news/leaked-sony-emails-reveal-jokes-about-obama-and-race-1201376676/.

Stein, Sam. "Donald Trump Suggest Obama May Be Sympathetic to Islamic Terrorism." *Huffington Post*, 13 Jun. 2016, http://www.huffingtonpost.com/entry/trump-obama-isis-terrorism_us_575ea346e4b00f97fba8c1d7.

Sumerau, J., and Sarah L. Jirek. "Post-Apocalyptic Inequalities: Race, Class, Gender, and Sexualities in *Firefly*." *Race, Gender, and Sexuality in Post-Apocalyptic TV and Film*, edited by Barbara Gurr, Palgrave MacMillan, 2015, pp. 71–83.

Sussman, Dalia. "Negative View of U.S. Race Relations Grows, Poll Finds." *New York Times*, 5 May 2015, https://www.nytimes.com/2015/05/05/us/negative-view-of-us-race-relations-grows-poll-finds.html?_r=0.

"What Is Bioengineering?" Bioengineering Department, University of California, Berkeley. 25 Mar. 2017, http://bioeng.berkeley.edu/about-us/what-is-bioengineering.

Zushi, Yo. "Scarlett Johansson in Ghost in the Shell: Why Hollywood Whitewashing Isn't Always Racist." *NewStatesman*, 18 May 2016, http://www.newstatesman.com/Scarlett-Johansson-ghost-shell-whitewashing-racist.

STAR TREK MEDIA CITED

"Space Seed." *Star Trek*, season 1, episode 22, written by Gene L. Coon and Carey Wilber, directed by Marc Daniels, 16 Feb. 1967.
Star Trek Beyond. Directed by Justin Lin, Paramount Pictures, 2016.
Star Trek into Darkness. Directed by J.J. Abrams, Paramount Pictures, 2013.
Star Trek II: The Wrath of Khan. Directed by Nicholas Meyer, Paramount Pictures, 1982.

Star Trek *into Colonialism*

Bart Bishop

Khan Noonien Singh, in the *Star Trek: The Original Series* (*TOS*) episode entitled "Space Seed," preys upon the audience's xenophobia. If the half-Vulcan, half-human Mr. Spock is the "Model Minority," a positive example of his race, then Khan personifies the "Other," everything different from one's self. A North Indian Sikh superman resulting from scientific experimentation, Khan was a rare sight on 1960s television, even if Mexican actor Ricardo Montalbán was problematically playing outside his race. Regardless, it was progressive for an ethnic actor on television to seduce a white woman and lead a crew of diverse races who claim to be an "improved breed of human," a clever inversion of the Nazi *Übermensch*. That he is defeated in physical combat in "Space Seed" and then in a mental game of wits in 1982's *Star Trek II: The Wrath of Khan* (*WoK*) by Captain James T. Kirk, however, points to the white man still being the victor in the end.

Casting Benedict Cumberbatch as Khan for 2013's *Star Trek into Darkness* (*STiD*), the second in director J.J. Abrams's rebooted film series, has consequently been accused of "whitewashing," and the filmmakers' reasons for the change are ambiguous. Co-producer and screenwriter Roberto Orci's reputation as a "Truther," someone who believes the September 11, 2001, attacks were executed by the United States government to instigate a war, would indicate an ulterior motive. By framing Khan as a white "terrorist" actually working for Starfleet, this positions *STiD* as allegory. This modern focus on terrorism and inside jobs is also in stark contrast to the benevolent imperialism of *TOS*.

That imperialism was emblematic of American Exceptionalism, the idea that the United States' "values, political system, and history are unique and worthy of universal admiration," and "that the United States is both destined and entitled to play a distinct and positive role on the world stage," thus justifying its "Manifest Destiny" to proliferate (Walt). A product of Cold War sensibilities and fears, *TOS* encouraged containment and deterrence with the United Federation of Planets diametrically opposed to the Klingons, a veiled stand-in for the Soviet Union. Starfleet not only discouraged interfering with alien civilizations, abiding by the Prime Directive, but more importantly preempted Klingon intervention, with several episodes devoted to this brinkmanship.[1] This reflects the proxy wars between the United States and Soviet Union, including the Korean War and the Vietnam Conflict.

But if *TOS* is frontier life meets the Cold War and Kirk is John F. Kennedy, in 2009's *Star Trek* (*ST09*) and STiD the "Kelvin" timeline is the Wild West and George W. Bush in the wake of 9/11. The generational aspect is emphasized between George Kirk and Jim Kirk, with a resulting dynamic not unlike George H.W. Bush and his son. *ST09* endows Kirk with the best traits of Bush—namely the intrinsic qualities of his father endowing him with instinctual leadership ability—while erasing the negatives. *STiD*, however, subverts this by showing the young captain's shoot-from-the-hip attitude to be ineffectual against an earlier, more refined, distinctly European form of whiteness: Khan.

This is a fascinating reversal of the original character, from Other to colonial conqueror. The lily-white, British Cumberbatch maintains his accent, is introduced in London, has adopted the Western name of "John Harrison," and describes himself as "genetically engineered to be superior in order to lead others to peace in a world at war." That the character once ruled part of Asia and the Middle East—as the timeline parallels the original until *ST09*, although this is not mentioned, with Khan now described as a genocidal maniac—takes on very different connotations. He is now aligned with the once massive British Empire, which used "othering" to differentiate itself from those viewed as inferior in order to legitimize forceful expansion. Except in *STiD* he ironically refers to his own "savagery," indicating the filmmakers are rewriting history by applying this concept to a Western conqueror rather than an Eastern one. It's this savagery that Admiral Marcus (Peter Weller), who personifies the worst traits of the second Bush Administration, attempts to exploit, but Khan retains control. He manipulates a black man, Lt. Thomas Harewood (Noel Clarke), and the Klingons (represented by a single actor of African descent), and even his blood is superior as it both heals a sick mixed-raced girl and brings the inferior Kirk back to life. And unlike previous encounters, in *STiD* Khan soundly defeats Kirk, proving the former is a better white man.

A close reading of *Star Trek into Darkness* reveals that the recasting of Khan as a white man is a reframing on a character and thematic level, not just for him but Spock as well. No longer the Other, Khan is the Great Britain once known as "the empire on which the sun never sets" viewed through a modern lens that declares him the barbarian. This is Abrams and screenwriters

Orci, Alex Kurtzman and Damon Lindelof interrogating whiteness as superior, personified by American Exceptionalism with Kirk, who inherited his traits, and the colonialist, personified by Khan who was engineered as such. Both are shown to be outdated in the face of utopia, and their replacement is a different vision than Gene Roddenberry conceived. Spock, the stand-in for all minorities, sheds the Model Minority archetype by being intellectually and physically superior. By the end of *STiD* he has become the co-lead alongside Kirk.

Spock as the Model Minority

TOS envisions a future of peace and prosperity among all peoples. This meant the USS *Enterprise* was composed of an ethnically-varied crew including an African woman, Uhura (Nichelle Nichols), and a Japanese-American man, Hikaru Sulu (George Takei). They are, however, still captained by a white man, Kirk (William Shatner). Spock (Leonard Nimoy) as the First Officer is a Model Minority, "someone who assimilates into mainstream American culture by moving from a working-class status to a middle-class professional one," is "allowed to interact with a predominantly white American society," and functions "as a controlling image that denigrates another minority group" (Chan 51). In this case, that would be any alien culture not of the Federation.

The son of Jewish immigrants from Ukraine, Nimoy was decidedly Other to U.S. audiences at the time. He is the only visible alien main crew member on *TOS*, and is often a soundboard against the predominantly white male crew. Although logic-based, his culture has practices coded as primitive, pagan and/or exotic. For instance, the most well-known is *pon farr* from the *TOS* episode "Amok Time," in which Vulcans can satiate a blood fever only through mating or battle. There is also *Kolinahr*, a ritual in *Star Trek: The Motion Picture* (1979) in which all remaining vestigial emotion is purged. His "jet-black hair and steep slant of the brows, combined with personality traits that seem to align with model-minority tropes—cerebral, emotionless, skilled in unusual submission holds" also lend Spock an air of Asian mysticism (Haruch).

What heightens his Model Minority status, however, is his unfamiliarity with Earth culture, imbuing him with a child-like naiveté. This allows him to be a recipient of exposition and point out humanity's flaws. This is evident during the discussion in "Space Seed" providing context for Khan:

> CAPTAIN JAMES T. KIRK: [looking at a library picture of Khan on viewscreen] Name: Khan Noonien Singh.
> MR. SPOCK: From 1992 through 1996, absolute ruler of more than a quarter of your world, from Asia through the Middle East.

DR. MCCOY: The last of the tyrants to be overthrown.
SCOTT: I must confess, gentlemen. I've always held a sneaking admiration for this one.
CAPTAIN JAMES T. KIRK: He was the best of the tyrants and the most dangerous. They were supermen in a sense. Stronger, braver, certainly more ambitious, more daring.
MR. SPOCK: Gentlemen, this romanticism about a ruthless dictator is…
CAPTAIN JAMES T. KIRK: Mr. Spock, we humans have a streak of barbarism in us. Appalling, but there, nevertheless.
SCOTT: There were no massacres under his rule.
MR. SPOCK: And as little freedom.
DR. MCCOY: No wars until he was attacked.
MR. SPOCK: Gentlemen…
[Everyone but Spock laughs]
CAPTAIN JAMES T. KIRK: Mr. Spock, you misunderstand us. We can be against him and admire him all at the same time.
MR. SPOCK: Illogical.
CAPTAIN JAMES T. KIRK: Totally.

Often, Spock encounters prejudice from his own crew members related to his race. This is best demonstrated by Lt. Stiles's suspicion in *TOS* episode "Balance of Terror" that Spock is a traitor because of his resemblance to Romulans. There is also tension throughout the series and the movies because Dr. Leonard "Bones" McCoy doesn't fully trust Spock, lashing out at him in particular in *WoK* as a "green-blooded, inhuman…" before being cut off. In the same movie, Kirk says in Spock's eulogy, "Of all the souls I have encountered in my travels, his was the most … human." From the perspective of his crew members, it is better to be human than Vulcan.

In the rebooted series, however, Spock is now co-lead with Kirk aboard a much more progressive *Enterprise*. Although they are still outnumbered by humans, he is accompanied by many more visible aliens in this incarnation. Spock, now played by Zachary Quinto, is also in a relationship with Uhura (Zoe Saldana) that is both interracial and inter-species. And finally, the destruction of Vulcan by the Romulan villain Nero leaves Spock, as he refers of himself, part of an "endangered species," evoking any number of cultures that have faced diaspora throughout history.

In *TOS* and the related films, Spock was always a supporting character, "indispensable to the team—and its white male leader, for his intelligence and resourcefulness, but never really considered captain material himself" (Haruch). Even when he's promoted to captain in *WoK* he still defers to Kirk. Instead he was always one facet of Kirk's personality, the logical side, with Bones as the emotional side. *ST09*, however, introduces young Spock concurrently with Kirk, and the Vulcan is even briefly captain. In *STiD*, he goes on to win the day. As co-lead, Spock as minority avatar is no longer subordinate to Kirk.

Khan: Whitewashing the Other

TOS Khan, however, is an intriguing literalization of the Other, "a person or group who are different from oneself" that not only justifies colonization, but helps "the West define itself as a superior, civilizing force" (Mountz 328–329). As opposed to the *Enterprise* encountering an analogue for Native Americans or the Soviet Union, they find a bit of home out in deep space: the *Botany Bay*, containing 73 frozen war criminals. Khan, a genetically engineered specimen, not only is dark of appearance and a Sikh but also has a decidedly non–Western name echoing Genghis Khan, the 12th and 13th century Mongolian ruler. There's also the naming of Khan's crew members, who are only briefly seen but are purposefully multi-ethnic: Rodriguez, Ling, Otto and Joaquin. In that way, they mirror the diversity of the *Enterprise* crew, but with an ethnic leader.[2] The ultimate message seems to be that a crew of minorities needs the steady hand of a white man to keep them in line; otherwise they will go astray.

Even Khan's prowess is measured against his association with great white thinkers. In "Space Seed," Khan asks Kirk if he's read John Milton, leading to the captain quoting *Paradise Lost*: "Better to reign in Hell than serve in Heaven." In *WoK* Khan quotes *Moby Dick* twice, equating him with both the obsessive Swedish whaler Captain Ahab and the author Herman Melville. It also sets Khan in line as a dark mirror of Kirk, who quotes from Charles Dickens's *A Tale of Two Cities*. Khan's knowledge of literature puts him in the company of Western figures, implying that his ability to rise above his background is predicated on his becoming more Western.

On the conceptualizing of Khan for *STiD*, however, it is hard to deny criticisms of whitewashing, or replacing a character of color with an actor who reads "white." Whitewashing is when a white actor is cast in a non-white role. This was once common in Hollywood, as "[f]amous white actors such as Mary Pickford, Katharine Hepburn, Shirley MacLaine, Jerry Lewis, Peter Sellers, and Joel Grey have all been in 'yellow face'" in movies, a practice that involves "[t]he use of heavy, yellow cream, exaggerated accents, and heavy wigs [that] results in an inauthentic representation" (Larson 68). The same is true of black face with, amongst many others, Laurence Olivier in *Othello* (1965), and continues today with brown face in *Prince of Persia: The Sands of Time* (2010) and *Gods of Egypt* (2016). The key difference is Cumberbatch does not wear brown face as Khan, and is not modified at all. In fact, his only resemblance to Montalbán in "Space Seed" is the jet-black hair.

Orci and Trutherism

This drastic departure signals Orci and collaborators distancing themselves from casting any person of color in order to craft a "Truther" treatise taking aim at who they believe to be the real villains. Truthers is a term for conspiracy theorists who dispute the documented history of the September 11, 2001, attacks in which terrorists hijacked four airliners and crashed them into the Pentagon and New York's Twin Towers, leading to their collapse. There are LIHOPS, believing the government "let it happen on purpose," and MIHOPS, believing the government "made it happen on purpose," both allowing them to justify wars in Afghanistan and Iraq and a clampdown on civil liberties (Rudin). *STiD*'s 9/11 angle is emphasized by the closing credits:

> THIS FILM IS DEDICATED TO OUR POST-9/11 VETERANS WITH GRATITUDE FOR THEIR INSPIRED SERVICE ABROAD AND CONTINUED LEADERSHIP AT HOME.

But is this commentary on the popularly accepted account or a Truther's screed?

As extrapolated by film critic Devin Faraci in his article, "How *Star Trek into Darkness* is a Crypto-Truther Conspiracy Movie," Orci gained a reputation for his conspiracy theories on Twitter. This usually involved calling people that disagree with him "coincidence theorists" who chalk up inconsistencies in the official 9/11 story to coincidence. When this Truther context is, therefore, applied to the movie a subtext that is deeply cynical and counter to the original intentions of Roddenberry is revealed. As the movie unfolds, at first it appears John Harrison is an agent of Section 31, an intelligence agency comparable to the CIA, who has gone rogue. He "radicalizes" a Starfleet officer into blowing up a Federation archive that is actually a secret research facility. This is because:

> Section 31 is hidden in what appears to be a regular office building that also contains a very boring governmental facility, an archive in this case. World Trade Center 7, the building that Truthers believe was "pulled," housed an administrative CIA office on the 25th floor. Truthers claim that WTC 7 was destroyed in order to cover the tracks of those who orchestrated the 9/11 attacks, tracks that could have started in that CIA office, just as Khan's tracks would have started at Section 31 [Faraci].

Then Harrison attacks an assemblage of Starfleet command officers at their headquarters in San Francisco, only to escape to Kronos, the Klingon homeworld, putting him in the "Neutral Zone" where Starfleet cannot enter. Marcus orders the *Enterprise* to assassinate Harrison, but this is actually a ploy to instigate war with the Klingons. Marcus has been working with Harrison, who is revealed to be Khan freed from cryosleep because his superior intellect and barbarism give him an uncivilized advantage during civilized times. This plays into the Truther belief that the Bush administration was responsible for 9/11, with Marcus representing the worst conception of Bush, a leader that draws his people into war for what he believes is the greater good. As Khan explains, "I helped him realize his vision of a militarized Starfleet."

At this point it must be considered why the filmmakers believed a person of color could not work within this Truther narrative. Orci addressed the issue of the casting, saying:

> Basically, as we went through the casting process and we began honing in on the themes of the movie, it became uncomfortable for me to support demonizing anyone of color, particularly any one of Middle Eastern descent or anyone evoking that. One of the points of the movie is that we must be careful about the villain within US, not some other race [boborci].[3]

A person of color would perpetuate stereotypes of what terrorists look like, either Middle Eastern or similar. And that's the key: Khan is not a terrorist. He's secretly working for Marcus, and in order for the metaphor to hold, he has to be visually associated with Starfleet. Also, his victims are people of color. The Starfleet officer he radicalizes is of African descent, reflecting a multicultural future London, and the one Klingon seen without his helmet is played by a person of color. This is a choice for the Kelvin series of movies, considering this is the first and only time Klingons are seen, so this one actor and character represents all Klingons.

Klingons, the Soviet Union and People of Color

Menacing, conniving and bloodthirsty, the Klingons were originally an allegory for contemporary totalitarian regimes. "If the Romulans were given the militaristic philosophy and military virtues of Nazi Germany, the Klingons became obvious stand-ins for the Soviets," explains Ace G. Pilkington (55). Much like the Cold War, instead of outright war with Starfleet the Klingons would use smaller, less technologically sophisticated civilizations against their enemies. This is hammered home by "A Private Little War," an episode of *TOS* in which the Klingons and *Enterprise* arm "two opposing sides on a primitive planet in a ritual of one-upmanship which Kirk specifically compares to 'the twentieth century brush wars on the Asian continent'" (56).

As the franchise evolved, however, so did the Klingons. Always oliveskinned, by *Star Trek: The Motion Picture* (1979), their complexion became darker along with additional forehead ridges and prominent teeth, and by *Star Trek III: The Search for Spock* (1984) their costumes resembled feudal Japanese garb. Although mostly white actors played Klingons, that changed with Michael Dorn on the television show *Star Trek: The Next Generation* in

1987. *TNG* reframes the 24th century Klingons as warlike but honorable, resembling stereotypical Native American and African tribal cultures. Dorn, an actor of African descent, redefined the modern image of Klingons as belligerent allies. This is bookended by *Star Trek VI: The Undiscovered Country* (1991) depicting a Klingon moon exploding not unlike the meltdown of Russia's nuclear plant in Chernobyl. When the Klingons make peace with the Federation, it's reminiscent of the dissolution of the Soviet Union and end of the Cold War in 1991 and 1989 respectively.

The brief portrayal of the Klingons in the Kelvin series, consequently amalgamates prior versions. The Klingons are only mentioned in the first movie, and in *STiD* they are described in ominous terms before briefly appearing. As Marcus warns, "All-out war with the Klingons is inevitable, Mr. Kirk. If you ask me, it's already begun. Since we first learned of their existence, the Klingon Empire has conquered and occupied two planets that we know of and fired on our ships half a dozen times." This certainly hints at behavior similar to *TOS*. But instead of a massive empire standing against a conglomeration of planets, along the lines of NATO opposing the massive Soviet Union and satellite states, these Klingons are more like a Middle Eastern or African country invading neighboring countries due to petty tribal hatreds, religious disagreements, or outright greed.

When the Klingons are encountered in person, Uhura goes out to reason with them as only she speaks Klingon. This conversation is very formal:

> UHURA: I am here to help you. With respect, there is a criminal hiding in these ruins. He has killed many of our people.
> KLINGON: Why should I care about a human killing humans?
> UHURA: Because you care about honor. And this man has none. You and your people are in danger.

As mentioned before, this Klingon, the only one that removes his helmet, is played by a person of color, Sean Blakemore, and bridges the gap between *TOS* and *TNG* while adding variations. He has head ridges, but less pronounced, and is adorned with facial piercings. "They mark their bodies with victories, either with piercings or scarification," explains Neville Page, Lead Creature Designer for *STiD* ("The Klingon Home World"). This is much more like already mentioned uncivilized and decidedly non–Western tribal cultures. Correspondingly, Khan breaks up the conversation by laying waste to the Klingons with not just his strength but advanced weaponry.

There are connotations, as well, to Uhura being the one to speak to them. She is adept at communications, and in the first movie it is her understanding of Klingon that allows Kirk to warn of a Romulan attack. But a black woman being the only one able to communicate with a black man speaks volumes. This is especially true in Uhura's depiction as obdurate against the rational and logic-based Spock, her love interest.

Her brief encounter with the hypermasculine Klingon male is also coded with misogyny. The conversation does not go well, with the implication that he doesn't respect Uhura because she is a woman, as well as a human. All in all, in *STiD* they are a tribal, dark-skinned culture concerned with honor but sexist and prone to invade other civilizations, if only on a small scale, aligning them with the worst stereotypes of non–Western cultures. Consequently, the Klingons do not come across in a positive light, but as relatively inadequate compared to Marcus's Starfleet, representing the dark side of American Exceptionalism, and Khan's superior mind and physicality, representing old British colonialism.

American Exceptionalism

If the previous Kirk was modeled on the likes of Kennedy and Starfleet was inspired by NASA's "Space Race" with Russia to the moon, then the Kelvin Kirk is modeled after a very different man and very different times. Abrams's fast pace, humor, and bright, pristine aesthetic led many to draw parallels with the sense of optimism in the United States during the run up to and election of President Barack Obama. A closer look, however, suggests Kirk's personality and Starfleet's ideology are modeled on the self-proclaimed "wartime president" George W. Bush and his two terms in office. This Kirk is a cowboy who acts on his gut rather than advice from trusted confidantes.

In *ST09*, the former trinity of Kirk, Spock, and Bones is broken as Spock is now Kirk's rival, "captain for the majority of the movie, so he is issuing orders, not proffering advice," and Bones's advice is mostly ignored (McVeigh 202). This Kirk grew up in the shadow of his father, and comes into power after a catastrophic event: for Bush it was 9/11, for Kirk it's the destruction of the USS *Kelvin* at the hands of the *Narada*, a Romulan ship crewed by fanatics. Consequently, Starfleet is now described by Captain Christopher Pike as a "peacekeeping and humanitarian armada," emphasizing the militaristic aspect over exploration. The Romulan crew are also akin to fundamentalist Islamic terrorists in their shock tactics and use of untraditional weapons of mass destruction to wage all-out war. In this movie when Kirk says of the *Narada*, "Either we're going down ... or they are," the filmmakers are decidedly on his side.

The sequel, however, flips the narrative on its head in its deconstruction of Kirk. *STiD* examines the moral grey areas of responding to a post–9/11 world and evolves Kirk from the former Bush-inspired character to something more resembling the original, reconciling the two in the process. As Laura Ammon describes, "Key moments in the film address Kirk's transformation from a reactionary to trying to 'do the right thing,' even though he is not certain what that is—killing Khan? Bringing him to trial for his actions?—to a recognition that there are people whose lives are in his hands and therefore he must act with care." From the start, Kirk's previous certainty is broken down. He violates the Prime Directive by saving Spock in the opening and exposes the *Enterprise* to a primitive species. He lies about this incident on a report, getting himself demoted to First Officer, subordinate to Captain Pike, in the process. Upon his first meeting with Khan, he beats the man, who has surrendered, to no avail. This is in stark contrast to his physically besting Khan in "Space Seed." Kirk is repeatedly outwitted by both Marcus and Khan, and subsequently "moves from his position of utter certainty and faith in his instincts to strike back at Khan, to doubt and to the consideration of a choice between less than optimum options" (Ammon). In the end, he saves the crew through self-sacrifice, but is revived through the healing abilities of Khan's blood.

Kirk's American Exceptionalism is summed up by *STiD*'s opening: "It is, in one scene, everything imperial and colonialist about the *ST* universe: all the criticisms of *ST* and manifest destiny displayed in a ten-minute introduction" (Ammon). Kirk lures the natives out of their temple by stealing a sacred scroll that, when unraveled, forces them to their knees in worship. Presumably, even with a volcano threatening annihilation, they would not have left the temple without being prompted. Kirk tricking them into abandoning their backwards tendencies is not indicative of *Trek*'s former Manifest Destiny sympathies, as he and the *Enterprise* are not intentionally intervening in this culture. Instead, it's more a polemic against modern American intervention, as the sighting of the *Enterprise* leaves the natives irreparably changed. This is a provocative paralleling between the new versions of Kirk and Khan.

Accusations of American imperialism, after all, stem from the United States denying such claims. The Cold War had the U.S. occupying territories with the excuse of stopping the tide of communism. The crew of *TOS*, as formerly mentioned, were similarly in opposition to the likes of the Romulans and Klingons, operating as "an advance party, explorers to be sure, but also scouts, looking to identify the direction of the next attack or manipulate the shape of the next conflict" (McVeigh 200). But the Kelvin *Trek* is a product of modern American imperialism, the kind that bullies its way into countries like Afghanistan and Iraq to secure resources like oil, and leaves them destabilized in the process. It's revelatory, therefore, that the Romulans are now fundamentalist radicals and the Klingons are petty tribal aggressors. But the entirety of *STiD* is a deconstruction of Kirk's triumphant ascension in *ST09*, and consequently of modern American imperialism. Trumped by an older form of imperialism that, as Spock accuses Khan, "involves the mass-genocide of any being [Khan] find[s] to be less than superior," Kirk is supplanted by Spock.

Spock Triumphant

The climax of the film, therefore, is a confrontation between British colonialism in Khan and Spock breaking the Model Minority mold to become the co-lead. This functions alongside Orci's Truther subtext, as Kirk's attempts to defeat and Marcus's attempts to control Khan are impotent. If Kirk is an idealized Bush, then Marcus is the worst possible conception of the man. He can't, however, stand against the old-fashioned power of Khan's British analogue. That leaves Spock encapsulating the whole of oppressed minorities. The battle between Khan and Spock, therefore, is on four levels: genetically, intellectually, morally and physically.

On a genetic level Khan believes himself "better" at "everything," demonstrated by his ability to heal the mixed-race little girl from the beginning with his blood. Bones replicates the process, reviving a tribble and Kirk, proving both to be inferior life forms. None of the other 72 supermen is considered because it would be difficult to whitewash the entire crew. Spock, however, struggles to reconcile his dual heritages. This is foregrounded in *STiD* as he faces death in the opening and accepts it by overpowering his human emotions with Vulcan rationalism. But being mixed race is what allows him to defeat Khan.

On the one hand, his Vulcan mind is a step ahead of Khan and wins the game of wits that was previously between the Sikh and Kirk. Unlike this Kirk who ignores the advice of others, Spock seeks out council. He contacts the original Spock for advice, and by doing so is able to formulate an informed plan of action against his opponent. Khan has hidden his fellow crew members, whom he calls his family, in the 72 torpedo tubes that have been stored onboard the *Enterprise*. When he betrays the *Enterprise* and demands the tubes be transported onto his ship, it turns out Spock had the crewmembers removed, and detonates the torpedoes. Khan's ship is destroyed, and Spock outwits him not just intellectually but, in contrast to Kirk's struggle, morally as the crewmembers are spared.

In order to beat Khan in a physical bout, however, he embraces his human passion. Kirk's death sends him into a rage that propels him into the wreckage of San Francisco where Khan's ship has crashed. Fisticuffs ensue that are relatively evenly matched, but in the end Spock prevails. The old-world mentality, represented by the genetically superior white man, is defeated by the mixed-race Spock, and Khan and his crew are put back into cold storage. They are relegated to history, replaced by a very different future that embraces diversity of culture and genetics.

Counter-Point

The problem with this argument is Hollywood is just more prone to cast white. This is because:

> Even today many white viewers choose not to see films starring non-white actors or films set in minority ethnic environments, allegedly because they feel they cannot identify with the characters. Because of that fact, Hollywood tends to spend more money on white stars in white movies, and far less money on non-white actors in overtly racial or ethnic properties. The very structure of classical Hollywood narrative form encourages all spectators, regardless of their actual color, to identify with white protagonists [Benshoff, Griffin 80].

Abrams's first choice for the role, however, was the Mexican actor Benecio del Toro, so he was not completely ignorant of the character (Fullerton). Once del Toro passed on the role, however, there are many capable actors of dark complexion working in Hollywood today. A POC in the role of Khan could have been a great opportunity, not unlike Javier Bardem's acclaimed villainous performance in *Skyfall* just the year before *STiD*. Crafting a political message indicting the white men in power, a message that was more than likely missed by mainstream audiences, is a hollow gesture. Although it is at the expense of diversity, it is commendable, however, for a creator to articulate his or her perspective in a work of art, and it can't be denied that *STiD* is Orci's perspective.

Similarly, Spock as Model Minority finally coming into his own is good-intentioned but unfortunately backwards in its thinking. It's understandable that Nimoy's Spock fifty years ago would be used to make a macro comment on racial politics, but in 2013 it's an odd choice when there are multiple characters, from Uhura to Sulu, who actually are specific minorities. These characters hardly even interact with Khan, and have mostly inconsequential roles. Quinto is, however, openly homosexual, and it could be argued this lends his performance verisimilitude as he would understand being an outsider. The fact is, however, he is still a white man playing a character in a heteronormative relationship, so any related pathos is entirely subtextual. In the end, Hollywood is still locked into white as the default. It is within the spirit of the original series, however, for Abrams et al to sneak in such commentary within the constraints of the studio system.

Conclusion

And that is how J.J. Abrams and Roberto Orci insert their perspective into what they view as the racism and colonialism inherent in the original *Star Trek*. Kirk's containment strategy is replaced in *ST09* by a Bush-esque cowboy course of action, but that's undermined on two levels in *STiD*. First, there is the more classical, elite form of colonialism that the whitewashed Khan now represents. And Spock acts as a stand-in for the Model Minority. By changing Khan to ersatz terrorist and white man, accusations regarding the former can be avoided, but the nature of the character is altered. Whether or not this is intended by the filmmakers, he now evokes an earlier, as he puts it, more savage time that embraced a façade of civilization. Kirk's a lesser version of this Khan and thus fails. Consequently, only Spock, representing every oppressed nation formerly under the boot of the British, can defeat the living relic of antiquity with his representation of a different kind of diverse future.

Notes

1. Along with "A Private Little War" discussed here, there's also "The Trouble with Tribbles," "Friday's Child," and "Errand of Mercy."
2. In *WoK* the entire crew is white and predominantly blond. The character of Joachim, not to be confused with Joaquin from "Space Seed," is strongly implied to be Khan's son, and that would mean his mother is white. Still, more than likely, this is a symptom of Hollywood's tendency to default to white.
3. While Orci would occasionally comment on TrekMovie.com, after the fan backlash against *STiD* he stopped posting. In September 2013, he also deleted his Twitter account.

Works Cited

Ammon, Laura. "Where We Have Gone Before: Star Trek into and Out of Darkness." Implicit Religion IMRE, vol. 17, no. 4, 2014, pp. 379–94.
Benshoff, Harry M., and Sean Griffin. America on Film: Representing Race, Class, Gender, and Sexuality at the Movies, 2nd ed., Wiley-Blackwell, 2009.
boborci. Comment on "Into Darkness Open Week Thread + Polls." TrekMovie.Com, 25 May 2013. Accessed 3 June 2013.
Chan, Jachinson. Chinese American Masculinities: From Fu Manchu to Bruce Lee. Routledge, 2001.
Faraci, Devin. "How Star Trek into Darkness Is a Crypto-Truther Conspiracy Movie." Birth. Movies.Death., 11 September 2013, https://birthmoviesdeath.com/2013/09/11/how-star-trek-into-darkness-is-a-crypto-truther-conspiracy-movie. Accessed 24 September 2016.
Fullerton, Huw. "Benecio Del Toro Has No Regrets About Being Replaced by Benedict Cumberbatch in Star Trek." RadioTimes, 8 Oct. 2015, http://www.radiotimes.com/news/2015-10-08/benicio-del-toro-has-no-regrets-about-being-replaced-by-benedict-cumberbatch-in-star-trek. Accessed 28 Sept. 2016.
Haruch, Steve. "Mr. Spock, Mixed-Race Pioneer." NPR, 1 Mar. 2015, https://www.npr.org/sections/codeswitch/2015/03/01/389543692/mr-spock-mixed-race-pioneer. Accessed 29 Sept. 2016.
"The Klingon Home World." Star Trek into Darkness. Directed by J.J. Abrams, Paramount Pictures, 2013.
Larson, Stephanie Greco. Media & Minorities: The Politics of Race in News and Entertainment. Rowman & Littlefield, 2006.
McVeigh, Stephen. "The Kirk Doctrine: The Care and Repair of Archetypal Heroic Leadership in J.J. Abrams' Star Trek." Star Trek as Myth: Essays on Symbol and Archetype at the Final Frontier, edited by Matthew Wilhelm Kapell, McFarland, 2010.
Mountz, Alison. "The Other." Key Concepts in Political Geography, edited by Peter Shirlow, Carl T. Dahlman, Carolyn Gallaher, Alison Mountz and Mary Gilmartin, SAGE Publications, 2009.
Pilkington, Ace G. "Star Trek: American Dream, Myth and Reality." Star Trek as Myth: Essays

on Symbol and Archetype at the Final Frontier, edited by Matthew Wilhelm Kapell, McFarland, 2010.

Rudin, Mike. "The Evolution of a Conspiracy Theory." BBC, 4 Jul. 2008, http://news.bbc.co.uk/2/hi/uk_news/magazine/7488159.stm. Accessed 28 Sept. 2016.

Walt, Stephen M. "The Myth of American Exceptionalism." Foreign Policy, 11 Oct. 2011, https://foreignpolicy.com/2011/10/11/the-myth-of-american-exceptionalism/. Accessed 5 Oct. 2016.

STAR TREK MEDIA CITED

"Amok Time." *Star Trek*, season 2, episode 1, written by Theodore Sturgeon, directed by Gerald Fried, 15 Sep. 1967.

"Balance of Terror." *Star Trek*, season 1, episode 14, written by Paul Schneider, directed by Vincent McEveety, 15 Dec. 1966.

"A Private Little War." *Star Trek*, season 2, episode 19, written by Gene Roddenberry, directed by Marc Daniels, 2 Feb. 1968.

"Space Seed." *Star Trek*, season 1, episode 22, written by Gene L. Coon and Carey Wilber, directed by Marc Daniels, 16 Feb. 1967.

Star Trek (2009). Directed by J.J. Abrams, Paramount Pictures, 2009.

Star Trek into Darkness. Directed by J.J. Abrams, Paramount Pictures, 2013.

Star Trek: The Motion Picture. Directed by Robert Wise, Paramount Pictures, 1979.

Star Trek II: The Wrath of Khan. Directed by Nicholas Meyer, Paramount Pictures, 1982.

Star Trek III: The Search for Spock. Directed by Leonard Nimoy, Paramount Pictures, 1984.

Star Trek VI: The Undiscovered Country. Directed by Nicholas Meyer, Paramount Pictures, 1991.

Uhura and Linguistics of *Star Trek*

OLGA A. PILKINGTON

"Xenolinguistics. You have no idea what that means." This is the first reference to the study of language in the 2009 *Star Trek* film. It is an insult Uhura throws at James T. Kirk in response to his unsuccessful flirting. The second sentence is also a set up for an explanation to the audience, who, if they are real science fiction fans, already know the answer, just like Kirk does, "The study of alien languages: morphology, phonology, syntax."

While *Star Trek*, as a science fiction franchise, is bound to expose its fans to alien languages and the ways humans handle them, it also explains to the audiences what Linguistics as a discipline is and what a linguist might do—in the future and today. This popularization of the study of language is so successful because The Original Series as well as the new films have a compelling and believable character as a face of the Linguistics community—her name is Uhura. The character's expertise and linguistic abilities are not mere embellishments to the plot lines but essential components of the story world created by *Trek*. On the *Enterprise*, a skilled linguist is just as vital as an expert engineer and an experienced captain.

Nichelle Nichols' (and later Zoe Saldana's) character plays a double role: that of a popularizer of linguistics and an expert in one particular field. Both facets deserve attention since both represent established traits of the science fiction genre. The very presence of Uhura allows for an examination of the *Trek* universe from the point of view of linguistics in many of its manifestations, be it historical or gender linguistics, technology assisted translation or foreign language acquisition.

The reset of the *Star Trek* franchise (*Star Trek*, *Star Trek into Darkness*, and *Star Trek Beyond*) follows the long-standing tradition of science fiction in its fascination with linguistics. Mary Shelley, whom many fans and scholars of the genre consider one of its progenitors, called the art of communication and language use "a godlike science" (140). Shelley, through the character of Frankenstein's monster, described human speech in the following way: "a method of communicating ... experience and feelings to one another by articulate sounds" (139–140). Science fiction writers ever since have turned to the study of language and communication as a means of enhancing their stories and creating their characters. As Walter E. Meyers observes in his book *Aliens and Linguists*, "Communication, with language as its chief discipline, is centrally important to an enormous portion of science fiction, and crucial to its understanding" (1). Some writers even devoted significant time and effort to unraveling the basic linguistics notions for themselves and those who would follow them. Thus, L. Sprague de Camp produced a *Science-Fiction Handbook* (1953); the book covered the use of language among other advice and focused specifically on historical variations in English.

De Camp asked an important question that the creators of the Kelvin timeline films should also have considered: "What if your characters are 'really' speaking a past or future variety of English?" (253). The films do not show any variation from present-day English except for a few instances of new vocabulary that reflect the technological changes of the twenty-third century. This is very unlikely. At present, English is experiencing several grammatical shifts associated with the cultural changes happening in the majority of Western societies. For example, as gender roles shift and gender neutrality becomes more acceptable, English is introducing new gender-neutral pronouns that are increasingly preferred by people who do not wish to disclose their biological gender. These include *ze*, *per*, *ve*, and a host of others. The pronoun "they" has been gaining popularity and recognition as a gender neutral form as well. In fact, 2016 saw singular "they" declared the word of the year "by a crowd of over 200 linguists at the American Dialect Society's annual meeting in Washington, D.C." (Guo). A year earlier, *The Washington Post* officially changed its copy editing guidelines to accept singular "they." As Bill Walsh, "a *Post* copy editor since 1997" explains, "What finally pushed me from acceptance to action on gender-neutral pronouns was the increasing visibility of gender-neutral people." Walsh also acknowledged the linguistic changes that are coming in this area, "Trans and genderqueer awareness will raise difficult questions down the road, with some people requesting newly invented or even individually made-up pronouns." *The Post*'s attempt at standardization is just that, an attempt.

Linguistic norms take centuries to get established. De Camp in his *Handbook* mistakenly suggests that the speed of linguistic change will slow down in the future "because of the spread of literacy and world-wide intercommunication" (253), but the opposite has been true so far. That means there is no excuse for the writers of the *Star Trek* re-set not to extrapolate the linguistic shifts happening today. Science fiction itself is not a novice to explorations of gender neutrality and equality, and the writers would have been well within the bounds set by the genre. On the other hand, as some critics have suggested (see, for example, Ace G. Pilkington's essay in this volume), the new films are not primarily science fiction but adventure/action movies.

What the new *Star Trek* probably does get right about English in the future is its status as a planet-wide language. For this prediction, however, the writers didn't have to go far. Again, there are clear indicators in the present of English's dominance over other languages. Former colonies of the British Empire, countries and areas currently under U.S. control, and even the former republics of the Soviet Union all are establishing their own, distinct linguistic relationships with the English language. It has been common among linguists to talk about "Englishes" as an acknowledgment of the contribution that non-native speaking countries make to the English language. From here, it is not hard to imagine English as a planetary language. In fact, science fiction writers in the past have gone further and made English the language of the cosmos (in an attempt to solve the communication problem between humans and aliens). In *The Caves of Steel*, Isaac Asimov has Lije Baley remark that the English of the future is "the final potpourri that was current over all the continents, and with some modification, on the Outer Worlds as well" (266).

Star Trek Beyond (2016) demonstrates just how important English is to the future Earth. USS *Franklin*, which went missing about one hundred years before the events of the film take place, used English as its language of operation—a usual situation for Starfleet vessels. When it crashed on the planet Altamid, the ship's remains served as a home and a language school for Jaylah—an alien who was imprisoned on the planet but later escaped. Because of her knowledge of the English language, she is able to help the stranded crew of the *Enterprise* much more effectively.

While this development highlights the prominence of English as a planet-wide (and even perhaps Federation-wide) language, it does not take into account that the English Jaylah learned from a hundred year-old ship might be somewhat archaic. In fact, when, near the end of *Star Trek Beyond*, Uhura examines the USS *Franklin*'s videologs, there is no difference at all between the language spoken by *Franklin*'s Captain and the language of the *Enterprise*'s crew. Granted, the differences would not have been so great as to impact understanding, but they would be present.

The wide use of English, of course, does not mean that other languages cease to exist. And there are clear indications of linguistic presences other than English in the new *Star Trek* films. Scotty retains his Scottish accent, and Chekov uses Russian in emotionally charged situations. In *Star Trek* (2009), after succeeding in beaming out Kirk and Sulu from Vulcan (a complicated procedure since he has to capture them midfall), he exclaims "ё моё!"—

a rough equivalent of "oh, my!" His accent is so heavy we are to believe even twenty-third century voice recognition technology can't quite deal with it. When Chekov has to initiate a ship-wide broadcast at Captain Pike's command, he is having trouble logging in his authorization code because he pronounces "v" as a "w"—a common confusion of sound for a native Russian speaker.

Star Trek (2009) should get due credit for preserving languages other than English as valid means of communication (if only on a communal and intraplanetary basis). As Richard R. Jones suggests in his essay "Course in Federation Linguistics," the linguistic diversity of *Star Trek* is not accidental. It is part of the Vulcan idea "'infinite diversity in infinite combinations'"— an overall vision of the franchise (130). Generally, in science fiction, however, it is very common to suggest that in the future all people of Earth speak only one language. David Samuelson in his book *Visions of Tomorrow: Six Journeys from Outer to Inner Space*, blames the scientists for this development, "The wishful thinking which lies behind the science fictional assertion of one common tongue in the future is, I suspect, related to the scientist's desire to communicate across international or interlingual borders as freely with words as with mathematical and technical symbols" (cited in Meyers 21). This line of thinking, though, does not automatically equal English as the Earth-wide language since a variety of languages have assumed the title of "the scientific language" at one point or another throughout history, for example, Latin, French, German, and Russian. Out of the languages popular with scientists, only one, other than English, has been used in science fiction as a planet-wide tongue—Russian (Myers 21).

With the linguistic variety of Earth in mind, critics of *Star Trek* (2009) have suggested that it is unrealistic that Romulus—a planet of eighteen billion—would have only one language with three dialects (Bigham). We first learn of the Romulan dialects when Uhura gets to demonstrate her "unmatched" (according to Spock) xenolinguistic abilities on board the *Enterprise* as it is about to warp into a Romulan trap despite Kirk's warnings. Uhura is the only one on board, it appears, who can speak Romulan fluently. She relieves the current communications officer after he admits to not being able to "distinguish the Romulan language from Vulcan." Uhura confidently declares that she speaks "all three dialects" of Romulan. Outrage from linguists around the world ensues.

For instance, D.S. Bigham, a professor of linguistics at San Diego State University, suggests *Star Trek* (2009) is well within the established traditions of science fiction when it denies linguistic variety to creatures other than humans. He points out: "As you look at language-users in science fiction, from the Kzinti of Larry Niven's *Known Space* to the bugs of *Starship Troopers* to all the aliens in *Star Wars* and beyond, though they may command a vast space-faring empire across many cubic light years of territory and billions if not billions of billions of sapient speaking beings, they never seem to command more than a handful of languages."

However, we need to keep in mind the history of Romulus before passing any harsh judgments. Romulans and Vulcans are essentially the same species. Jones calls them "distant cousins to the Vulcans" (132). And in the "Balance of Terror" episode of *The Original Series*, Spock says, "Romulans are an offshoot of my Vulcan blood." In the *Star Trek: The Next Generation* episode "Unification part 2," Ambassador Spock tells Captain Picard that the two races have been "apart for centuries." That is hardly enough time for a host of new languages to develop on Romulus. This situation is similar to the colonization of America by the British. Centuries later, when the colonies have become the sovereign United States, the people still speak English, with very slight modifications and a handful of dialects. So Romulans essentially speak Vulcan. That is why the lieutenant responsible for *Enterprise*'s communications in *Star Trek* (2009) can say without major embarrassment that he cannot tell the two languages apart. This is also why everyone is impressed with cadet Uhura's abilities. Not only can she distinguish Romulan from Vulcan (which will probably be like distinguishing Russian and Ukranian or Belarusian), but she knows all three dialects of Romulan.

Bigham, on the other hand, offers more elaborate linguistic explanations. The first one is based on Chomskyan Universal Grammar. That is, all Earth languages share similarities because they all come out of a universal set of principles innate to each human. The same, presumably, applies to some alien languages as well. After all, "within the *Star Trek* universe, by virtue of shared biological history, humanoids have linguistic structures ... that are similar enough to allow communication to be possible" (Jones 131). And to us (as to Uhura), the languages of Romulus may well appear as one language with several major variations. In fact, Mark Lasbury suggests that "*Star Trek* takes a strong Chomskyan viewpoint" (189).

Bigham's other solution to the "three dialects" problem involves the research of "linguistic anthropologists Charles Hockett and Terrence Deacon, who believe that language ... is best described by ... its surface features, not its hypothetical mental structure. Along this line of thinking, if aliens have something we recognize as language ... then it's probably going to be a language much like any other, with arbitrary association between symbols and meanings." From here, Bigham suggests it is possible to argue that what Uhura means by "three dialects" is actually three distinct ways of exercising language. "Here on Earth ... we could say that we have ... two distinct ways of doing language—one auditory (spoken language) and one visual (signed language). Maybe on Romulus they've figured out a third way, like using touch, smell, taste, or another sense that humans don't even have?"

In fact, Bigham is not far from the truth (at least the linguistic truth of the *Star Trek* universe) in his second explanation. As Meyers notes, even if alien beings might have a communication system that "is similar to human speech," they might not use the same "method of producing that speech." He suggests that "their organs for phonation [production of sound]" may not always be "lungs and larynxes." Alternatively, the common voice production organs can be supplemented with other parts of the body to create linguistic meaning. For example, in the 1998 *Star Trek* novel *War Dragons* (#1 in *The Captain's Table* series) by L.A. Graf, Lt. Uhura comes across the Anjiri language, which she describes this way, "There's a detailed physical component to the Anjiri language.... The position of the body—and various body parts—in space can change the very definition of a word."

With all of Uhura's xenolinguistic prowess, the crew of the *Enterprise* still relies on the technology of a universal translator from time to time; however, we do not see Uhura herself use the device. The issue of the universal translator is complicated in the new films. It appears that it does not exist in *Star Trek* and *Star Trek into Darkness* but is used in *Star Trek Beyond*. In *Star Trek* (2009) the crew of the *Enterprise* repeatedly relies solely on Uhura's knowledge in critical situations, which would be unlikely had they had a universal translator. First of all, Uhura intercepts and translates a Klingon message about an attack in space. Next, she is the only one capable of scanning for transmissions in Romulan. Third, in *Star Trek into Darkness* she is part of an away mission with Kirk and Spock that encounters Klingons and has to negotiate with them using their native language.

In fact, the scene of Uhura's interaction with the Klingons is quite impressive. It allows her to display not only her linguistic abilities but also leadership and bravery. Even Spock does not dare to go against her ideas. "You brought me here because I speak Klingon," she tells Kirk, "Then let me speak Klingon." Kirk is not convinced that Uhura's talking with the Klingons will lead to the survival of the landing party and prepares some phasers just in case. Yet Spock is more resigned, "If you interrupt her now, you will not only incur the wrath of the Klingons but that of Lieutenant Uhura as well," he warns Kirk.

This scene embodies the aspirations that Nichelle Nichols had for her original series character. In her autobiography, *Beyond Uhura: Star Trek and Other Memories*, she reminisces, "One of my particular complaints revolved around who got to 'beam down' onto the planet. Considering that the communications officer was the sole crew member with a vast knowledge of alien languages and communications technology, you would think Uhura might be useful" (190). *Star Trek into Darkness* offered Uhura the very opportunity Nichols wanted for her character.

To return to the issue of the universal translator, it is unlikely that Uhura would not have used it at least as a backup in some of these life-and-death situations. Originally, as we see in the *Star Trek: Enterprise* series, the universal translator was designed not to replace a human linguist but to be a tool for a capable communications officer. It needed time to accumulate enough information about a language in order to be able to translate it, and it was incapable of translating alien writing that appeared on "control panels, hatches, and displays" ("Universal Translator"). Thus, it was never intended as a substitute for a human linguist and would not have undermined Uhura's characterization. If anything, the universal translator could have been used to showcase her linguistic intuition and technical abilities, as the device does in the novel *War Dragons* when Lt. Uhura has to adjust the translator manually to allow it to take into account body movements of the Anjiri as well as the sounds they produce.

In *War Dragons*, after explaining to Kirk "the inherent problem with all field-style translators ... that they're almost entirely dependent on audio and electromagnetic input," Uhura spends "more than an hour" modifying the device. The result is a "partially gutted" translator "nestled against the bottom of her tricorder, held in place by a wrap of wire and an umbilicus of data cables and conduits." Uhura was "letting [the tricorder] mate the audio portion from the universal translator to its own visual input to create a single English output, then ... reverse the process to take the English back into visual and audio Anjiri components."

Nowhere in the films does Uhura get to do anything similar. And when the universal translator appears in *Star Trek Beyond*, we do not see her interact with that technology. It is the alien Kalara whom we see as undeniably using the universal translator. When she first communicates with Kirk, asking for help, there is a dual audio—with English being spoken over her native language—an obvious use of the universal translator. Later on, when Kalara reveals her true traitorous nature aboard the crashed *Enterprise*, the translating device on her collar beams red as she speaks, again with dual audio. She does not bother turning the translator off when she communicates with her party and lets them know she got the artifact they are after. This is the most we see of the universal translator in use in the Kelvin timeline films. In the opening scene of *Star Trek Beyond*, Kirk is presumably using the technology to communicate with the Teenaxians, but we hear only English from both the aliens and the human. As Mark Lasbury rightfully points out, "So the audience sees the UT [universal translator] when it is an integral part of the story, and accepts that the UT is there and working properly when it isn't pertinent to the storyline" (169).

On some level, it is not surprising that it is *Star Trek Beyond* (the third film) that explicitly reintroduces the universal translator. Directed by Justin Lin, it is more in line with the spirit of The Original Series than the previous two movies and as such is more interested in the technological advancements of the future (for more on this, see Ace G. Pilkington's essay).

In fact, there are serious attempts being made to produce the universal translator, and several simplistic prototypes already exist. As Parker Wilhelm, a writer for the website *TechRadar*, points out, "Instant translation is quickly becoming commonplace. Skype has had its own on-the-fly translation software since October [2015], Google Translate can interpret text and voices across 37 languages, and Microsoft's voice translation mobile app ramps that number to 50." He also mentions a device called The Pilot, "a wearable produced by Waverly Labs, [it] is inserted in the ear like a hearing aid and then synced to an app. The device then takes in the speech of the other user and translates it instantly, resulting in the recipient hearing the original phrase in their native language." The downside, as Wilhelm notes, is that The Pilot requires two ear sets—unlike the universal translator of *Star Trek*, which works with only one unit.

The two-piece set is, very likely, the least of the problems that a fully functioning universal translator will need to overcome. As Mark E. Lasbury suggests in his book *The Realization of Star Trek Technologies*, "There are many components to language that must be recognized and analyzed in order to receive all the meaning" (170). If a universal translator is to become the fully and seamlessly functioning linguistic aid we see on *Star Trek*, it needs to be able to deal not only with the sounds but also with the brainwaves and physical appearances of the speakers. In fact, Lasbury's interpretation of the universal translator's technology supports a Chomskyan approach to language: "There are many universal concepts common to all intelligent life, including language. The UT tracks brainwaves of the speaker and teases out the common language aspects inherent in their brainwaves ... the machine's software then adds grammar to put the thoughts into a form the crew can understand" (170). This means that the universal translator would need to use "a non-contact form of electroencephalography (EEG)" (170).

In addition to getting the information directly from the brain, a universal translator needs to decipher nonverbal communication clues such as emotions, tone, level, etc., of the speakers. Nearly 40% of the meaning comes from "nonverbal and paraverbal communication" (Lasbury 173). Lasbury points out that the universal translators on *Star Trek* are capable of "kinesthetic ... and cultural pattern analysis" (173).

It might appear that a universal translator is just too challenging a technology to emerge yet. However, Lasbury proves that the technology necessary is here and it is not that complicated: "Twenty-first century engineering is managing the hardware/software matters with skill and innovation.... Current technologies for recognizing speech and text and for reproducing speech ... [are] amazing" (195). He even claims that a proper universal translator can be created without the help of artificial intelligence, "The software coding would be much more involved without AI, yet it could be accomplished" (195). The only problem that stands in the way is the nature of language itself. The idea of linguistic universals gets shattered from time to time as specialists examine newly found or newly decoded languages. What is inherent is that the patterns of language are extremely hard to generalize, and as Lasbury points out, just as in *Star Trek*, we will need the expertise of human linguists even when universal translators become commonplace.

The connections between *Star Trek* and linguistics, however, go beyond this optimistic message. The shows and the films are well known for their contributions to real-life science and technologies. *Star Trek*'s promotion, celebration, and ultimately popularization of linguistics as an academic discipline that will play a role in the future is not mentioned as often, yet it is paramount. The universal translator is just the most famous example.

Over the span of its various series and films, *Star Trek* has made contributions to several fields of linguistics. First of all, *Star Trek* is invaluable to sociolinguists. It provides a sample of language covering over twenty-seven years and a number of social changes. One example, is Jennifer M. Rey's study of male and female language in *Star Trek* and how it changed (along with gender roles) from 1966 to 1993. She came to the conclusion that the language assigned to the characters was "contrived" yet "relatively close to ... face-to-face conversation" (142). She also uncovered that the language of the female characters was more emotional than that of the males throughout the years, and in that way reflected the stereotypical gender roles of American culture.

Second of all, the study of artificial language has never been the same since *Star Trek* introduced Klingon. Its creator, Marc Okrand, went out of his way to use the most unusual existing language patterns. According to Dr. Tracy Canfield, a computational linguist and an expert in Klingon, that language uses the Object-Verb-Subject word order, while the Subject-Verb-Object is the most common syntactical order (This is what English uses, for example). "Klingon vocabulary is hard to learn because Okrand made sure it doesn't match any known language set" (Lasbury 194). Before Klingon, Esperanto was an artificial language that received a lot of attention—this hasn't changed—however, Klingon provided an example of an engineered language that does not embrace the conventions of the widely-spoken tongues. "Esperanto uses common roots and words from several languages and all the pronunciations are phonetic" (Lasbury 194). Kilngon has a fan base that creates a market for translations from Shakespeare into an artificial language. As representative nerds, Leonard, Sheldon, and Howard on *The Big Bang Theory* all speak Klingon and use it to play word games. *Star Trek VI* includes something of an in-joke about the popularity of the language when Chancellor Gorkon says, "You have never experienced Shakespeare until you have read him in the original Klingon."

The most important service, however, that *Star Trek* does for linguistics is popularizing the discipline and offering opportunities to talk about real linguistic theories and problems, as Bigham, Jones, and Lasbury do, for example. *Star Trek* allows for intelligent discussions about the origins of human language and its developments, the methods of translation, the role technology plays in linguistics, and many more aspects that for many non-professionals would go undiscovered if not for the *Star Trek* franchise.

The University of Arizona's course in general linguistics titled Meaning and Language in Society offers an excellent example. Professor Cecile McKee, who teaches the course, suggests that *Star Trek* (specifically the film *Star Trek VI: The Undiscovered Country*) can be an excellent gateway into such areas of linguistics as articulatory phonetics, for instance. She tells her students the story of how Okrand got involved with the franchise: He was "working at the National Captioning Institute when first hired.... His task was to make Vulcan dialogue that could be dubbed into an already-filmed scene where the actors were actually speaking English ... his challenge was to make speech that matched the actors' mouth movements but sounded so different that the audience would accept it as alien." This is where Okrand's knowledge of phonetics became very useful and where students get a glimpse into a more unusual practical application of linguistic knowledge (Everett-Haynes).

McKee is not alone in suggesting that *Star Trek* can help us "learn about linguistics." As Lasbury shows, *Star Trek*'s popularization of the theory of linguistic universals "impacts our space programs in real life" (189). In 1977 when space probes *Voyager 1* and *Voyager 2* were launched by NASA, they contained "two plaques and two records encoded with the sounds and imagery of Earth." Among the sounds, the records "represented more than 87 percent of Earth's languages" (Davidson 210, 307). The messages were sent to the stars "in hopes that a species with the ability to decode unknown languages would find and understand it" (Lasbury 189).

In its approach to language and communication, *Star Trek* is true to its overarching optimistic view of the future. We will meet intelligent aliens, and we will be able to communicate with them efficiently. In the process of creating this future, the contributors to the franchise sometimes do not take into account all the developments and existing knowledge of today's linguistics. They are punished unduly harshly for their mishaps by fans and language experts alike. However, it is important to keep in mind that *Star Trek* produced a significant segment of the general population that is interested in linguistics in the first place. It is an audience who otherwise would probably not care one bit about universal grammar, the linguistic sign, or the underlying principles of human language and would certainly not be interested in morphology, phonology, and syntax. The very "mistakes" that *Star Trek* makes allow linguists to introduce ideas and theories that would otherwise never appear in the pages or websites dedicated to laymen. *Star Trek* makes it possible for linguists to go where few language experts have gone before—into the hearts and minds of confirmed monolinguals—and, perhaps, recruit a few future experts along the way.

WORKS CITED

Asimov, Isaac. *The Caves of Steel*. Doubleday & Company, Inc., 1964. Print.
Bigham, D.S. "One Planet, One Language: How Realistic Is Science Fiction Linguistics?" *Slate*, 8 Sep. 2014, http://www.slate.com/blogs/lexicon_valley/2014/09/08/one_planet_one_language_science_fiction_versus_earth_linguistic_diversity.html.
Davidson, Keay. *Carl Sagan: A Life*. John Wiley & Sons, Inc., 1999. Print.
De Camp, L. Sprague. *Science-Fiction Handbook: The Writing of Imaginative Fiction*. Hermitage House, 1953. Print.
Everett-Haynes, La Monica. "Studying the Linguistic Relevance of *Star Trek*." *UA News*, 15 Mar. 2013, https://uanews.arizona.edu/blog/studying-linguistic-relevance-star-trek.
Guo, Jeff. "Sorry, Grammar Nerds. The Singular 'They' Has Been Declared Word of the Year." *The Washington Post*, 8 Jan. 2016, https://www.washingtonpost.com/news/wonk/wp/2016/01/08/donald-trump-may-win-this-years-word-of-the-year/.
Jones, Richard R. "Course in Federation Linguistics." *Star Trek as Myth: Essays on Symbol and Archetype at the Final Frontier*, edited by Matthew Wilhelm Kapell, McFarland, 2010. Print.
Lasbury, Mark E. *The Realization of Star Trek Technologies: The Science, Not Fiction, Behind Brain Implants, Plasma Shields, Quantum Computing, and More*. Springer, 2017. Print.
Meyers, Walter E. *Aliens and Linguists: Language Study and Science Fiction*. University of Georgia Press, 1980. Print.
Nichols, Nichelle. *Beyond Uhura: Star Trek and Other Memories*. G.P. Putnam's Sons, 1994. Print.
Rey, Jennifer M. "Changing Gender Roles in Popular Culture: Dialogue in Star Trek Episodes from 1966 to 1993." *Variation in English: Multi-Dimensional Studies*, edited by Susan Conrad and Douglas Biber, Routledge, 2001. Print.
Shelley, Mary Wollstonecraft. *Frankenstein: Or, the Modern Prometheus*, edited by D.L. Macdonald and Kathleen Scherf, Broadview Literary Texts, 1994. Print.
"Universal Translator." *Memory Alpha*, http://memory-alpha.wikia.com/wiki/Universal_translator. Accessed 27 May 2017.
Walsh, Bill. "*The Post* Drops the 'Mike'—And the Hyphen in 'E-Mail.'" *The Washington Post*, 4 Dec. 2015, https://www.washingtonpost.com/opinions/the-post-drops-the-mike—and-the-hyphen-in-e-mail/2015/12/04/ccd6e33a-98fa-11e5-8917-653b65c809eb_story.html?utm_term=.80b2a64b3c87.
Wilhelm, Parker. "This Earpiece Could Be the Universal Translator of the Future." *TechRadar*, 17 May 2016, http://www.techradar.com/news/world-of-tech/this-earpiece-could-be-the-universal-translator-of-the-future-1321563.

STAR TREK MEDIA CITED

"Balance of Terror." *Star Trek*, season 1, episode 14, written by Paul Schneider, directed by Vincent McEveety, 15 Dec. 1966.
Graf, L.A. *War Dragons. The Captain's Table: Books One Through Six (Star Trek)*. Pocket Books, 2000. Amazon Kindle.
Star Trek (2009). Directed by J.J. Abrams, Paramount Pictures, 2009.
Star Trek Beyond. Directed by Justin Lin, Paramount Pictures, 2016.
Star Trek into Darkness. Directed by J.J. Abrams, Paramount Pictures, 2013.

Star Trek VI: The Undiscovered Country. Directed by Nicholas Meyer, Paramount Pictures, 1991.
"Unification Part 2." *Star Trek: The Next Generation*, season 5, episode 8, written by Michael Piller, directed by Cliff Bole, 9 Nov. 1991.

All Talk and No Action
What's a Girl Gotta Do to Get Noticed Around Here?

TERESA CUTLER-BROYLES

"It is the modus operandi of myth to tell similar stories in a multitude of ways"—Kapell 217

Stardate 313650.8349

It's May 2009. Movie theaters across the country fill up, buzzing with excitement, expectation, elation, and more than a little bit of trepidation. Popcorn bought, seats found, everyone settles but for a slight murmur. The lights dim; the screen darkens. The requisite Paramount introduction sequence plays, and a profound silence settles over the theaters as house lights go dark and flashing lights whip by onscreen. Diegetic beeps and buzzes—sounds from within the story of the film, i.e., diegetic sound is that which story characters can hear—and snatches of conversation fade in, barely audible, filling the space of silence. The flashing lights resolve into a spaceship, recognizable as a Federation Starship. Its name, the USS *Kelvin*, flashes by just as a voiceover offers the same information. Less than three minutes later the ship is in dire straits: gravity isn't working, a mysterious vessel has appeared from nowhere, crew members are dying, shields aren't functioning, and the captain orders an evacuation.

Audiences were captivated, and while many were at this moment still reserving judgment, the first test was passed: at least it wouldn't be boring. But would it deliver on other levels?

From the beginning, Jeffrey Jacob "J.J." Abrams' *Star Trek* is adrenalin fueled, dark, and strangely confusing. At four minutes, ten seconds in, the

Kelvin's Captain Robau designates his First Officer, a Mr. Kirk, as Acting Captain and leaves him the ship. Captain Kirk. This situates audiences a bit. It's something familiar, a name they know, though die-hard Trekkers have no real clue about where he is or why he's there. But at least he's a Kirk. Approximately one minute later Captain Robau on the enemy ship is asked whether he knows Ambassador Spock, and audiences thrill. Another familiar name and a familiar face—the older Ambassador we last saw in 1991 interacting with *Star Trek: The Next Generation* (*TNG*) crew.

Yet, though audiences knew Spock, Captain Robau does not ... and when he states the date, 223304, Trekkers twitch. This is too early. The Kirk they know wasn't even born yet, and Spock certainly shouldn't be that old....

Moments later, this Captain Kirk's name is revealed: it's George, not James T. Audiences give a collective gasp, unsure where this new timeline is taking them—for surely that must be what is happening. This is all counter to the *Star Trek* canon, and yet the fast action and George Kirk's heroics keep most audience members in their seats. He holds the enemy off long enough for his wife to escape, and when she gives birth to their son amidst the chaos, they name him Jim and audiences stay put, drawn in by curiosity and, frankly, a desire to see just what Abrams would do with a James T. Kirk born in space instead of Iowa, in what is now obviously a new timeline with infinite new possibilities.

For countless viewers since the late 1960s, *Star Trek: The Original Series* (*TOS*) and its spin-offs, the overarching mega-text—"a relatively coherent and seemingly unending enterprise of televisual, filmic, auditory, and written texts" (Bernardi 7)—have functioned not solely as entertainment, but as both myth and social commentary. As a result, these 2009 viewers had high expectations of the Kelvin reboot; perhaps the most important was that the franchise would continue one of Gene Roddenberry's signature goals: to confront social issues. While the issues of 2009 were different from those that faced the world in the 1960s, since the beginning *Star Trek* has confronted viewers with their prejudices and fears while fulfilling its mission to explore strange new worlds and new civilizations ... going where no one had gone before. And even when this formulation of the original five year mission was revealed to be frankly imperialistic, fans of *Star Trek* were happy to overlook it so long as the continuing flights of the *Enterprise* and her fellow ships and their crews kept us entertained, visually and pseudo-technically stimulated, and at some level titillated.

One way *Star Trek* accomplished this was by offering viewers images that challenged cultural norms and asked important questions. The presumed devil-like connotations of Spock's ears were thought by network execs to be highly suspect; putting a Japanese helmsman on the bridge was highly controversial; and the gratuitously short skirts and revealing costumes of just about every female character encountered in space was if not exactly shocking in the era of the mini-skirt, an expression of the blatant sexist attitudes of the time. But perhaps none of those images was quite so powerful or potentially ground-breaking as the presence of Lieutenant Uhura, a black female communications officer played by Nichelle Nichols.

In a mid– to late 1960s America steeped in civil rights issues, Uhura was an in-your-face statement. She was a black, recurring, omni-present female character who was not subservient to those around her. Additionally, she was shown to be capable, respected, intelligent, and beautiful. All of which added up to something unfamiliar to the American television viewing public. Much has been noted about Roddenberry's insistence on placing a black woman on screen, and Nichols has been quoted relentlessly as saying that though she had few lines and was often frustrated, her decision to quit after the first season was reversed in a conversation with Dr. Martin Luther King in which he noted her vital role as role model for young black girls who were finally seeing a black woman on screen who was more than sex object, mammy, or entertainer. "You are our image of where we're going, you're 300 years from now," King reportedly said, "and that means that's where we are and it takes place now. Keep doing what you're doing, you are our inspiration" (Speigel). In large part it was this very dynamic that threatened many, predominantly white viewers.

For them, Uhura's role as a communications officer helped mitigate the impact of her physical presence. Yes, she was also capable of assisting on away teams, manning (!) the transporter in a clinch, helming the bridge when called upon, or performing pinch-hitter duties for others. She was beautiful, and while this was not made a factor in the way the crew interacted with her, she could be sexual when necessary—though only in pursuit of distracting others or while under the influence of alien control. She occasionally sang a song, and once or twice flirted with Spock. But ultimately her job was to listen, to translate, and to open hailing frequencies so others could speak— i.e., she was a mediator, a go-between, a conduit through which others could interact. A direct descendant of the ubiquitous telephone operator, hers was a traditional female screen role, calming potential anxieties of viewers who were unsettled by her physical reality, and she did not threaten the virility or ability of the male characters marked as white by whom she was surrounded.

Roddenberry's faith that in the future, humankind would overcome racial prejudice and sexist attitudes was admirable, and his attempt to make Uhura an important character went farther than anything on television at the time. While Roddenberry's testosterone-laden vision is problematic, as is the fact that it was white, or white-coded men who led the way to the stars. Nonetheless, his vision deserves credit for its attempts at inclusion in the 1960s. What he neglected, and what has continued to be problematic in the

Kelvin universe, is figuring out what this black female character would actually do other than *exist*. It's almost as if having a doubly-marked black woman on the bridge was enough; agency was secondary, and action was barely on the radar.

As noted elsewhere in this volume, *Star Trek: The Original Series* (*TOS*) ran for three years and 79 episodes, ending in 1969 just after the first actual landing on the moon by American astronauts Neil Armstrong and Buzz Aldrin. Throughout its 79 episodes *TOS* commentated on, critiqued, and contested the milieu in which it was created in areas such as: race relations in the U.S. and the burgeoning and continuing Civil Rights Movement; perpetuation of the continuing Cold War with Russia; the concurrent Space Race also with Russia and the rise of NASA as a key player in ongoing myth-making in—and the mythos of—the U.S.; and gender performance and sexist expectations of women.

Star Trek Producer Gene Roddenberry's vision for the future of his Federation was one in which prejudices, wars, hunger, and inequality of all kinds had been eliminated by humans and their allies. He saw the twenty-third century toward which the human race, and others, were moving as one of inclusion, equality, peace, and scientific superiority. The relative success or failure of this has been explored at length by Bernardi and others. He termed this vision "infinite diversity in infinite combinations," and the *TOS* crew was to some extent multi-racial, and certainly bi-species. It consisted of an American, white male captain (with a middle name of Tiberius ... how much more militant and imperial could you get?); a Scottish, white male engineer; an Irish, white male doctor; a Russian white male flight engineer; a Japanese coded-white male flight engineer; a half-human, half–Vulcan first officer, also coded white; and an African female communications officer.

In an America in the throes of the Civil Rights Movement with its attendant riots, upheavals, marches, and new laws, and in which black characters on TV and in film were typically written and portrayed as less-than their white counterparts, Uhura was a black woman in full view, part of a command team and, significantly, she was not a love interest, a victim, a maid, or a sassy, joke-telling entertainer. While she often was left out of the action, she was never demeaned, nor was there any overt note taken by her fellow officers that she was a woman, nor the object of their interest. Not so great for character development, maybe, but in terms of television and other media representations of beautiful women, a leap forward.

For the most part she stayed non-sexual. She projected virtually no come-hither vibe, and she dressed without cleavage and sans skin, aside from the no-more-than-other-female-characters revealing short skirt. There were exceptions. In "The Man Trap," the very first episode, she flirted just a bit with First Officer Spock while Captain Kirk was away, attempting to engage

Spock in a conversation about his home's romantic allure. In the second, "Charlie X," she danced and sang as Spock played the Vulcan lyre. In Season Three's "Plato's Stepchildren," she was dressed in an arm-baring shimmering purple dress with quite a bit of cleavage, and she and Captain Kirk were forced to kiss in what has been called the first interracial kiss on prime time television. (This claim is often made, but it turns out that the first one on American TV was either in the 1950s between Desi Arnaz and Lucille Ball, or in 1960 between two characters in the series *Adventures in Paradise*.) And in Season Two's "Mirror, Mirror," Uhura was transported with the Captain, Chief Engineer Scott, and Chief Medical Officer Dr. McCoy into an alternate universe where she was transformed by necessity into a midriff-baring distraction, playing a key role in the group's escape by keeping Mirror Sulu's attention with sexual advances and then a rough rebuffing of his subsequent response.

Throughout *TOS*, she had moments in which she showed her humor, her approachability, and her brains, but for the most part, Uhura acted as mediator, conduit, translator. That is, as her title would suggest, an expert in communications. Despite efforts to round out her role made by Roddenberry, the show's writers, and Nichols herself, she was not a complete character.

Daniel Bernardi posits that her presence was less-than, essentially "relegated to the spatial and narrative background for most of the episodes" (40) though it could be argued that in the context of the 1960s, and of science fiction at the time wherein black characters were non-existent or killed as a matter of course, Uhura's longevity was at least notable, even commendable. Her presence on the bridge and on television screens spoke in some ways for itself, and it certainly commented on social issues in the broader context. She was the one consistently visible female character in the series, and though she didn't get many lines in relation to her male counterparts, she got screen time.

However, ultimately Uhura's meaning depended in large part on those broader contextual issues for its power, and viewers understood her based on their own beliefs, understandings, and expectations; finally, her mere presence wasn't quite enough to make the intended statement. Despite Roddenberry's vision and admirable intentions for the series as a whole, Uhura quickly became one-dimensional. The message offered to viewers boiled down to: you can be black and female and competent, but you can't exist outside that rigid role. You can't have desires and hopes, or failures. You can flirt ("The Man Trap" and to some extent "Charlie X"), you can sing and dance ("Charlie X"), and under duress you can kiss the Captain ("Plato's Stepchildren"), but you can't have agency. Not really. Not the kind that allows you to do more than taste the possibilities of action.

In the series of *Star Trek* films that followed, starting ten years after *TOS* went off the air, with *Star Trek: The Motion Picture* in 1979, through *Star Trek*

VI: The Undiscovered Country in 1991, Uhura gets promoted from Communications Officer to Lieutenant Commander, then Commander. But these events happen offscreen; for the most part, the action on screen is effected by the men. She does get a chance to help rescue whales and she makes important decisions, but her role is essentially the same throughout: she is support, she translates and interprets language, she mediates.

Reboot

Enter J.J. Abrams and the 2009 film *Star Trek*, the one that rebooted the entire franchise. He offers us a new Uhura, now with the first name Nyota. (I refer to her as Nyota from this point forward to distinguish her from the pre–Kelvin Uhura. While this has echoes of the ever-present diminishment of women in power by referring to them more familiarly than their male counterparts, in this case the differences between the original Uhura and the Kelvin Nyota necessitate clearly differentiating the two.) This was an attempt to make her character more than just a token. Attempts were made to update her role in other ways as well, by rounding out her character and giving her a life before the *Enterprise*, a relationship with Mr. Spock, arguably the most desirable and certainly the most emotionally unavailable character of *TOS*, and a prominent visual presence onscreen. She is the third canonical character we see, after Kirk and (two incarnations of) Spock. This sets up a familiar triad, one that the franchise's slash fiction writers recognized and reacted to, many negatively (Scodari). In the broader fandom, her relationship with Spock has been discussed and arguments have been put forward that she might better have been paired with Scotty given their interaction in *Star Trek V*. However, as much as societal norms have changed since the 1960s, it is still more acceptable for American audiences to see a black woman paired with a half human/half Vulcan than with a white Scottish human. I return to this point later.

In any case, in the first Kelvin film and into the second, *Star Trek into Darkness*, Nyota and Spock are in a relationship, dealing as all couples do with communication issues and emotional tangles and misunderstandings. Not surprisingly, given her skills, Nyota susses out their problems and, through empathy and understanding, allows Spock space and time to figure things out. This story of course runs as a second plot through the larger one that involves life and death situations and the fighting of enemies, but Nyota's role as Communications Officer does not change. In other words, she slides nicely into the role Uhura has always had: she's background color, a bridge between beings who need to communicate with each other. And while it is her translation of a message that ultimately allows the new *Enterprise* to be prepared for its encounter with the Romulan Captain Nero, she is not the one who puts together the translation's import; that falls to Kirk to decipher and for Spock to support.

This pattern continues in the third installment *Star Trek Beyond*, directed by Justin Lin, even though this has been called the most feminist of the new *Star Trek* films (Truffaut-Wong). This is true only if you believe that one female character kicking some serious butt is enough to make a film feminist. And this has nothing to do with Uhura. The female character with serious skills is Jaylah, an alien with black markings on her whiter than white face. She rescues Scotty from certain death, transfixes Kirk and Chekov in a trap, and has technical skills that rival any trained engineer's. She is indeed formidable, and as the only other female role of import, her skills are important to note, but Nyota in this film is less prevalent, less vocal, less active, and far less relevant than in the first two Kelvin films. In one scene she chooses to sacrifice herself and thereby saves the ship, so to say she does nothing important is an overstatement. But sacrifice for others is less an active role than a martyr's, and even the villain asks her why she did it; her answer serves only to pay tribute to the valor of her superior officer—important for story movement and interrelationships, but not so much for her agency.

For this and other reasons, I contend that it is in this third film that the entire franchise loses its direction in an important way.

Assuming that one of the most important functions of *Star Trek*, second only to being entertaining storytelling, was and should continue to be to comment on social issues, Uhura's role is a nice window into how and why this disconnect occurs. To return for a moment to her relationship in this new universe, if indeed the fact that seeing a black Nyota with a Scottish Montgomery Scott would have been less familiar or less acceptable to viewers, then that is exactly what Abrams should have done. Viewers' comfort is not the best measure, especially when *Star Trek*'s legacy is at stake. And it was in the first few seconds of the first episode of the original *Star Trek* series that that legacy began, when viewers were introduced to Lieutenant Uhura. From the beginning, audiences knew that business was not as usual in the twenty-third century, and maybe it shouldn't be usual in their own, either.

Back to the Beginning

"The Man Trap" starts with a space ship sweeping majestically from left to right, in front of a planet in the near background. A Captain's Log voiceover establishes date and location; the unknown Captain is the voice of authority. As he continues speaking, noting that "on board the *Enterprise*" are people he's left in charge, an interior establishing shot presents the bridge of the ship that has just flown past, an assumption audiences would make due to film logic, specifically due to what's called the Kuleshov Effect. This effect explains that viewers will attach meaning to shots depending on how they are assembled. Or, in simpler terms, when one shot follows directly after another, viewers assume they're related.

The bridge is clean, primarily of three colors, red, blue and black, filled with blinking lights and a low-level hum, and three crew members. So far, while little is known about them other than that they are not the Captain and that they are on board the *Enterprise*, film logic again tells viewers more than simply those basic facts. Because viewers would have had no idea who these characters were, they would have looked to filmic language for clues to identity and importance, using mise-en-scène, cinematography and editing. Mise-en-scène is essentially everything viewers can see in a shot; cinematography is how the camera moves and captures the action; editing is how the various shots and scenes are spliced together.

Reading from left to right, a motif established from the first by the ship's motion across the screen, a viewer would see: farthest left and *closest to the camera* a black female dressed in a strikingly red dress seated at what looks like a command center; slightly behind her and partially eclipsed by her body, in a chair raised on a dais, sits a visually marked white male with pointy ears, dressed in blue to differentiate him from the others; and finally at the far right of the command center sits another white male dressed in red.

The voiceover continues, introducing the ship as the *Enterprise*, and Mr. Spock as the acting commander about fifteen seconds in. A cut to the pointy-eared man in blue makes it clear that this is Spock. While only he gets named at this point and the next scene goes to the planet, the positioning of the characters suggests that the woman (known soon thereafter but not yet named as the Enterprise's Communications Officer Lieutenant Uhura) is vitally important. In this relatively deep-space and deep-focus interior establishing shot, she features prominently.

To an audience in the 1960s, wherein fights over where black women were allowed to sit in public were recent history, and in which black students had less than ten years earlier staked a radical claim to equality by sitting next to white customers at a lunch counter, this opening scene proffered something remarkable. A brand new television show was taking big risks from the start by placing a black woman closest to the camera in a position of obvious power, her figure visually overlapping a white man's. The length of the take is just a few seconds but it resonated and was, and continues to be, significant.

After the close-up on Spock, the Captain's Log continues. The next person named is Ship's Surgeon McCoy, and as the Captain states that they are beaming to the surface of an ancient planet, three figures appear on screen, reverse-dissolving into corporeality. Again, reading left to right, the assumption is that McCoy is far left, in blue—like Spock—and the Captain must be the one in gold, and in the center of the screen. Audiences didn't yet know what soon became evident: the Kirk, Spock, McCoy triad is the main one, and Uhura fills out the fourth role. Scotty enters later. The story continues, mostly involving the three men and the people on the planet, but *Star Trek* with all its intended diversity and controversy was born.

Lieutenant Uhura is in almost every episode of the original series, and in the following six films that dealt with the original crew and their adventures. (*Star Trek: The Motion Picture, Star Trek II: The Wrath of Khan, Star Trek III: The Search for Spock, Star Trek IV: The Voyage Home, Star Trek V: The Final Frontier, Star Trek VI: The Undiscovered Country*.) As noted earlier, though she gets less action than her male, white-coded characters, she is present, she participates, she gets promoted (off-screen) and she endures.

Warp Speed Ahead, Fifty Years. Enter J.J. Abrams.

As described earlier in this essay, in 2009 Abrams killed George Kirk in the first ten minutes of *Star Trek*, essentially breaking the Prime timeline and birthing a new trajectory at the same moment as a newly positioned James T. Kirk came into the world. This new trajectory offered exciting possibilities for character development. No longer constrained by the facts or events of the Prime universe, writers Roberto Orci and Alex Kurtzman, and director Abrams, arguably gave the main characters more depth, more back-story, more reasons for their actions, more emotional range, and consequently more connections with each other.

This essay opened with a quick look at the first ten minutes of the 2009 *Star Trek*. The next ten minutes offer viewers a young James T and a young Spock in their respective worlds, with enough information imparted to understand their relative positions and attitudes, and feel comfortable with these new versions of familiar characters. A young-twenties version of Spock is shown deciding to enter Starfleet Academy.

At almost exactly twenty minutes into the film, a similarly-aged Nyota arrives onscreen. As befits a young cadet studying xenolinguistics at an elite academy, she is obviously intelligent, she banters with the handsome young man at the bar who introduces himself as Jim Kirk—not an Academy student—and she is shown as a well-known, well-liked individual in the bar in which they find themselves. When she introduces herself as "just Uhura" a running joke is established that nods toward the Prime universe, and the fact that she never actually had a first name before is made starkly clear.

Immediately thereafter she tells Kirk her name is Nyota, differentiating her in an essential way from the Prime version of herself. Star Trek blogs and fan sites offer the translation Star or Freedom as the meaning of Nyota in Swahili, while many baby name sites say Warrior is the translation. Character names are the subject of a forthcoming essay that specifically asks and attempts to answer the question: why do ethnically coded characters' names so often mean something? For instance, Penda, another contender for Uhura's first name, means *loved*. But Tiberius—Captain Kirk's middle name—doesn't mean anything. It refers to a Roman emperor and possibly also to a Roman general; Kirk is named after a historic figure, Uhura is named after a concept. This new Nyota is more than her predecessor. She is a realized person, the name intimates, not a token. However, she is not given a new back story; viewers learn nothing of her life before this moment, as they did of Kirk and Spock. And why would they? This new timeline only affects her once she comes into contact with the two of them at Starfleet Academy.

Significantly, again using filmic language, she is the third canonical character audiences see. Arguably, Spock's parents are canonical, and the first twenty minutes does offer them onscreen. In terms of the *Enterprise*, however, and the formation of the *TOS* crew, they matter less than Kirk, Spock, and Uhura. The next is Christopher Pike in a nod to the Prime universe, and the next, Leonard McCoy, the fourth crewmember of *TOS Enterprise*, and we assume, in this new universe, too. Characters, situations, running jokes, plots, underlying issues all show up in new form in the Kelvin universe. Without taking away from the experience of anyone who doesn't know the Prime universe and its stories well, these moments give those of us who might be considered Trekkers / Trekkies recurring moments of delight.

Essentially the Kelvin universe has set up the same configuration of main characters who were offered in "The Man Trap." The difference is that this new Nyota, despite the demotion in terms of her order of arrival onscreen, already has more screen presence, more personality, more attitude, and more sense of self than she was ever allowed in the Prime universe. She is not daunted by Kirk, nor is she willing to accept whatever fate was doled out to her as she often seemed to be in *TOS*. Moreover, at thirty-seven minutes in she confronts Spock—making what turns out to be a sexually-laden joke in the process when she reminds him that he has "often" complemented her on her "exceptional oral sensitivity"—and sways him to her desire to be on board the *Enterprise*, and viewers are given a hint that something more than meets the eye might be going on between them. As divergent timelines go, this is a doozy. After all, in *TOS*, Spock was only ever emotional when under duress of some kind. Forty minutes in, Sulu and Chekov are presented, rounding out the crew.

To this point Nyota has been active in her scenes. She speaks her mind, she goes where she wants, she rebuffs advances by men she is not interested in. Viewers would have had reason to hope that she would continue to grow and expand her role. What this would look like is debatable, but some level of being involved in the action would be one probable and important option. However, for the next hour and more, Nyota essentially offers only linguistic and emotional support. As with the initial promise of the Prime universe, Nyota is offered as a potentially fully-realized character, but then fades into the background. Where, arguably, she always was in the Prime universe.

The last minute of the film shows the characters performing their duties, and the last scene is of Spock and Kirk joining forces as Captain and First Officer. To round out the triad, Spock walks by Nyota, and she smiles.

In the second film in the Kelvin universe, *Star Trek: Into Darkness* released in 2013, Nyota is visually demoted from the beginning. Instead of being the first person introduced, as in *TOS*, or even the third as in the 2009 *Star Trek* film, she is the fourth person viewers see this time, after a high-action scene involving Kirk and Bones in danger and running from aliens, and Spock suiting up for a dangerous mission. The same four main characters are presented, yes, but the order has changed. Film language tells us this matters. And the action she's taking in her first scene? Unlike *TOS* where she was at the helm of a Starship, and unlike *Star Trek* 2009 where she entered a loud, busy bar space and was greeted by many and held her own with Kirk, in *Into Darkness* she is helping Spock dress, and telling him she believes he's capable of doing the dangerous mission he's embarking on; i.e., she's performing duties of support, emotional and sartorial.

When things don't go as planned and Spock's life is in danger, Nyota stays brave, as a woman who is in this film already coded as *support* should be. Soon thereafter the camera leaves her to follow the men doing very active, important things to move the story forward, and it isn't until almost forty minutes in that Nyota gets another full scene. And in this one? She is offering comfort again, this time to Captain Kirk.

Soon thereafter she gets to kill a Klingon on an away mission with the others and then she essentially disappears again for another forty minutes or so, until called upon to establish communications with an outside person. Staying true to the unfortunate pattern that has developed, she offers comfort to another crew member, the only other woman in the film. Finally at almost two hours in, she jumps into action, putting herself in danger to save her boyfriend, Spock. She manages to connect with a blow to the bad guy's head, and for a moment viewers could believe she is being pulled into a level of importance equal to that of the men in the film, but in the end, it is the emotional bond between Spock and Kirk that is reinforced while she once again fades into the background. The film's last scene gives us those three main characters as a unit, true, but she stands behind the two men. And she once again smiles.

Despite the promise and the possibility of more, in the first two films of the Kelvin universe Nyota, updated and more three-dimensional than her *TOS* counterpart, is still relegated to being little more than a character who steps in and steps up when she's needed for a specifically gendered role: talking, communicating, soothing. Interestingly, she isn't asked to carry all the emotion in the film—most of that happens between Kirk and Spock, setting up a love triangle the film nods at but does not pursue—much to the chagrin of the fan-fic crowd whose long-standing gay subtext and explicit fiction exploring their relationship is well-known.

And in the third Kelvin universe film, 2016's *Star Trek Beyond*, Nyota's character fades even more. The first four characters introduced to viewers are Kirk in a long sequence involving aliens, and then Scotty, Spock, and McCoy in that order when Kirk returns to the ship. Through a voiceover Captain's Log, he notes what's been happening on the ship in the nearly three years of their five-year mission, and he interacts with Dr. McCoy in emotionally-laden conversation, made acceptable by a stolen bottle of whiskey, coding it as masculine interaction instead of merely emotion. As screen-time and placement go, Nyota has been demoted again, to fifth.

It isn't until ten minutes in that she has a scene. Following the tone set up earlier by Kirk and McCoy, she is upset, seems off her game as she offers to give back to Spock a gift she had obviously received from him in the past, a necklace that was his mother's. Through this interaction we learn that they are no longer together and her emotional state is explained. While it doesn't affect her ability to do her job, it is notable. The film saves her from being its token carrier of emotion, however, by setting Kirk up first as being in a funk, and showing Spock following suit as he learns of Ambassador Spock's fate.

Notwithstanding some impressive bravery in the face of a very nasty villain when she races to separate the saucer of the Enterprise from the rest and thereby save her fellow-crewmates by sacrificing herself, Nyota mainly opens channels of communication, translates alien languages into English—including one particularly humorous moment in which she translates for Spock, telling Kirk that what Spock means by a characteristically obtuse statement is a method for kicking their enemy's ass—and makes intuitive leaps. As noted earlier, however, sacrifice is less action or agency than it is plot device and martyrdom. So while she is not simply a receptacle in this film for emotion, nor is she a passive follower of orders, she doesn't get much action beyond, again, communicating, emoting, sacrificing, translating and interpreting.

And the last scene? After Kirk turns down a Vice Admiralship, and

Spock chooses to stay on the *Enterprise* as well, everyone attends a surprise party for Kirk. The very last scene with dialogue is between McCoy, Kirk, and Spock—Kirk centered in the screen. And the last shot shows Nyota walk up beside Spock, hand him a drink, and smile as they reach a kind of détente. And while in this move to his side she has once more claimed her place as a vital part of the Enterprise, Scotty begins his move up on the other side of the group just before the camera cuts away to an over-the-shoulder shot of the Enterprise being rebuilt, again. Nyota is still in fourth position as viewers read this last scene left to right but Scotty looks poised to move into place in a way that will push her to fifth, exactly where she was positioned in the first few minutes of the film. And in any reading of this last few moments, Nyota is still in the support role she cannot seem to break out of.

Familiarity for Trek viewers is part of what each new incarnation of the mega-text has striven for as much as anything else. It's a delicate balance creating something new out of something very familiar whose fans might rebel and reject anything too far afield. And it could be argued that Nyota's role is right in line with her role on board the original *Enterprise* in *TOS*, and destabilizing this too much could cause a disruption in believability. After all, she's already been given a love life—with Spock, no less. And valid arguments could be put forth that her role of translator, her ability to decode and make intuitive leaps, and even sacrifice, are in large part what allow the plots of these new films to move forward.

But in *TOS* her existence made a statement audiences couldn't help but notice. Her presence on the bridge, in the series, and in living rooms in 1967, across a country riddled with struggles for equality by people who looked like her, embodied important concepts and conveyed important messages. *Look to the future*, her appearance promised, *believe that this is possible*.

In the Kelvin universe, for audiences of the twenty-first century, that message is lost.

Meaning in films inheres in the viewers' minds, and is made up of subject position and context. Fatimah Rony, James Snead, Toni Morrison, and others have discussed the importance of seeing oneself onscreen. Television and film are America's collective mythology, the way we see ourselves, the vision we have for the future. When entire groups of people are left out, or coded as less-than by only being represented in particular ways relative to other characters, the effects are many-fold and potentially devastating. For instance, if the only black characters on screen are criminals or maids, an entire group's possibilities are curtailed. So when Uhura arrived onscreen in 1967 in a position of power and in a potentially utopian future she presented another possibility, one that Whoopi Goldberg has famously stated inspired her to be an actor, and that inspired African American astronaut Mae Jemison to reach for the stars. But in the twenty-first century, Nyota simply by being present doesn't speak to race relations as she did then. Too much time has passed, and the fact that the mere corporeal presence of a strong black woman on screen doesn't mean as much is perhaps a testament to what America might be getting right in some ways. But that's the problem.

Star Trek's continuing mission should be to create stories and character arcs that challenge the status quo the way Roddenberry intended, not to simply reinforce stereotypes or keep audiences comfortable. Abrams in 2009 launched Trekkers old and young into a new universe filled with infinite possibilities of a brand new kind. He managed to round out familiar characters in ways that stretched but did not break the boundaries of long-time fans' willingness to believe, and he successfully broke through the resistance they might have had to changing canonical facts.

But, despite early promise, in the end he kept the triad of Kirk, Spock, and McCoy as the center around which the Kelvin universe revolves. Nyota was christened but demoted from the start visually and by the third film left adrift as Scotty is poised to usurp her place as the fourth member of the core. The male crew members of the *Enterprise* are ready to take on the galaxy, and Nyota is poised to offer them drinks and translate their desires.

But perhaps Roddenberry's future is even now working on the makers of the next, fourth installment. Infinite possibilities, after all, could include Lieutenant Nyota Uhura breaking out of her traditionally female role as communicator, consoler, and conveniently passive linguist. Maybe she can assert herself as not only Spock's lover with a first name but an essential member of the *Enterprise* crew who has real agency, can kick butt while wearing her short red skirt and cursing in Klingon, and instead of sacrificing herself to save her crewmates by dismantling the ship, maybe she can fly the *Enterprise* out of danger instead while the Captain and Spock and Bones are busy emoting and making grand plans.

If she can finally step into the foreground instead of providing background color as a screen against which others are measured, the Kelvin universe might be able to nod to both the past *and* the future by challenging viewers anew with social issues more in keeping with the twenty-first, and the twenty-third centuries.

In other words, let the woman do something. Because translating and sacrifice aren't action enough, and a name isn't agency at all.

Works Cited

Bernardi, Daniel Leonard. *Star Trek and History: Race-ing Toward a White Future*. Rutgers University Press, 1998.
Kapell, Matthew Wilhelm. *Star Trek as Myth: Essays on Symbolism and Archetype at the Final Frontier*. McFarland, 2010.
Morrison, Toni. *Playing in the Dark: Whiteness and the Literary Imagination*. Vintage, 1993.
Rony, Fatimah. *The Third Eye: Race, Cinema, and Ethnographic Spectacle*. Duke University Press, 1996.

Scodari, Christine. "'Nyota Uhura Is Not a White Girl': Gender, Intersectionality, and *Star Trek* 2009's Alternate Romantic Universes." *Feminist Media Studies*, vol. 12, no. 3, 2011, pp. 335–351.

Snead, James. *White Screens Black Images: Hollywood from the Dark Side.* Routledge, 1994.

Speigel, Lee. "Gene Roddenberry's Son Reveals Unhappy 'Star Trek' Family Life." *Huffington Post*, 12 Mar. 2017, https://www.huffingtonpost.com/2011/11/29/gene-roddenberry-son-star-trek_n_1119119.html.

Truffaut-Wong, Olivia. "*Star Trek Beyond* Is the Most Feminist Movie in the Franchise." *Bustle*, 22 Jul. 2016, https://www.bustle.com/articles/173531-star-trek-beyond-is-the-most-feminist-movie-in-the-franchise.

STAR TREK MEDIA CITED

Star Trek (2009). Directed by J.J. Abrams, Paramount Pictures, 2009.
Star Trek Beyond. Directed by Justin Lin, Paramount Pictures, 2016.
Star Trek into Darkness. Directed by J.J. Abrams, Paramount Pictures, 2013.
Star Trek: The Original Series. Rodenberry, Gene, creator. Desilu Productions and Paramount Television, 1966–1969.

"Throw a punch and kiss a girl"
Gender and Sexualization in the Kelvin Timeline

ANDREA WHITACRE

The scene in which the Kelvin Timeline *Star Trek* reboot introduces Lieutenant Nyota Uhura acts as a microcosm for the central duality that characterizes the way these films portray their female characters: competent professionalism tied to sexual objectification. The scene opens in a crowded bar in Iowa, with a shot following Uhura through the room as she breezes past tables, greets friends, and orders several drinks at the bar. She is constantly in motion, confident and vibrant, qualities that are emphasized by the swift tracking movements of the camera. As she orders at the bar, James T. Kirk appears and tries to buy her a drink, which she declines. The two banter playfully as Kirk hits on Uhura and she deflects his advances with an air of amused annoyance—both dismissive and flirtatious. She tells him her professional specialty, xenolinguistics, as a way of scaring him off, and is surprised and impressed when he knows what it is. Her conversation with Kirk draws a group of male Starfleet cadets who ask if Kirk is bothering her. "Beyond belief, but it's nothing I can't handle," she says, but the cadet doesn't leave, picking a fight with Kirk over Uhura's objections. From the background, Uhura chides them to stop. The fight escalates, and Kirk is thrown around the room by a series of punches from the group of cadets. Kirk is thrown into Uhura, and his hands land, palms open, on her breasts, and the camera captures shots of his face, surprised and pleased, and hers, affronted, as she pushes him backwards. The cadets get the upper hand, and one of them hits Kirk repeatedly in the face. Uhura again calls for the cadet to stop ("He's had enough!") and is ignored. Instead, it is the arrival of Captain Pike that ends the fight, his command signal stopping the cadet's fist in midair.

The scene demonstrates the complicated nature of the portrayal of women in the rebooted timeline: Uhura's status as a professional is explicitly emphasized and her role expanded, but she also remains a subsidiary and sexualized figure, serving the narrative arc of the central male character. The film emphasizes her confidence, intelligence, and devotion to her work. Her position on the ship, as this scene takes care to introduce, is upgraded from "communications" to "xenolinguistics." Following on the heels of introductory scenes devoted to young Kirk and young Spock, this scene also shows Uhura in a role significantly expanded from that of *Star Trek: The Original Series* (*TOS*). Her reboot introduction shows the film's efforts to establish her as a character who is the professional and personal equal of her crewmates. However, Uhura's introduction scene is all about Kirk, initiating his story arc by setting him on the road to Starfleet captaincy. In context, the dialogue that establishes Uhura's credentials as a xenolinguist is crafted to highlight Kirk's unexpected intelligence through his knowledge of her field. Through Kirk's pursuit of Uhura and the Starfleet cadets' reaction to it, the scene works to reveal his personality: intelligent, flirtatious, reckless, arrogant, funny. Uhura herself is ignored through the second half of the scene. The juxtaposition of her own futile commands with the instant efficacy of Pike's establishes his authority and fatherly leadership role.

And then, of course, there is the boob grab, as Kirk's accidental lurch lands his hands on Uhura's chest. While the rest of the fight scene between Kirk and the cadets emphasizes the gravity of punches and crashing tables, this moment veers briefly into a comedic mode. Kirk is sent flying as the camera follows him, he catches himself on Uhura, and they both look down at his hands as Uhura gasps. Then the camera shows us a close-up of Kirk's face, blank surprise turning to a dopey grin. Another close-up shows Uhura as she shoves him away with a grunt and clenched teeth. Kirk is thrown back into the fray. The slapstick framing of this moment allows Kirk access to her body as a sexual object, reinforced by the close-up of Kirk's enjoyment. Like Kirk, the viewer is granted a moment of sexual access to Uhura that is innocently unintentional.

The dualism of the female role calls for a more nuanced understanding of where *Star Trek*'s liberal and conservative impulses originate. It would be easy to render these films in terms of the contrast between their creators: one might praise J.J. Abrams's portrayal of the reboot Uhura and other female characters as a leap forward from their soft-focus secretarial role in *TOS*. Likewise, one might criticize Abrams's reboot for not holding true to Roddenberry's utopian idealism, as female characters remain sexualized figures and their roles consistently revolve around relationships to men. On the surface, both representations of female characters also seem distinct products of their eras, one emblematic of the sexual revolution of the 60s, the other a "Strong Female Character" in the mold of so many fictional women of the early 2000s. Both praise and censure on these grounds would be supported by the evidence of the films and television show. But both of these modes of critique rely on a creator-centric model of understanding *Trek*'s liberal and conservative elements: the mixed results on screen are usually understood as the products of a battle between progressive, visionary creators and traditional, commercially-driven networks and studios. A close review of the reboot films in comparison to the original Roddenberry television series and films shows that this conflict is not the driving force behind the dualistic representation of women in the reboot. Instead, the seemingly contradictory qualities of professionalism and sexualization are a consistent feature of *Star Trek*'s women as a whole, and a symptom of its larger ideological commitments, which consistently center male characters.

In the first section, I will show that the first two reboot films, *Star Trek* (2009) and *Star Trek into Darkness,* approach female representation in male-centered and individualistic terms, an approach that inflects both the empowering and disempowering aspects of these characters. Second, I will argue that this portrayal is a result of the films' adherence to a humanist approach to diversity that has been consistent across the properties of the *Trek* franchise. In other words, neither the reboot's successes nor its failures in the representation of women are the result of a departure from the ideals of the original Roddenberry series; instead, both of these dualistic elements are a result of the reboot's faithfulness to the series and its liberal humanist philosophy. This suggests that the problems with female representation (as well as the representation of other kinds of marginalized figures) in the reboot films are not the result of a conflict between visionary creators and more conservative commercial studios, but rather an inherent ideological feature of *Star Trek* as a franchise.

The Roddenberry Mythos

It has become a Trekkie truism that *TOS* creator Gene Roddenberry was the sole visionary figure responsible for *Star Trek*'s progressive idealism, hampered in his visions of a television utopia by a conservative network at NBC. This Roddenberry mythos carries over into evaluations of Abrams' *Star Trek* films. Both fans and detractors tend to frame their evaluations of the film in terms of creative authorship versus profit-based production. A 2009 *Telegraph* article positions the new director as the visionary successor to Roddenberry: "Before the film started, the head of Paramount—the producers of the film—

came on and talked tremblingly about joining 'The Paramount Family,' and about the 'incredibly visionary film-maker' who had directed it. Then a small, black-haired, bespectacled, 42-year-old man bounded up to the microphone. This was J.J. Abrams, the incredible visionary himself, and for once, the hype didn't seem out of place" (Preston). In her article, "A New Vision: J.J. Abrams, *Star Trek*, and Promotional Authorship," Leora Hadas shows how the promotional material for the first reboot film was well attuned to the need to portray Abrams as both a successor to Roddenberry and an independent creative mind. This positive emphasis on Abrams as a fellow visionary to Roddenberry fed positive reviews of the films themselves.

Negative evaluations of the reboot films and Abrams as director also draw on the assumed conflict between creators and executives by associating Abrams with the latter: an agent of the studio's commercial formula who doesn't truly understand *Star Trek*'s ideals. Criticizing the films for their failure to represent LGBTQ characters, a 2013 *Wired* article blames Roddenberry's loss: "In a post–Roddenberry world, there's no philosophical visionary on *Star Trek* projects pressuring the studio to push the sociopolitical envelope, so there hasn't been much—or any, really—burden to continue challenging norms." A 2016 *New York Times* op-ed, "Who Stole My *Star Trek*?" argues that commercialism has corrupted the simple idealism of *Star Trek* with empty action: "Recently, the original series' casting director, Joseph D'Agosta, told me that he hated this summer's *Star Trek Beyond*. 'There was no heart or soul that Gene brought to the original series,' he said, 'in story or character development'" (Vinciquerra). Such negative appraisals of the reboot films, especially those that criticize their lack of political progressiveness, consistently attribute their failures to a conflict between the creative and the commercial.

Yet the narrative of creative staff versus the television network doesn't fit *TOS* neatly, especially when considering the show's treatment of female characters. Roddenberry famously included a female first officer in his original pilot for *TOS*, the otherwise unnamed Number One. The character was conceived as a hyper-professional woman, competent and analytical, with a stoic affect. When NBC ordered a second pilot of the show, they asked that Roddenberry cut two characters: Number One and Spock. Roddenberry fought for Spock and won, recasting Majel Barrett as Nurse Chapel instead of Number One. Spock absorbed much of Number One's role and personality, including her analytical absence of emotion, which would become his defining trait. Another female bridge officer, Yeoman Janice Rand, was cut from the show in season two at the request of the network executive board. Roddenberry again backed off and allowed it: "And I had said no so many times to the network that I thought I maybe should give them a yes this time. But looking back now, I would've kept Rand on the show and I'm sorry I didn't. I know what a disappointment it was to Grace Lee Whitney as it was to Majel to be the number two in line and then be gone. But producing is not a science and sometimes we make mistakes" (Gross and Altman 111).

While there was pressure from the network to change many aspects of *TOS*, Roddenberry was able to pick his battles and keep the elements that mattered most to him, and those priorities consistently slighted female characters. He himself said that during *TOS*, he "didn't pay attention to women" and *TOS* was known for its use of female guest stars as sexual objects for Kirk (37). Moreover, the narrative of "Roddenberry versus the network" was one that Roddenberry himself pushed in public appearances throughout his tenure as showrunner of *TOS* (120–121). To be sure, there were tensions between Roddenberry and NBC, and the network pushed *TOS* to be more conservative and commercial. But the framework of creator/network conflict obscures the subtler conflicts within the show's commitments to liberal ideals, and the small, significant ways in which creators compromise with network demands. Instead of clear-cut battle between progressive creators and conservative networks and studios, *TOS* has a set of ideals that are filtered through its male-centered priorities: the presence of women as professional crewmembers furthers the utopian message of the show, but women characters also remain subject to the priorities of male characters—and their creators.

Masculinity in Star Trek

The *Star Trek* reboot also displays this prioritization of male characters. To understand the complex portrayal of female characters in the reboot, it is first necessary to understand its portrayal of masculinity, especially that of Kirk. The female characters in many ways take their cue from Kirk, in roles that accentuate the masculine values that he embodies. The young Kirk of *Star Trek* (2009) is brash, arrogant, rebellious, charismatic, prone to fistfights, and a persistent flirt, all characteristics that play up a kind of frat boy masculinity that matures into a leadership role in the later movies. Former *Star Trek* writer and producer Ronald D. Moore, who is also known for his work on *Battlestar Galactica* and now on *Outlander*, praises Kirk's reboot characterization as closer to the first-season *TOS* portrayal of Kirk: "The early and younger Kirk who was a little edgier, a little more dangerous. A little bit more willing to throw a punch and kiss a girl. *That* was the take in the movie, and I liked that" (Altman and Gross 768). This emphasis on masculinity is consistent with Roddenberry's vision of the character: his Kirk also emphasized masculinity, albeit of a slightly different nature: a naval-style commander (Gross and Altman 218). Not only does Moore articulate the importance of Kirk as a masculine character to both the reboot and *TOS*, but he associates this core masculinity with two characteristic actions: "throw a punch and kiss a girl." These twin characteristics of violence and heterosexuality are the exterior symbols of his key personality trait. As such, women become an important tool for communicating Kirk's masculinity to the viewer.

Some of the sexualization of female characters in the reboot therefore comes from a need to establish Kirk's aggressive heterosexuality. Uhura's introduction scene serves this purpose, kicking off a minor plotline/running joke in the film about Kirk's hapless pursuit of Uhura. After a scene between Kirk and fellow cadet Leonard "Bones" McCoy ends with Kirk leaving to go "study" ("Yeah, right," responds Bones with an eyeroll), a hard cut shows Kirk in bed with a green-skinned female Starfleet cadet named Gaila. The cut from Kirk "studying" to Gaila's bedroom, combined with Bones' obvious disbelief, further establishes the pattern of Kirk's personality and virile masculinity. That Gaila is the only female Starfleet character besides Uhura speaks to the consistent use of female characters as subsidiaries to male characters: she exists in the film as a woman because the plot and characterization requires Kirk to sleep with a cadet; additional female characters are unnecessary to the plot's priorities. In *Star Trek into Darkness*, this character motif is reestablished with a short scene that shows Kirk in bed with two cat-like alien women. Even absent women can be summoned as reinforcement for Kirk's masculine trait of casual sexual conquest: in *Into Darkness*, Marcus mentions Nurse Chapel as one of Kirk's flings, saying that she left the crew to take a post on the outer frontier—to get away from Kirk, she implies. Kirk does not remember her.

At other times, the use of sexualization to characterize Kirk overlaps with its use as audience voyeurism. Here the reboot prioritizes and centers not just Kirk, but the male viewer. In the first two reboot films, nearly every named female character (the only exceptions are the mothers of Kirk and Spock) is shown at some point in her underwear, Kirk voyeuristically watching. The first is Gaila, described above: a literal sexual encounter. The other two are different from this, and very similar to one another: in *Star Trek* (2009), Uhura walks in on her roommate Gaila and begins undressing, unaware that Kirk is hiding under the bed, avidly watching; in *Star Trek into Darkness*, Doctor Carol Marcus instructs Kirk to turn around while she changes out of her uniform, but he sneaks a peek. In both instances, the camera colludes with Kirk's voyeurism, giving the audience a view of the women's bodies. These scenes play into the conception of Kirk as an aggressively heterosexual character, who can't help but look and enjoys it when he does. Like the opening scene where his hands accidentally fall on Uhura's breasts, these scenes frame Kirk's voyeurism as playful and funny—not innocent, exactly, but harmless. More particularly, though, these scenes enable audience voyeurism through Kirk, a choice that signals the films' prioritizing of a (presumed straight) male audience. The films' crew does little to conceal the role that these female characters play in establishing Kirk as a womanizer and titillating the audience through blatant fanservice. In a 2013 interview, costume designer Michael Kaplan told the *Guardian*, "Last time, Zoe needed to wear underwear, and this time it was Alice Eve's turn. You know, it's a rather large male fanbase, and J.J. wanted to appeal to that" (Godfrey). Like Roddenberry's *TOS*, the reboot films center male characters, male viewers, and male desire, and these priorities inform the way both use female characters.

Uhura as Case Study

Nowhere are the doubled effects of these conflicting priorities—the representation of an egalitarian future and the demands of a male-centered narrative—more apparent than in the character of Uhura. While much of the popular conversation surrounding the new incarnation of Uhura has focused on the reboot's decision to place her in a romantic relationship with Spock, I see this aspect of her character as less relevant to the overall issue of female representation in the films. As Christine Scodari has pointed out in her article "'Nyota Uhura Is Not a White Girl': Gender, Intersectionality, and *Star Trek* 2009's Alternate Romantic Universes," Uhura's role in the film must be considered from an intersectional perspective: the choice to portray a woman of color in a romantic relationship with a male lead is a much different issue than a similar portrayal of a white woman, one that expands Uhura's scope as a character rather than limiting it (Scodari 337–340). Instead, I would like to focus on the duality that attends Uhura's role as a strong female character in the reboot—both a capable professional and an eroticized body. As with Kirk's trenchant masculinity, Uhura's doubleness is a consistent feature of both *TOS* and the reboot.

In *Race-ing Toward a White Future*, Daniel Bernardi describes Uhura's role in *TOS* as one of scopophilic consumption: both the audience and other characters within the show derive pleasure from the act of looking at her, the visual consumption of her body. This is true from the earliest description of the character in "The *Star Trek* Guide," a writer's guide for the staff of *TOS*. In the guide, Uhura is described as "a warm, highly female female off duty," who sings and does impressions to entertain her crewmates (Bernardi 40). Bernardi's analysis shows that *TOS* Uhura is subject to scopophilic consumption both through her gender and her race:

> As a singing, "highly female female" African, Uhura is written as a performance, an icon, of black beauty. This translates to the broadcast text. In "Mirror, Mirror," (1967), for instance, she is eroticized by the camera, as several scenes show her scantily clad body in tight close-ups: her long legs, smooth stomach, and large breasts—

scopophilic fragments of her body—are emphasized for their womanly and "exotic" features. It is as if her blackness is made safe and appealing when it is performing in fragmented and fetishized forms—when, in other words, it is as exoticized as it is eroticized [41–42].

This scopophilic lens on Uhura is magnified in proportion to the size of her role in the episode. "Mirror, Mirror," for instance, is one of the few *TOS* episodes where Uhura has a featured role, with increased dialogue and a key role in the central plot. But in this episode the eroticism and exoticism with which she is viewed also intensifies, reinscribing the character's narrative power within a context of fetishized consumption. The role has an implicit doubleness: on the one hand, there is the powerful impact of her presence on the show as a black woman and a bridge officer; on the other, the price that the character pays for that presence through scopophilic consumption. The two sides of this duality, as shown in "Mirror, Mirror," are reciprocally linked.

Similarly, the reboot films show a version of this doubleness in their reconception of Uhura's character, one that draws an implicit connection between her professional authority and her feminine sexualization. April Webster, the casting director for *Star Trek* (2009), says they were looking for "someone who could give us that 'I'm smarter than you' quality without being obnoxious." She praised Zoe Saldana for her ability to play the role with humor and without defensiveness: "She has to have an attitude of 'I've got to set these guys straight'" (Altman and Gross 771). These statements frame the reboot's version of Uhura as competent without being threatening: she is a crewmate but also a corrective figure, her professionality deployed in service to the male crew. Saldana's own appraisal of the character is even more ambiguous and double-edged:

> There's an androgynous essence to Uhura. Even though she's very beautiful and her feminine presence is obvious, there's this energy and leadership to her that sort of gives you the feeling that her sex appeal is probably observed and admired by the audience, but her coworkers just acknowledge her energy and authority.... Here you've got Kirk, who is a very cocky young man who was born to do this. It's a gift. Whether he wants it or not, he possesses it. Things are very easy for him, whereas a character like Uhura is someone who has had to work really hard for everything that she's earned. There's just an awareness of each other, and she's like, "Why is he so the boss of it all and so disrespectful and so funny?" And I'm pretty sure Kirk goes, "She's sexy, she wears that little dress, she knows what she's doing." Maybe he's not used to dating smart girls or something [Altman and Gross 772].

In this description, Saldana describes Uhura as a highly gendered character—much like the original Uhura, she is a highly female female—and yet simultaneously gives her an "androgyny" that equates to leadership potential. Saldana claims that the character is not sexualized within the storyworld, yet she describes her character's personality in terms of her sexual appeal to another character, Kirk. Uhura can be playfully combative ("Why is he so the boss of it all and so disrespectful and so funny?") only within the context of this flirtation, of setting the boys straight. Kirk's assessment of Uhura's competence also exists within this sexual context ("She's sexy, she wears that little dress, she knows what she's doing"). Moreover, the two characters' differing leadership potentials are communicated through this sexually-coded exchange: while Kirk is "born to do this," destined to command, Uhura has had to work hard for her skills and commission, a distinction that renders her less fit for the charismatic command position. Like *TOS*-Uhura, she has both power and presence, but both are carefully mitigated by her sexualization and subordinate narrative role. As she gains significance within the narrative, she must be recontextualized to preserve the hierarchical status of the male characters.

Both the reboot and the original television series and films have a complicated view of women. They present women as professionals and crewmates, the equals of the male characters in name if not in narrative emphasis. But both reboot and original also prioritize men and portray a masculinity that is dependent on the sexual objectification of named and unnamed female characters—even if said woman also has a doctorate in applied physics, or is an expert in xenolinguistics. The reboot is not, then, a failure to live up to the standard of progressive representation set by Roddenberry's *Star Trek*— both productions tend to cast women primarily as the subsidiaries and scopophilic objects of men. And the reboot is also not a clear-cut triumph over the regressive gender politics of *TOS*—both emphasize women's professional roles and work to portray them as the social equals of their crewmates. Instead, they tend to represent women in very consistent, similar ways. The next question to ask, then, is why: if neither the liberal nor the conservative impulses of the reboot can be explained as a case of creator versus network, or Roddenberry versus Abrams, then what are the key reasons for the pattern of female representation across both *Star Trek* iterations?

Humanism and the Star Trek *Subject*

Instead of framing *Star Trek*'s strengths and weaknesses in representation in terms of a conflict between progressive creators and conservative studio institutions, the pattern of representation must be understood as part of the underlying structure of the franchise: *Star Trek*'s liberal humanism. Humanism, often associated with a secular worldview, places value on the human as opposed to the divine, emphasizing human needs as well as human rationality. Within humanism, the ability to have rights, such as a right to self-determination, or a right to bodily autonomy, is based on one's human status: you are human, therefore you inherently deserve rights. Since human status is the basis for rights, humanism is left with a thorny, difficult question at its heart: who gets to be human?

Roddenberry's humanism is the philosophical premise of the *Trek* utopia. Through this humanism, *Star Trek* tends to express liberal values by gradually incorporating more women and racial minorities into a crew that revolves around a center of whiteness, maleness, and heteronormativity, practicing inclusion while maintaining a tacit hierarchy. Within humanism, in other words, some people are always "more human" than others, occupying the center even as others are brought within the larger circle. This trend is present from the beginning in *TOS*, which employed de facto tiers of importance for its characters: Kirk at the center, then Spock and then Bones, forming the core trio, and then an outer fringe of diverse minor characters, such as Uhura, Sulu, Chapel, Rand, and even Russian Chekov. The first two Kelvin films stay true to this conception of the series. It is this approach to diversity, based in an individualistic understanding of humanist ideals, that informs the consistent pattern of gender representation across franchise installments in *Star Trek*.

In Deborah Tudor's "Twentieth-Century Neoliberal Man," she examines the Abrams *Star Trek* films as an example of the revised kind of masculine hierarchy that results from a compromise between patriarchy and feminism. Through such a compromise, capitalist structures of power seem to adopt feminist ideals: women are presented as equals, and masculinity shifts to accommodate and accept, rather than resist, such equality. Feminism in the reboot is a common-sense truism, and gendered problems are always already in the past (Tudor 63). Absent any structural inequality shaping the role of gender in society, people can be assumed to be individually responsible for their position in the ship's power structure. At the same time, the compromise between existing power structures and feminist ideals doesn't actually change those power structures in a major way: Kirk remains at the center of both the narrative and the starship's command structures. Instead of blatant sexism predicated on inequality and defended through hostility toward women who try to gain power, a more outwardly benign form of exclusion is instituted: women still exist on the margins of the narrative, but now their exclusion is attributed to individual and internal forces rather than systemic ones. In other words, the position of women in the film is attributed to the women themselves rather than to external forces that keep them from command.

The reboot's exclusions therefore go unvoiced, and are present in the films' silences and assumptions more than any explicit discrimination. One can see this process in the assumptions that are made about Uhura's character behind the scenes, as Saldana reimagines her character's position as an inherent personality trait of Uhura. She rationalizes Uhura's position on the ship not as an effect of exterior forces holding Uhura back from command, but as the result of Uhura's "hard worker" personality contrasted with Kirk's status as a born leader. This makes her position the result of internal forces and individual preference rather than external systematic forces. Silence and omission mark the subtle ways in which women are kept from power. In *Star Trek* (2009), Kirk assigns junior officer Chekov to take command of the bridge, rather than Uhura, as he and Spock exit; the framing of the shot places Uhura out of view on the screen. David Greven writes about the framing of this moment as an example of how the film elides the question of sexism while continuing to center male characters (207–208).

In *Star Trek* (2009) and *Star Trek into Darkness*, the women's uniforms enact another subtle omission. While male crewmembers wear long-sleeved uniforms that display rank insignia on the wrists, the cap-sleeved female uniforms lack insignia, tacitly omitting women from the marked chain of command. Women are also absent from major action scenes in this action-heavy reboot. Saldana requested an action scene from Abrams in the second film, in which she was shown briefly firing a phaser at the conclusion of a lengthy fight scene between Spock and Khan (White). In isolation, these silences and unspoken assumptions about female roles in the reboot appear as minor issues, but together and in the context of the franchise as a whole, they add up. They speak to the larger problem that Tudor identifies: *Star Trek*'s surface-level embrace of feminist ideas obscures the continued problems in the representation of women—and the source of those problems. *Trek*'s liberal humanism is the structural limit to the franchise's progressive vision.

As Tudor points out, the reboot works to portray feminist ideals of equality and empowerment in its female characters, but is unwilling to dislodge Kirk as the center of the narrative. In this way, the Abrams films remain faithful to the humanist approach to diversity practiced by Roddenberry and inculcated into the *Trek* franchise. This center position occupied by Kirk is an expression of the humanist idea of the subject. This "subject" is the answer to the question of who gets to be human. The humanist subject, in classical Enlightenment terms, is one who stands outside of nature and observes it, one who has a consciousness and a unified, unchanging identity. The human subject commands nature through the use of reason. The subject, in other words, is an individual—complete, natural, and unique—and from this status as a human subject flows the individual's claim to human rights.

Historically, the answer to "who is a human subject" has depended on a variety of factors, and things like gender, race, or disability could jeopardize one's human status. This means that the human is always a contentious category, and only a particular kind of subject has an unquestioned claim to humanity and the rights and privileges that come with it. Since gender, race, disability, or sexuality, for instance, have been used to question a group's claim to full human status, the humanist subject tends to be conceived first and foremost as white, male, able, and straight. Because this subject position defines what is human, other non-normative categories of identity become "the Other," and this dichotomy produces an us/them way of thinking about identity. "Others" become marginalized, distanced from the powerful position of rationality and observation at the center, while the normative, "most human" human stands at the center.

As Lynne Joyrich notes in her article, "Feminist Enterprise? *Star Trek: The Next Generation* and the Occupation of Femininity," the franchise as a whole tends to express its commitment to diversity and humanist ideals by gradually bringing "Others," including women and aliens, into the circle of human subjectivity already occupied by the white maleness. The different iterations of *Star Trek*, from *TOS* onward, operate on a spectrum of humanist inclusion that is always careful to leave the very center subjectivity in place (Joyrich 67). Bernardi provides a powerful critique of *Star Trek*'s treatment of racial difference and representation, showing how racial diversity in *TOS* and *Star Trek: The Next Generation* works to center whiteness and marginalize people of color. When considered as part of the franchise as a whole, even the series that use the captain's seat to center identities outside of this central subject position remain linked to a foundation of white masculine humanism.

Star Trek: Deep Space Nine, with its black male captain, and *Star Trek: Voyager*, with its white woman captain, begin only after the originary subject position is reestablished through Captain Jean-Luc Picard on *Star Trek: The Next Generation*. *Deep Space Nine* and *Voyager* each take one and only one step away from this center: a white woman, a black man. Not until *Star Trek: Discovery* (2017) does this decentering become intersectional, and then the black female protagonist's relation to the hierarchy of power remains ambiguous—a complex and still-developing narrative position that I will touch on below. The humanism at the heart of the franchise champions human rights and dignity for all, but it never—yet—dislodges the normative identity of its subject from the hierarchy of power. It is this commitment to an individualistic humanism that informs *Star Trek*'s most progressive impulses as well as its consistent shortcomings.

Boldly Going Beyond: The Future of Star Trek

How, then, can *Star Trek* escape the limits of its own humanist ideals and address its attendant exclusions? A first step might be leaving behind the reboot structure entirely. In the Abrams films, this structure encourages a repetition of elements that often uncritically transfers features forward and lends them an air of inevitability. While assumptions about diversity and the human subject inform the entire *Trek* franchise, the reiterative reboot structure gives them the force of destiny. In *TOS*, Kirk is the unspoken center of a humanist hierarchy (Bernardi), but the reboot films make that position of authority a plot directive—the focus of the entire plot of *Star Trek* (2009) is that Kirk *must* become captain of the ship in order to save the Federation and fulfill his personal destiny. Captain Pike encourages Kirk to enlist in Starfleet by citing his unique destiny: "You can settle for a less than ordinary life, or do you feel like you were meant for something better? Something special?" Even his friendship with Spock becomes predestined, as Spock Prime implies at the end of the film: "I could not deprive you of the revelation of all that you could accomplish together, of a friendship that will define you both in ways you cannot yet realize." In this nod to the original timeline of *TOS*, the film gives these character relationships the force of necessity: it has already happened, so it must happen again. This use of repetition retroactively reinforces the *TOS*-era restrictions on female characters: recall Saldana's rationalization of her character as a hard worker and Kirk as "born to do this." Even when the plot doesn't play into this implication of destiny so directly, the repetition of characters and story necessarily reproduces the basic power structures and roles of the original.

However, both *TOS* and the reboot offer possibilities for critiquing *Star Trek*'s humanism and moving beyond the reiterative centering of Kirk as the classical humanist subject. The entire premise of the final *TOS*-era film, *Star Trek VI: The Undiscovered Country*, pokes at the humanist foundations of *Star Trek*'s world. As disaster forces a longtime enemy, the Klingon Empire, to sue for peace, the Federation—and Kirk himself—must grapple with their identity and its ugly roots. What is Starfleet if there is no war, and no Klingon menace to counter? Who is Kirk if he must give up his deeply ingrained hatred of the other? At a formal dinner with Klingon dignitaries, the already tense conversation turns to the Federation's embrace of its own normative subject position. Azetbur, the Klingon chancellor's daughter, challenges the way Starfleet justifies and distributes its power. Azetbur's own subject-position is Othered several times over: she is a Klingon visiting a Federation vessel; she is an alien, a metaphor that *Star Trek* frequently employs to encode racial division; she is exotified by her alien costuming, forehead ridges, and striking makeup. Further, she is a woman among men, the only woman in the Klingon delegation, and the only woman at the table besides Uhura—each the sole representative of the female Other in their respective groups. It is significant, then, that the most direct challenge to the Federation's claim to political and moral authority comes from her. Chekov voices the show's humanist rhetoric, unselfconsciously exclusionary ("We do believe that all planets have a sovereign claim to inalienable human rights"). Azetbur responds: "Inalien. If only you could hear yourselves. Human rights. Why the very name is racist. The Federation is no more than a *Homo sapiens*-only club." Through Azetbur, the film questions and critiques its own humanist foundations, taking the viewer outside of *Trek*'s typical subject position and illuminating its blindnesses. Azetbur's challenge to Chekov's humanism makes visible *Star Trek*'s commitments to exclusionary philosophical traditions as the basis for representation.

The third reboot film, *Star Trek Beyond*, also works to correct, if not critique, the earlier films' myopic focus on Kirk and Spock. By distributing the screen-time more evenly among its core cast, the film works against the tendency to center Kirk as the sole driver of the narrative. In distributing more of its plot agency, the film relies less on a destined uniqueness for Kirk's character, and thus has less pressure to emphasize Kirk's masculinity. As a result, *Beyond* resists sexualizing its female characters, while at the same time giving Uhura and newcomer Jaylah more active roles in the plot. In addition, the film places greater emphasis on Sulu as a leader and includes *Star Trek*'s first (very subtle and still marginal) onscreen queer representation in Sulu and his family. The film demonstrates that the hierarchical dynamic that has dominated *Star Trek* shows and movies and often placed women in stereotypical roles can be circumvented—not, as some might argue, by simply replacing the director of the film with a more progressive creator, but by de-centering the focus of the franchise from Kirk and the captain's seat.

Working within an assumption that equality has always already arrived, *Star Trek* is unlikely to ever explicitly address the gender inequalities it perpetuates through its liberal humanist lens, but through tacitly expanding the roles available to women and reconfiguring the dynamics of the characters and plot, it can change the subject position through which we view the series and films. Even within a reboot, options are available for creators who prioritize gender equality, in ways that *Star Trek Beyond* demonstrates. Creators can avoid stereotypes of the nurturing woman and the sexualized woman that tie female characters' significance to larger male roles. They can make full use of the source material by developing minor characters, such as Chapel, Rand, or Marcus. They can create new characters, such as Jaylah and Sulu's husband, to expand the world of the source material. Just as importantly, they can be mindful of the kind of directors, producers, and writers they hire behind the scenes—not to ensure a visionary creator to recreate the mythic influence of Roddenberry, but to diversity the subject positions from which *Star Trek* is viewed.

As *Star Trek* boldly launches a new series, the future of the franchise and its representation of women remains in question. *Star Trek Discovery* promises to upend many of the franchise's established centralities—yet it also maintains a complicated relationship toward women in power. Main character Michael Burnham, played by Sonequa Martin-Green, is *Trek*'s first woman of color lead, and the first who is not a captain. With the show unanchored from "throw a punch and kiss a girl" masculinity as its narrative center (and introducing queer main characters as part of the new crew), the opening episodes are free of the kind of scopophilic, sexualizing gaze through which so many previous *Trek* women are viewed. But the pilot episodes also strip Burnham of her institutional power within Starfleet and reestablish her under the command of a white male captain, Gabriel Lorca, played by Jason Isaacs. In turn Lorca, through his ambiguous morality and hawkish utilitarianism, subverts the traditional position of the captain as the objective center and expression of humanist subjectivity. *Discovery* so far is a *Star Trek* reflective of its own origins, seeking both to reiterate and question the franchise's guiding principles and the nature of its utopian subjectivity—a balancing act that is as ambitious as it is delicate. Only time (and the next twelve episodes) will tell how their narrative will handle *Trek*'s traditional views of human nature. Over the course of the first season, Burnham may earn her way back toward the center from the brink of total disenfranchisement, or remain on the fringes of official command. The nuances of these two characters, Burnham and Lorca, and the way the show navigates their relationship to power will determine to what extent they ultimately support, critique, or destabilize the franchise's liberal humanist subjectivity.

As a franchise founded on a humanist philosophy that both encourages diversity and maintains the status quo, *Star Trek* will always be at odds with itself. But it also has the capacity to self-critique and self-correct, and the direction of its most recent film and upcoming series tease further development and discovery, the potential for unsettling its own entrenched subject position and rethinking the position of women within it.

WORKS CITED

Altman, Mark A., and Edward Gross. *The Fifty-Year Mission: The Complete, Uncensored, Unauthorized Oral History of Star Trek: The Next 25 Years: From the Next Generation to J.J. Abrams*. St. Martin's Press, 2016.
Bernardi, Daniel. *Race-ing Toward a White Future*. Rutgers University Press, 1998.
Godfrey, Alex. "*Star Trek into Darkness*: How It Was Made, by the People Who Made It." *The Guardian*, 11 May 2013. Accessed 12 Feb. 2017.
Greven, David. *Gender and Sexuality in Star Trek: Allegories of Desire in the Television Series and Films*. McFarland, 2009.
Hadas, Leora. "A New Vision: J.J. Abrams. *Star Trek*, and Promotional Authorship." *Cinema Journal*, vol. 56, no. 2, 2017, pp. 46–66.
Joyrich, Lynne. "Feminist Enterprise? *Star Trek: The Next Generation* and the Occupation of Femininity." *Cinema Journal*, vol. 35, no. 2, 1996, pp. 61–84.
Maloney, Devon. "*Star Trek*'s History of Progressive Values—And Why It Faltered on LGBT Crew Members." *Wired*, 13 May 2013, https://www.wired.com/2013/05/star-trek-lgbt-gay-characters/. Accessed 20 Jan. 2017.

Preston, John. "J.J. Abrams: *Star Trek* Director." *The Telegraph*, 6 May 2009, https://www.telegraph.co.uk/culture/star-trek/5284141/JJ-Abrams-Star-Trek-director.html. Accessed March 1, 2017.

Scodari, Christine. "'Nyota Uhura Is Not a White Girl': Gender, Intersectionality, and *Star Trek* 2009's Alternate Romantic Universes." *Feminist Media Studies*, vol. 12, no. 3, 2011, pp. 335–351.

Tudor, Deborah. "Twenty-First Century Neoliberal Man." *Neoliberalism and Global Cinema: Capital, Culture, and Marxist Critique*, edited by Jyostna Kapur and Keith B. Wagner, Routledge, 2011.

Vinciquerra, Thomas. "Who Stole My *Star Trek*?" *New York Times*, 8 Sep. 2016, https://www.nytimes.com/2016/09/08/opinion/who-stole-my-star-trek.html. Accessed March 1, 2017.

White, Cindy. "Saldana Seeks More Trek Action." *IGN*, 13 Sep. 2009, https://www.ign.com/articles/2009/09/14/saldana-seeks-more-trek-action. Accessed March 16, 2017.

Star Trek Media Cited

"The Battle of the Binary Stars." *Star Trek Discovery*, season 1, episode 2, written by Gretchen J. Berg and Aaron Harberts, directed by Adam Kane, 24 Sep. 2017.

"Context Is for Kings." *Star Trek Discovery*, season 1, episode 3, written by Gretchen J. Berg, Aaron Harberts and Craig Sweeny, directed by Akiva Goldsman, 1 Oct. 2017.

"Mirror, Mirror." *Star Trek*, season 2, episode 4, written by Gene Roddenberry and Jerome Bixby, directed by Marc Daniels, 6 Oct. 1967.

Star Trek (2009). Directed by J.J. Abrams, Paramount Pictures, 2009.

Star Trek Beyond. Directed by Justin Lin, Paramount Pictures, 2016.

Star Trek IV: The Undiscovered Country. Directed by Nicholas Meyer, Paramount Pictures, 1991.

Star Trek into Darkness. Directed by J.J. Abrams, Paramount Pictures, 2013.

"The Vulcan Hello." *Star Trek Discovery*, season 1, episode 1, written by Bryan Fuller and Akiva Goldsman, directed by David Semel, 24 Sep. 2017.

Science Fiction and the New *Trek* Timeline

Ace G. Pilkington

The 2009 reset of the *Star Trek* franchise (at three movies and counting) has been called the Abramsverse (from the producer of all three films and director of the first two), the Kelvin Timeline (from the alternative timeline that established the reset), and at least a few equally descriptive but less complimentary things. In an article titled "Star Trek: How J.J. Abrams ruined everything," Megan Leigh says, "While I perfectly understand that Paramount ... wants to commercialize their product as much as possible... what I don't understand is why they have to gut the original concept to do so. They have moved the series completely away from its original premise."

In Gerry Canavan's words, "J.J. Abrams ... wore his lack of interest in the original *Star Trek* as a badge of honour during publicity for *Star Trek* (US 2009)" (321). In one of his longer disquisitions on the original series, Abrams said, "Star Trek ... always felt like a silly, campy thing. I remember appreciating it, but feeling like I didn't get it. I felt it didn't give me a way in. There was a captain, there was this first officer, they were talking a lot about adventures and not having them as much as I would've liked. Maybe I wasn't smart enough, maybe I wasn't old enough. But The Twilight Zone I was obsessed with. Loved it" (Rose). Nicholas Meyer seems to have had a similar problem, but he puts it in fewer words, "I'm not a science fiction fan, I didn't watch the show as a kid—I didn't get it. It's only to the degree to which I understand the earthbound human aspects of the stories that I can create or relate to them" (Schepis). The fact that Nick Meyer co-wrote *Star Trek IV*, co-wrote and directed *Star Trek VI*, and is currently working on scripts for the new *Star Trek Discovery* television series set in the Prime (original) Timeline suggests that J.J. Abrams is not the first major player in the franchise to have a problem with science fiction.

Unfortunately, Abrams' trouble with the series runs deeper than possibly not being old enough when he first saw it. He seems to have been unable to connect with characters such as Kirk and Spock who knew what they wanted to do with their lives and qualified themselves through hard work to do it. In an interview for *The Fifty Year Mission: The Next Twenty-Five Years*, Abrams laid out the kind of hero he found appealing, "When I first saw Star Wars, and even now when I watch those original movies, they were wonderful adventures that were completely relatable, because Luke Skywalker was you. Luke was this kid who didn't know where he was going to go, didn't know what his life was going to be. He was an average farm boy" (Altman and Gross 756). About Shatner's character he says, "Kirk was always a cocky, brilliant, shoot-from-the-hip guy who I never felt connected to ... his character was objectified to me because I just didn't connect with who that guy was." Nor did he find Nimoy's character any more appealing, "The other main guy was Spock, and he was obviously wildly logical and incredibly deliberate in his consideration, yet I never was really him." And he concludes in a startling failure of empathy, "So I was disconnected from these characters even though I could appreciate them" (Altman and Gross 756–757).

The qualities that Abrams finds alien—intelligence, decisiveness, careful deliberation, all of that informed by ostentatious scientific training—are common in works of science fiction. And those qualities were meant, on some level, to show what it would take to reach the future which Roddenberry was suggesting in *Star Trek*. They were tied very closely to real science, a connection that Abrams seems not to have understood. He says, "Science fiction has questionable at best science" ("Gene Roddenberry's Vision"). No wonder Abrams went in a different direction entirely. As Gerry Canavan writes about the Abramsverse, "*Trek* only in name: Roddenberry's utopia was replaced by a paranoid and militaristic Federation, scarred and traumatised by loss, seeing space as a site of horror, threat and murder rather than wonder" (321). Or in Dr. McCoy's words from *Star Trek* (2009), "Space is disease and danger after darkness and silence." That sounds more like horror than SF, with the tagline from *Alien*, "In space, no one can hear you scream." It's a long way from the words on the screen at the end of *Star Trek: The Motion Picture*, "THE HUMAN ADVENTURE IS JUST BEGINNING."

Of course, not all of the resistance to complicated characters can be traced to Abrams. Roberto Orci and Alexander Kurtzman, the screenwriters for the first two films of the reset, seem to have been working to create an essentially simple narrative. Roberto Orci explains how someone unfamiliar with the material is meant to respond to *Star Trek* (2009), "Oh look, human kid, alien kid get together and they become best pals. Amazing. Great Story" (Altman and Gross 789). In addition, because various *Trek* series have been moving away from Roddenberry's initial vision for decades, it can be hard to appreciate the size of the gulf that exists between the Original Series and the reset. *Deep Space Nine* had already scrapped, undermined, or overwritten most of Roddenberry's version. To quote Canavan again, "Viewers of the *DS9* spin-off, come to know ... that the entire Federation governmental apparatus has always been a kind of obscene fraud, secretly manipulated and at times directly controlled by a secret black-ops division called Section 31 that dates back as far as the signing of the Federation charter and which has been manipulating its history ever since" (322). In light of that, it's hard to condemn Abrams for besmirching paradise.

Nevertheless, the point to a reset and a prequel is to lose those decades of baggage and return to the characters of the original series. In fact, it means seeing them when they were younger and, one might expect in the normal course of human development, more optimistic than they were when we first met them. We might also have expected, since the speed of technological change is increasing at an ever greater rate, an emphasis on science and science fiction equal to or much greater than that in Roddenberry's series. Imagine a reset that had had as its goal the kind of scientific and technological excitement that came with those original episodes for many viewers—even if not for Abrams.

It may seem that I am painting an unrealistic picture of what the Original Series was like. But it helps to look at it on its own terms, and from the perspective of people who wrote, read, watched, and liked science fiction. And it's good to remember that Gene Roddenberry was one of them. *Time Star Trek* describes him as "a science fiction buff since junior high school" (Zoglin). An enormous part of *Star Trek* came straight from science fiction. One of the best SF films in the decade before Roddenberry created his series was *Forbidden Planet* (1956). Keith Booker says about it, "*Forbidden Planet* is a virtual compendium of pulp science fiction themes from the 1950s" (43). It was also a source of big ideas and stunning visuals. In an August 10, 1964, memo, Roddenberry wrote, "You may recall we saw MGM's *Forbidden Planet* with Oscar Katz some weeks ago. I think it would be interesting for Pato Guzman to take another very hard look at the spaceship, its configurations, controls, instrumentations, etc. while we are still sketching and planning our own" (Alexander 202). However, the *Forbidden Planet* vessel was the first flying saucer piloted by humans in a film, and Roddenberry decided he needed additional inspiration. He had consulted "think tanks such as the Rand Corporation," and he now turned to Sam Peeples, a friend, "a fellow writer" and "owner of a huge collection of old science fiction magazines." Roddenberry said, "Our problem is simply we're too far ahead of what scientists are planning, or even speculating. After many days of wasted research ... I've decided I've got to go back to science fiction in this area too" (Alexander 203). What he asked for and got was a chance to go through Peeples' extensive library.

In the event, "Gene took somewhere between fifty and a hundred photographs of old science fiction magazine covers, searching for ideas for the design of the *Enterprise*" (204).

"Five days before the show premiered on NBC" Gene Roddenberry was a guest "at the 24th Annual World Science Fiction Convention in Cleveland, Ohio" (Alexander 256). He showed the audience the *Star Trek* Episode "Where No Man Has Gone Before." According to Allen Asherman, who was there, "We gave him a standing ovation. We came close to lifting Gene Roddenberry upon our shoulders and carrying him out of the room" (quoted in Alexander 256–257). For Roddenberry it was "a tremendous boost" (256). It was also there that he first met Isaac Asimov, and "a friendship was formed" (Shatner *Star Trek Memories* 189). The science fiction community was always important to Roddenberry. He turned to them for help and inspiration. He was comfortable with them, and they accepted him as one of their own.

He was happy to use major authors and new SF talents to write scripts for the series. As William Shatner puts it, "Instead of just hiring veteran TV writers, they also contacted some rather well-known names from the world of literary science fiction, ultimately luring many of them to the show" (*Star Trek Memories* 92). These included Jerome Bixby, Robert Bloch, Max Ehrlich, Harlan Ellison, David Gerrold ("Tribbles" was his first sale), Richard Matheson, Jerry Sohl, Norman Spinrad, and Theodore Sturgeon. Ray Bradbury isn't on that list, but he would have been if Roddenberry had had his way. Bradbury says, "We'd been friends for many years when he asked me to write for Star Trek more than 25 years ago. But I've never had the ability to adapt other people's ideas into any sensible form" ("Playboy Interview"). The science fiction writers who helped to save *Star Trek* from cancellation (and who received thank you telegrams from Roddenberry) read like a Who's Who of the genre: "Poul Anderson, Isaac Asimov, Robert Bloch, Lester del Rey, Harlan Ellison, Philip José Farmer, Frank Herbert, Richard Matheson, Theodore Sturgeon, and A.E. Van Vogt" (Solow and Justman 307).

But perhaps the most important service ever provided for the series by any science fiction writer was that performed by Isaac Asimov himself. By June 19, 1967, the success of the series in general and Spock in particular was causing difficulties for William Shatner, and those difficulties radiated outward to Leonard Nimoy and the rest of the show. As Roddenberry explained in a letter to Asimov, "Bill is ... generally rated as fine an actor as we have in this country. But we're not getting the use of him that we should.... It's easy to give good lines and good situations to Spock. And to a lesser extent the same is true of the irascible Dr. McCoy." The trouble was "Star Trek needs a strong lead, an Earth lead. Without diminishing the importance of the secondary continuing characters" (Solow and Justman 309). Roddenberry also laid out the problem—one that he undoubtedly understood well from his time as an airline pilot and police officer—that if Kirk appeared too professional and unyielding, he would "seem unlikeable," but if he were too likeable, he would not be believable (309). Meanwhile, Shatner was counting lines and insisting that he had to have more than Nimoy in every episode (Van Hise 24). George Takei, who was one of those who got caught in the struggle, says, "When the final shooting script was delivered, the eagerly awaited scene or line would now be in someone else's mouth, and invariably, it was Bill's.... And gallingly, he always managed to keep up that smiling, charming façade ... that smile as bright, as hard, and as relentless as the headlights of an oncoming car. You just had to get out of the way" (259). Asimov had indeed contributed to the overall problem with an article he wrote for the April 29, 1967, *TV Guide* titled "'Mr. Spock Is Dreamy.'" In fact, Shatner was in danger of becoming the "straight man" for a more idiosyncratic character, and Asimov's title indicates an additional problem. Unlike the usual situation with a comic and a straight man, where the straight man is the romantic lead (e.g., Martin and Lewis), Mr. Spock had sex appeal too.

Asimov, who would, by the end of his career write nearly five hundred books, was often approached by people in the science fiction and scientific communities when they couldn't find an item of information or a solution anywhere else. Asimov would search his eidetic memory and find the answer. He is listed, for instance, in the credits of *Star Trek: The Motion Picture* as "Special Science Consultant," largely, he says, for answering "some questions by phone and mail" for Roddenberry (Stanley Asimov 180).

In the case of Kirk and Spock, though he asked for time to think, Asimov didn't need to look far to find a solution. His most important suggestion was, "It might be well to unify the team of Kirk and Spock a bit, by having them actively meet various menaces together with one saving the life of the other.... The idea of this would be to get people to think of Kirk when they think of Spock" (quoted in Alexander 310). Roddenberry immediately saw the point, "I think the most important comment is that of keeping them a close team. Shatner will come off ahead by showing he is fond of the teenage idol [Mr. Spock]; Spock will do well by displaying great loyalty to his Captain. In a way it will give us *one* lead, the team" (quoted in Alexander 311).

Asimov's advice came not from prescience but from experience. He was an expert on unifying disparate heroes. His 1954 novel *Caves of Steel* and its 1957 sequel *The Naked Sun* had paired a detective from Earth and a humaniform robot from the planet Aurora to solve science fiction mysteries. They had been forced to work together, had begun with great difficulties because of their differences, and had ended (after a series of perilous adventures) as friends. It had been hard for an emotional Earthman and a coldly logical robot to understand each other, but by the end of the third novel (*The Robots of Dawn*), Lije Baley and Daneel Olivaw had reached the same point in their shared character arc as Kirk and Spock would in theirs. The Earthman Baley, who has just told Daneel how happy he is to see him again and been assured by the robot that the feeling is mutual, asks, "You feel emotion, do you?" And Daneel responds, "I cannot say what I feel in any human sense.... I can say, however, that the sight of you seems to make my thoughts flow more easily, and the gravitational pull on my body seems to assault my senses with lesser insistence" (29–30). Both pairs of disparate heroes had become best friends.

Of course, Asimov and Roddenberry were not trying to set up the central emotional bond in *Star Trek*. Nor were they trying to make it easier for Nicholas Meyer, J.J. Abrams, and others like them to relate to the franchise. They were trying to find a way to keep the actors happy and the mechanism of the show running so that it could continue to produce what Asimov repeatedly called "the first piece of adult science fiction to appear on television" (*I. Asimov* 369). In fact, Roddenberry was concerned to get his science fiction right. In commenting on "the illusion of the remarkable speeds necessary to the U.S.S. Enterprise," he writes, "One answer is suggested in the *Journal of the British Interplanetary Society*, an article by Dr. I.E. Sanger, 'Some Optical and Kinematical Effects in Interstellar Astronautics.'" And he asks in an aside, "Impressed? I wasn't kidding about research" (Alexander 201). Here too Roddenberry turned to his friend Sam Peeples, "an expert on science fiction," and "the two often had heated discussions over the definitions and limitations of hard science fiction as opposed to fantasy" (Alexander 229).

Whatever Roddenberry's idea of Hard SF may have been, his practice for much of the series comes very close to a standard definition: Hard SF is science fiction that extrapolates from science and provides rational (and often detailed) technical explanations for its wonders. In James Gunn's definition, it is "Science fiction based on accepted scientific principles and reasonable extrapolation of those principles into the future." He adds, however, "The way science is expanding its horizons of the possible, hard SF seems limited only by the imaginations of its creators" (iii). Brian Stableford makes some large claims for Hard SF, "Hard science fiction aspires to serve as a medium of thought experiments, significant not merely as a means of popularising scientific ideas but also—and primarily—as a means of their philosophical investigation" (228). *Star Trek* managed to do pretty much all of that.

As is usual with genre definitions (and as it seems to have been with Roddenberry and Peeples), the arguing is at least half the fun. On one hand, the lines blur, and it's easy to include most people, but on the other, it sometimes seems as though no one is pure enough, and besides, writers are not consistent. The early H.G. Wells, by his own admission, could not possibly have qualified, but later on, he made successful predictions, always a badge of honor in Hard SF as it has been in *Star Trek*. For those who want to be too strict in their definitions and exclusions, I point out that Isaac Asimov's creation of the positronic brain (used for Data in *Star Trek: The Next Generation*) was much closer to fantasy than to physics, and yet it may turn out to be in its own non-scientific way, one of Asimov's most successful prognostications, not because he provided a blueprint but because he set a nearly irresistible goal. This is a claim that may also be made for some of Roddenberry's most difficult technologies, such as teleportation and warp speed. (Parts of this definition and some other portions of the essay first appeared in my *Science Fiction and Futurism: Their Terms and Ideas*.)

One of the most extraordinary things about Roddenberry's SF was that he seems to have incorporated it effortlessly into the business of building a television show. For instance, in a memo from July 24, 1964, Roddenberry lays out what would become one of *Star Trek*'s most innovative thought experiments. It predated both Captain Kirk and Captain Pike, "More and more I see the need for some sort of interesting electronic computing machine designed into the U.S.S. Enterprise, perhaps on the bridge itself. It will be an information device out of which April and the crew can ... extract information on the registry of other space vessels, space flight plans for other ships, information on individuals and planets and civilizations" (quoted in Alexander 200). Roddenberry also suggested something to be used with that powerful computer system, "a Tricorder ... an instrument of the future whereby wherever the Captain is, he can make log reports or records of any kind ... which later are fed into the ship's computer system" (Alexander 240). In "The City on the Edge of Forever," Spock indicates how powerful the technology is, "I am a fool. My tricorder is capable of recording even at this speed. I've missed taping centuries of living history." And, most famous of all, there was the "communicator ... the hand-held device used to talk from person to person or ground to ship" (240). Perhaps there is an explanation for this in the following, "One writer commented that Gene had spent so much time in the twenty-third and twenty-fourth century that he would argue with you about the merits of an idea as if he had been there" (Alexander 245).

The list of technologies predicted, inspired, or encouraged by *Star Trek* is lengthy. Harold Kaufman constructed the first ion drive in 1959, but Marc Rayman, chief mission engineer of Deep Space 1, which launched on 24 October 1998, gives an excellent example of the Trek connection, "I worked on a mission called Deep Space 1, which was the first interplanetary mission to use ion propulsion to travel around the solar system. And the first time I ever heard of ion propulsion was in the *Star Trek* episode 'Spock's Brain....' So the opportunity to connect what I saw in *Star Trek* as a little kid to what I'm doing now as an adult is very, very exciting" (Shatner *How William Shatner Changed the World*). A similar story involves the original *Star Trek* and Martin Cooper, inventor of the cell phone. As Cooper tells it, "And suddenly, there's

Captain Kirk talking on his communicator, talking with no dialing. That was not a fantasy to us, although to the rest of the world it was, but to me that was an objective" (Shatner *How*). According to Shedroff and Noessel, "The connection was made even more apparent by the product's name: the Star-TAC. The phone was a commercial success, arguably aided by the fact that audiences had been seeing it promoted in the form of *Star Trek* episodes and had been pretrained in its use for three decades" (6).

In the words of Brent McDonald, "Take a look around your house. Do you have a personal computer? How about a cell phone? What about a Bluetooth headset.... Gene Roddenberry first envisioned all of these devices in *Star Trek*.... Even the simplest inventions demonstrate this, such as the automatic sliding doors seen throughout the original ... series. Roddenberry used the trends that were current in the 1960s to create more advanced technology in the show" (194–195). Automatic sliding doors already existed, but Roddenberry assumed they would be everywhere in the future, especially on starships (even though the sliding doors on his set were anything but automatic, no matter how they looked). A similar use of existing technology as futuristic is transparent aluminum in *Star Trek IV*, where Scotty and McCoy supposedly hand over the formula in exchange for materials to build a whale tank. A related use of the material as SF can be found in the opening words of the *Star Trek* novel *War Dragons*, "Transparent aluminum spun a delicate membrane between the spindly green of transplanted Martian foliage and the blue-black Martian sky" (Graf).

McDonald also says, "Roddenberry created for the show many things we currently take for granted. One important example of this is the plasma-screen television" (195). McDonald continues, "Whenever the crew hails another ship, they receive a crisp, clear, real-time image of whoever they are speaking to. Not only does this mean that the bridge of the Enterprise has a large plasma-screen TV but also that Roddenberry envisioned the creation of teleconferencing" (196). McDonald's book was published in 2013. I would strongly suggest that Roddenberry's technology is more advanced than a plasma screen, but that's only to be expected. Another Roddenberry innovation or inspiration "is removable computer memory" which is "done by using crystals and 3 × 3-inch squares in *Star Trek*" (197).

And there are more recent demonstrations of the impact of the original series. Dr. McCoy's medical tricorder (with the term licensed from CBS) became the model for an X Prize. On April 13, 2017, after five years of competition to make a mechanism that could "non-invasively diagnose 13 medical conditions without assistance from health professionals" (Karlin), the $10 million Qualcomm Tricorder X Prize made a decision. In the words of Jonah Comstock, "Final Frontier Medical Devices ... won the top prize of $2.6 million. Runner-up Dynamical Biomarkers Group will walk away with $1 million" (Comstock). Nor is that all. Comstock writes, "The X Prize foundation also announced the ways it will continue to support these teams and the other five finalists in bringing their tricorder devices to market, even though the competition is officially over." Plus, Comstock says, "The Roddenberry Foundation, established by the son of Star Trek creator Gene Roddenberry, pledged an additional $1.6 million toward the goal of getting tricorder devices into hospitals and communities."

A better known example is "Alexa, Amazon's digital voice assistant that responds to your commands on their Echo speaker, has a brand-new feature: instead of having to tap it awake, or call it by its name, you can ... just say, 'Computer.'" Cause and effect could not be clearer, "This is all because of Amazon founder Jeff Bezos, who happens to be a huge Star Trek fan. He watched the show as a kid, and role-played the characters with his friends. The Echo, it turns out, was inspired by the show, and part of Bezos' lifelong dream to integrate voice commands into technology, mirroring the pre–Siri computer voice on the U.S.S. Enterprise" (Ulster). Bezos, who also appears briefly as an alien Starfleet officer in *Star Trek Beyond* (Boyle "Get a Look"), was far from the only one to be inspired. In the words of Ray Ramadorai, principal avionics engineer at Planetary Resources, "By tying the future to that view of a diverse society, it created the expectation that society would change to match as the people who watched Star Trek grew up. That expectation extended beyond the society to the technology as well. So much of the technology we have now reflects the assumption that it could be developed and should exist. That was set in the minds of many technologists and entrepreneurs by watching the series and imagining how to get there" (Boyle "'Star Trek' at 50"). Even Abrams has experienced the impact. He says, "I can't tell you how many people I've spoken with who are in the space program who literally can point to *Star Trek* as the reason they do what they do" ("Gene Roddenberry's Vision").

McDonald puts Gene Roddenberry's role in context, "Roddenberry's contemporaries saw him as more than an author of science fiction." I point out that calling Roddenberry "an author of science fiction" and not a television producer is an important distinction or at least an important addition to his credentials. McDonald continues, "He was a futurist—someone who is seen as knowledgeable about future technological advancements. His papers on the future of technology opened doors for him and brought prestigious invitations.... NASA invited him to speak on his thoughts and ideas, and he gave lectures at universities and colleges" (195). This is a typical career path followed by creators of Hard SF. In 1992, Roddenberry posthumously received the National Space Society's Robert A. Heinlein Memorial Award which "honors those individuals who have made significant, lifetime contributions to the creation of a free spacefaring civilization" ("NSS"). Others who have been similarly honored include Arthur C. Clarke, Wernher von Braun, Robert H. Goddard, Carl Sagan, and Neil Armstrong.

I do not mean to suggest by all this that Roddenberry was the only person in the original *Star Trek* who was interested in SF or involved with space exploration. For example, he was not the only one to work with and be honored by NASA and similar organizations. Nichelle Nichols recounts "some amazing, eye-opening experiences such as flying an eight-hour mission aboard the Kuiper C-141 Astronomy Observatory (with an all-Trekker crew of serious scientists and astronomers thrilled to have Uhura aboard." She says that in 1976 she "was honored to be invited to the Jet Propulsion Laboratory to witness the touchdown of the Viking lander on Mars and delighted in receiving a copy of the first photograph it transmitted." Also, as a result of the work she did "to promote the program through Women in Motion, Inc." she "was appointed to the Board of Directors of the National Space Institute, a civilian organization founded by Wernher von Braun" (219).

By comparison, the Abramsverse is a smaller and less interesting place, and it tends to be far more violent, frequently using the threat of genocide or genocide itself as entertainment, a strategy Abrams had repeatedly employed in his television series *Person of Interest* and that he used again in *Star Wars: The Force Awakens*. Gerry Canavan says, "The new film universe begins by killing off the Romulus-Remus double planetary system before killing Kirk's ... parents, Kirk himself (he got better), Captain Pike ... (he did not), a huge portion of the population of 2259 San Francisco, and, perhaps most famously and most gratuitously, all but a tiny sliver of the entire Vulcan race" (320). Except for James Kirk's mother, Winona, who survived, that account of the death toll is correct. It is a species of disaster porn. Here's Alan Dean Foster's description of the end of Vulcan from the novelization of the film, "Soundlessly crumpling in upon itself like a candy wrapper in a child's hand, Vulcan imploded. Deserts, atmosphere, oceans—all the familiar geological features that combined to give the surface of a world its character—vanished, along with cities and infrastructure and the people who had built them."

At the beginning of *Star Trek into Darkness*, Captain Kirk is demoted for stopping the destruction of yet another race. He incurs this punishment because his interference supposedly violates Starfleet's Prime Directive, the metalaw that prevents the Federation from interfering in the natural development of other civilizations. Let us for the moment assume that enforcement of the Prime Directive is insane enough to require the death of an entire sentient species and call it non-interference. Such a thing would be completely ridiculous and would discredit the Federation and its laws, and perhaps that is part of the movie's point. However, even if it were true and we were meant to take it seriously, we would also have to believe that Spock, who had suffered through the near-extinction of his own race, and Kirk, who had witnessed that destruction and had come close to witnessing the end of the Earth as well, would have been expected to stand passively by and watch the death of another sentient species not long after. Even if standing aside for such a catastrophe could be required in some (admittedly unimaginable) circumstances, who could demand it from a captain and first officer who had so recently suffered through something so much like it themselves? Are we to believe that no one in Starfleet sees or feels the connection? Clearly, inside the Abramsverse, genocide and its parallels are entertainment. They have no emotional resonance. They generate no sense of horror and grief. Even sympathy seems absent. There are similar problems in *Star Wars: The Force Awakens*. As Lili Loofbourow notes, "Take, for example, the annihilation of several planets, and the way we're invited to regard them as so marginal to the story that no one even seems to remember it happened by the end." As she identifies the problem, "When you've actually invented a tragedy that's hundreds of thousands of times bigger than the Holocaust (in a film that prominently references Nazis) only in order to threaten that they're about to do it again, in a matter of seconds, YOU CANNOT ASK YOUR AUDIENCE TO CARE THAT SOME GUY AND HIS SON ARE WASTING THOSE ESSENTIAL SECONDS HAVING A MOMENT ON A BRIDGE." Nor can you expect Kirk to learn to obey Starfleet rules so that next time he will allow the population of an entire planet to die the way they should.

Now, it is unfair to place all or even a significant amount of the blame for this escalation of destruction in films on Abrams. If violence is an important element in entertainment (and that is certainly true), then there will be (and indeed there has been) a steady increase in that commodity as movies evolve. The difference between an early R-rated film such as *Dirty Harry* (1971) and almost any similar recent example more than proves my point. Nor, obviously, is the increase in violence limited to a particular type of film. Science fiction makes it possible to kill far more people since we are dealing with galactic civilizations, and so we might expect slaughter on a truly unprecedented scale. Nevertheless, individual movie makers are responsible for their own choices, and repeatedly employing genocide is, I think, a bad one, if for no other reason than that it damages the film's narrative structure and characterization. Either the enormous subject of genocide will engulf whatever story the film is trying to tell and trivialize any other emotional issues, or it will itself be pushed into the background, destabilizing the foregrounded narrative by its own weight and opening the moviemakers up to just the sort of charges that have been leveled against Abrams.

However, genocide is not the only source of or expression for extreme violence in the three Kelvin films. All have revenge as a major theme and all have a villain who is presumed to be psychologically unstable at best. Far from providing us with an optimistic vision of coming technological attractions, *Star Trek* (2009), for example, presents a nightmare substance called Red Matter that seems to be more a species of black magic for creating black holes than an example of plausible science. In fact, the red stuff in the movie turns out to be a kind of recurring in-joke between Abrams and his production designer Scott Chambliss. Chambliss says, "In the containment field in the ship is a big red ball. The 'big red ball' has a lot of resonance for J.J. and I [sic]: we have one in virtually everything we do. It started with the *Alias* pilot. I always look at a script and wonder what the big red ball is going to be this time" ("Star Trek Magazine").

The "big red ball" is not only good for committing genocide but also for time travel. However, as is only to be expected, the science fiction explanations and explorations are kept to a minimum. Briefly (though still at greater length than the film manages), the issues are that travel to the past makes three relatively plausible outcomes possible. The first (and, most people think, the most likely) possibility is that the past is fixed and everything that can happen has already happened. By that argument, time travelers to the past will do what they have already done, and the past will not be changed. The second possibility is that the past can be changed, and the future from which the time traveler came will be altered or even eliminated by those changes. This is what previous Trek films and television series have endorsed. In the first two seasons of the original series, three episodes—"Tomorrow Is Yesterday," "The City on the Edge of Forever," and "Assignment Earth"—took the *Enterprise* or members of its crew into the past and made it clear that their actions could alter the future from which they came. In "The City on the Edge of Forever," McCoy's accidental journey to Brooklyn in 1930 and his saving of Edith Keeler meant, in the words of the Guardian of Forever, "Your vessel, your beginning, all that you knew is gone." The third possibility is that time travelers can make changes, but those changes will not affect the timeline from which they came. Instead, the changes will create an alternate (alternative) or parallel timeline in which the time travelers may or may not be trapped. This is the version of time travel which Abrams' "big red ball" seemingly creates. But beyond Spock's statement that "Nero's very presence has altered the flow of history, beginning with the attack on the USS *Kelvin*, culminating in the events of today, thereby creating an entire new chain of incidents that cannot be anticipated by either party," and Uhura's labeling it "an alternate reality," there is little explication.

Other science fiction elements in the movie—such as they are—are handled with careless unconcern. Most movies, however they may have been written and assembled, end up being individual scenes strung together in the hopes of producing a narrative. The danger comes when the narrative is turned into a vehicle for the scenes. This can make real science fiction difficult as well as interfering with characterization and the creation of a believable secondary world or world building as it is often called. For example, we are asked to believe that a civilization which can disassemble humans down to the quark level and then reassemble them again as a means of transportation is still using live viruses in vaccines. After all, Kirk looks hilarious as he suffers through the ridiculous symptoms. There is a scene where Luke is attacked by a monster on the Ice Planet Hoth. No wait, Kirk is attacked by a monster on the ice planetoid Delta Vega, and the very large monster is eaten by an even larger monster. It's a standard trope, it is usually good for a visual shock and a laugh, and it appears in various forms in *Star Wars: The Phantom Menace* (1999), *Jurassic Park* (1993), and the *Star Trek* send-up *Galaxy Quest* (1999), among many other places. Unfortunately, to get to this particular punch line, Kirk has to be banished from the *Enterprise* by Spock, which is highly unlikely, the rest of the crew has to stand by while the Vulcan maroons the second in command on an ice planetoid, which is nearly unbelievable, and an escape pod fired from the Federation's most advanced ship has to be far less accurate than a bomb dropped by a B-2, which is impossible. We are also asked to believe that Spock Prime has been sitting passively fourteen kilometers from a Starfleet outpost instead of doing what he can to save Vulcan. Again, it seems more important for two guys to have a moment (and for the movie to work in some exposition) than to interfere with genocide.

While time travel is the main SF issue in *Star Trek* (2009), in *Star Trek into Darkness* (2013) it is genetic engineering. Unfortunately, at a time when the possibilities for such things are greater than they have ever been before and are about to become more extraordinary still, Abrams' second *Trek* film did little more than repeat the simple story from "Space Seed" with a footnote about conflict with the Klingons from the *Star Trek: Enterprise* episode "The Augments." There were appropriate special effects upgrades and, of course, far more casualties.

There were always superhumans in *Star Trek*, just as there have always been superhumans in science fiction in general. From Olaf Stapledon's *Last and First Men*, "a book that was instrumental in the development of the *Star Trek* format" (Alexander 229), to A.E. Van Vogt's *Slan*, from Harry Kutner's *Mutant* to Gordon R. Dickson's Dorsai series, from Nancy Kress's *Beggars in Spain* to Lois McMaster Bujold's *Cetaganda*, from the X-Men franchise to the *Heroes* series, to *Gene Roddenberry's Andromeda*, there has been a parade of possibilities, a series of suggestions of what human beings might be with just a little transformation. There were even two television series about mutants created by geneticists, albeit, not kind and responsible ones, *Mutant X* and James Cameron's *Dark Angel*. As long ago as 1921 in *As Far as Thought Can Reach*, Bernard Shaw was looking forward to humans who had evolved themselves "to the vortex freed from matter, to the whirlpool in pure intelligence that, when the world began, was a whirlpool in pure force" (261). They had gone beyond "flesh and blood," saying, "It imprisons us on this petty planet and forbids us to range through the stars" (255). Roddenberry's Organians in the original series episode "Errand of Mercy" might have said the same.

However, for some time it seemed that such stories, unless they could be explained by the strange impact of radiation (or Shaw's version of creative evolution), were impossible. Now, though, those other forms of transformation, those other mutants, the kind we choose to create, are nearly within our reach. We will not, perhaps, produce vortices freed from matter, but the time when there is one and only one human species may be rapidly nearing its end. There was a point in the past when there were multiple hominins. "At least three of the 'other species' were alive when our ancestors emerged from Africa 50,000 to 80,000 years ago: Denisovans, Hobbits, and Neanderthals" (Enriquez and Gullans 228). Many modern humans have DNA from Neanderthals and Denisovans. The day may be coming when transhumans will talk about having DNA from Homo sapiens sapiens. Today, "We can design, build, and transfer new genes into humans within months.... Millions of years' of evolution is being reformulated, redirected by humanity in just a few years" (Enriquez and Gullans 259).

The speed will increase, the possibilities will multiply, and there is even a vanishingly small chance that we might reach Bruce Sterling's unsettling future when "not only is humanity extinct but, strictly speaking, pretty much everyone alive today should be classified as a unique, postnatural, one-of-a-kind species" (442). Or we might be looking at the future outlined by Michael Goldblatt, then head of DARPA, the Defense Sciences Office of the United States' Defense Advanced Research Projects Agency (Garreau 19). He described it as "science action, not science fiction" and said, "Imagine if soldiers could communicate by thought alone.... Imagine the threat of biological attack being inconsequential. And contemplate, for a moment, a world in which learning is as easy as eating, and the replacement of damaged body parts as convenient as a fast-food drive-through" (cited in Garreau 22–23).

It may be, instead, that we will not view the future through a military lens but that there will be benevolent superhumans and paradises beyond imagination. It is very likely that the future holds life forms beyond our dreams because scientists have already built a new form of DNA with "two new base pairs" that "turned a four-letter code of life into a six-letter code" (Enriquez and Gullans 255). As Juan Enriquez says, "This Lifecode stuff ... is the single greatest superpower humans have ever had" (Enriquez). Soon, it will indeed be true that a suite of mutations can leap into being in one sudden event in a lab, that the resulting mutant can be a new species, better than the one that came before, and perhaps, as Dylan Hunt says in the *Gene Rod-*

denberry's *Andromeda* episode "A Symmetry of Imperfection," it will "be nice to be genetically perfect."

On a more mundane note, as early as 2001 Julian Savulescu was arguing in an article of *Bioethics* called "Procreative Beneficence: Why We Should Select the Best Children" that we have a moral obligation to make a "eugenic selection of embryos" (413). He has since become professor of practical ethics at Oxford and moved beyond the selection of embryos to advocating gene editing, "Humans have a lot of limitations.... When science offers us the opportunity to overcome these limitations, we should ask the ethical question: 'should we?'" And his answer is, "In many cases we have a moral obligation to overcome those limitations." He points out that "You're not allowed to test for things that are obviously beneficial, such as genetic dispositions for higher intelligence, in most of Europe and Australia; whereas the Chinese have a billion-dollar project for these sorts of genes and will be using that information in their reproductive decisions." His sympathy is obviously with the Chinese, "We will need some rules and some regulation, but much less than we have today in some parts of the world" ("As a Species'"). It may be that his advocacy is making positions such as his more widely accepted. He says, "We should treat gene editing as we would any other medical intervention" (Savulescu "Why We Should").

It was a tremendous opportunity for an SF film. New technologies are here or almost here. Predictions and encouragements would have been—if not easy—at least easier than usual. And yet *Star Trek into Darkness* gives us little more than the slightly smarter, somewhat stronger, much more aggressive creatures of the original series episode. There are no speculations or explorations. There are no questions about what might be possible for future humans, and there are certainly no answers. There is again a magical red substance, only this time it is the blood of Khan Noonien Singh. McCoy uses it to bring a tribble and then Captain Kirk back from the dead. Dr. McCoy says, "Once we caught him, I synthesized a serum from his superblood." And that's it as far as scientific explanations go. There is a last reminder that this movie is more horror than SF, one of those films where blood transfusions or organ transplants may result in a transference of personality. McCoy asks Kirk (admittedly as a joke), "Tell me, are you feeling homicidal? Power mad? Despotic?" Other problems include a Federation unbelievably riddled with conspiracies and the fact that Earth seems to have no planetary defense system whatsoever.

Unlike the first two Kelvin timeline films, *Star Trek Beyond* was not directed by J.J. Abrams. In a video provided by *The Huffington Post*, Abrams said, "It was clear that having made two of these movies, that having another director come in to bring his or her point of view and voice to the proceedings was the right move." He calls Justin Lin, the director of the third film, "an incredibly strong storyteller, filmmaker" but adds, "What struck me more than that was his love of *Star Trek*. He grew up a lifelong fan of what Gene Roddenberry created. And when he spoke about the characters he talked about them in a way that felt very much from the inside out, so I felt really excited to see how he was going to bring his love of these characters to life" (Van Luling). To his credit, Abrams strongly endorsed a point of view quite different from the one with which he had started.

While *Star Trek Beyond* has many of the troubling characteristics of its siblings—a revenge-driven plot that twists back on itself to the point of incoherence, violence as its most important means for entertaining the movie audience, and a tendency to see disaster rather than opportunity in the future—it is arguably the one that looks most like it belongs in the *Trek* family, the one that most obviously comes from the same *gene* pool as the original series. Of course, it has its problems. What *Star Trek Beyond* describes as a nebula actually seems to be much more like an asteroid belt. Alan Boyle writes, "The Enterprise has to negotiate an obstacle course of crashing rocks as it passes through what's called a nebula in 'Star Trek Beyond.' In the real world, however, the clouds of gas and dust that make up a nebula are so thin that a starship would have no place to hide—and nothing to dodge except for protostars" ("5 Tech Tidbits"). Additionally, it sometimes seems that the crew of the *Enterprise* should all be wearing red shirts to signal their imminent demise, and that the ship itself should be painted that color as well. Clearly, such repeated devastation results in desensitizing the audience in a way that would have been unthinkable for the original series. Let me give just one example of how much things have changed. Years ago, I asked a student in a science fiction class how he felt about the destruction of the *Enterprise* in *Star Trek III* (the first time the ship was destroyed), and he replied, "It was the most traumatic thing that happened to me during the eighties." Even Admiral Kirk, who is at least partly responsible for that first elimination, says, "My God, Bones, what have I done?" Of course, no reset could restore such innocence, but we might hope for a little less carnage as the franchise continues, and the third film in the Kelvin timeline does show some small signs of improvement, including a lower body count.

In terms of science fiction, *Star Trek Beyond* is better than the first two films. Alan Boyle cites two important developments in contemporary scientific research that the film extrapolates into the Federation's future, cloaking devices and swarm weapons. Boyle says, "Captain Kirk describes the cloaking technology as a type of 'holographic camouflage' that can also create illusions. That sounds more like the projection-based invisibility cloaks that military researchers are developing." About swarm weapons, Boyle says, "Almost every trailer … shows the Enterprise being attacked by a hail of tiny spacecraft, like a swarm of killer bees." He continues, "In the real world, military planners are also thinking about creating swarms of low-cost battle robots that could overwhelm an enemy's defenses. In February, Defense Secretary Ashton Carter said the Pentagon was working on fleets of 3-D-printed micro-drones" ("5 Tech Tidbits").

There is also the space station Starbase Yorktown. It's another in a continuing series of such things from Deep Space 9 to Babylon 5 to the city/starship Atlantis in *Stargate Atlantis*. Alan Boyle says its "thoroughfares ... stick out in all directions like an M.C. Escher print." Dr. McCoy declares it "looks like a damn snow globe in space just waiting to break." While it's unlikely to suggest a new direction for technology or to endorse one that currently exists, Simon Pegg (Scotty as well as the co-writer of the film) says, "Yorktown also has a very unique design, a sort of round and transparent enclosed structure that seems to generate artificial gravity on its curved, interior surface (kind of like a very small Dyson sphere)" (quoted in "Yorktown Base"). More important for the film and for its more positive message is the notion that, as Scott Collura argues, "It sounds like the writers were shooting for a classic Star Trek feel to Starbase Yorktown, a place where the many species that make up the United Federation of Planets can meet to pursue a better, common future for all." Or in the words of Simon Pegg, "It's a kind of diplomatic hub.... It's where all the most recent Federation inductees can come and mingle with each other and learn about each other. It's kind of lovely" (quoted in "Yorktown Base").

There are also lighter, more humorous elements in this movie, in some sense a revival of the mixed tone of the original series. In Zachary Quinto's (Spock) words, "I definitely feel like there's this return to some of the nature of the original vision of the franchise. It's funny, it's got a sense of humor, it doesn't take itself too seriously. Gene Roddenberry, I think, really understood the balance of that in a lot of ways" ("To Live Long and Prosper"). As Captain Kirk returns to the ship early in the film, he says, "I ripped my shirt again." That's not only a reference to William Shatner's frequent difficulties in the original series, but also to the fact that here the shirts and uniforms become something of a running gag. At one point Kirk opens a closet to reveal seven identical shirts. Toward the end of the film when Jaylah is informed that she has been accepted by Starfleet Academy, she asks, "Will I have to wear that uniform?" And Kirk replies, "Afraid so." And there's one last mention of such things. Kirk says to a small alien on Yorktown who is wearing some version of the outfit, "Kevin, still not wearin' pants, I see." Even serious situations have lighter moments. In response to McCoy's complaint that the Yorktown base "looks like a damn snow globe in space just waiting to break," Captain Kirk says, "That's the spirit, Bones!" After the crash of the *Enterprise*, McCoy and Spock find themselves separated from the rest of the crew and in danger. Dr. McCoy has just told Spock, "At least I won't die alone." At that instant Spock is beamed away, leaving McCoy behind. The doctor says, "Well, that's just typical." Later, as Kirk and company play "Sabotage" by the Beastie Boys to disrupt the communications of the swarm bots and save Yorktown, McCoy asks, "Is that classical music?" And Spock replies, "Yes, Doctor, I believe it is."

Finally, the message *Star Trek Beyond* sends from in front of the camera and behind it is one Roddenberry might have approved. Indeed, it is clearly one that Roddenberry inspired. Justin Lin tells us about his childhood, "The reruns of the original series—you know—I think of it being on in our living room every day. The crew of the *Enterprise* became kind of our family" ("To Live Long") Kirk puts it in similar fashion in the original series episode "A Private Little War," "Beam us up home."

Not surprisingly at the end of a movie whose director grew up with *Star Trek* and whose screenwriters are also fans, Captain Kirk, who had considered leaving the *Enterprise* to become a vice admiral, decides that exploration is more important and for that matter, more fun. Spock too rethinks leaving the ship (and Uhura), and the film concludes with the rebuilding of the *Enterprise* followed by the crew taking turns speaking Roddenberry's "These are the voyages" opening accompanied by the music of Alexander Courage. It is certainly the most traditional and therefore the most optimistic ending for any of the three Kelvin films. And there are equally optimistic messages from writers, director, and cast in "To Live Long and Prosper," an extra video on the Blu-ray. Karl Urban (Bones) says, I think *Star Trek* is hugely important. It's a vision of humanity that is done with warring, with global environmental destruction. There's a unity in mankind. Mankind's come together, and we're out there; we're exploring space." For Simon Pegg, "It's a universe where we're all accepted.... It's all about hope. It offers us the idea of our own future writ large." Doug Jung (co-writer of the film and Sulu's spouse) puts everything in a larger context, "Ultimately, Roddenberry presents this hopeful universe. We are the answer. You know, like we are the thing that will evolve and bring about a better way of living." If *Star Trek Beyond* is not the perfect continuation of Roddenberry's science fiction universe, it is at least a continuation. It answers Abrams's question about what would happen when Justin Lin brought his love of the characters to life. Nor was Lin alone in his affection for the material. It may be safe to say that the Abramsverse, which began in darkness, has reached a place of hope. And if hope has arrived, can real science fiction be far behind?

Works Cited

Alexander, David. *Star Trek Creator: The Authorized Biography of Gene Roddenberry*. Roc Books, 1994. Print.
Alien. Directed by Ridley Scott, Brandywine Productions, 1979.
Altman, Mark A., and Edward Gross. *The Fifty-Year Mission: The Complete, Uncensored,*

Unauthorized Oral History of Star Trek: The Next 25 Years: From the Next Generation to J.J. Abrams. St. Martin's Press, 2016.
"'As a species, we have a moral obligation to enhance ourselves.'" TED.com, 19 Feb. 2014, http://ideas.ted.com/the-ethics-of-genetically-enhanced-monkey-slaves/.
Asimov, Isaac. *I, Asimov: A Memoir.* Doubleday, 1994. Print.
Asimov, Isaac. *The Robots of Dawn.* Doubleday, 1983. Print.
Asimov, Stanley, ed. *Yours, Isaac Asimov: A Lifetime of Letters.* Doubleday, 1995. Print.
Booker, M. Keith. *Alternate Americas: Science Fiction Film and American Culture.* Praeger, 2006. Print.
Boyle, Alan. "5 Tech Tidbits from 'Star Trek Beyond.'" *GeekWire,* 22 Jul. 2016, http://www.geekwire.com/2016/tech-tidbits-star-trek-beyond/.
Boyle, Alan. "Get a Look at Amazon CEO Jeff Bezos as an Alien in 'Star Trek Beyond.'" *Geek-Wire,* 20 Jul. 2016, http://www.geekwire.com/2016/jeff-bezos-alien-star-trek-beyond-amazon/.
Boyle, Alan. "'Star Trek' at 50: How a Space Saga Inspired a Generation of Scientists, Engineers, and Writers." *GeekWire,* 8 Sept. 2016, http://www.geekwire.com/2016/star-trek-memories-50-year/.
Canavan, Gerry. "*Star Trek* at 50, Or, *Star Trek* Beyond *Star Trek.*" *Science Fiction Film and Television* vol. 9, no. 3, 2016, pp. 319–324.
Comstock, Jonah. "The Qualcomm Tricorder X Prize Has Its Winner, but Work on Tricorders Will Continue." Mobihealthnews.com, 13 Apr. 2017, http://www.mobihealthnews.com/content/qualcomm-tricorder-x-prize-has-its-winner-work-tricorders-will-continue.
Enriquez, Juan, and Steve Gullans. *Evolving Ourselves: How Unnatural Selection and Nonrandom Mutation Are Changing Life on Earth.* Current, 2015. Print.
Enriquez, Juan, perf. *TED Talks Science and Wonder.* Directed by Linda Mendoza, ITVS, 2016. Television.
Forbidden Planet. Directed by Fred M. Wilcox, MGM, 1956.
Foster, Alan Dean. *Star Trek into Darkness* [Film novelization]. Pocket Books, 2013. Amazon Kindle.
Garreau, Joel. *Radical Evolution: The Promise and Peril of Enhancing Our Minds, Our Bodies—And What It Means to Be Human.* Doubleday, 2005. Print.
Gunn, James. "Introduction." *Tomorrow and Tomorrow,* by Charles Sheffield, The Easton Press, 1997. Print.
Karlin, Susan. "More 'Star Trek' Tech in Real Life: The Qualcomm Tricorder XPrize." Fastcompany.com, 13 Apr. 2017, https://www.fastcompany.com/40406304/more-star-trek-tech-in-real-life-the-qualcomm-tricorder-xprize.
Leigh, Megan. "Star Trek: How J.J. Abrams Ruined Everything." *Pop-Verse,* 1 May 2013, http://pop-verse.com/2013/05/01/star-trek-how-J.J. -abrams-ruined-everything/.
Loofbourow, Lili. "The 'Star Wars' Fandom Menace: The Glaring Emotional Blind Spots That Power 'The Force Awakens.'" *Salon,* 21 Dec. 2015, http://www.salon.com/2015/12/22/the_star_wars_fandom_menace_the_glaring_emotional_blind_spots_that_power_the_force_awakens/.
McDonald, Brent. "Information Technology in *Star Trek*: Android Versus Android, Ipads Versus PADDs, Facebook Versus the Borg." *Star Trek and History,* edited by Nancy R. Reagin, Wiley, 2013. Print.
Nichols, Nichelle. *Beyond Uhura: Star Trek and Other Memories.* G.P. Putnam's Sons: 1994. Print.
"NSS Robert A. Heinlein Memorial Award." National Space Society, 21 Oct. 2015, http://www.nss.org/awards/heinlein_award.html.
Pilkington, Ace G. *Science Fiction and Futurism: Their Terms and Ideas.* McFarland, 2017. Print.
"Playboy Interview: Ray Bradbury." Raybradbury.com, 1996, http://www.raybradbury.com/articles_playboy.html.
Rose, Steve. "J.J. Abrams: 'I Never Got Star Trek.'" *The Guardian,* 6 May 2009, https://www.theguardian.com/film/2009/may/07/J.J. -abrams-interview-star-trek.

Savulescu, Julian. "Procreative Beneficence: Why We Should Select the Best Children." *Bioethics*, vol. 15, no. 5/6, 2001, pp. 413–426.
Savulescu, Julian. "Why We Should Fine-Tune the DNA of Future Generations." *Cosmos*, 17 Aug. 2016, https://cosmosmagazine.com/biology/build-your-own-baby.
Schepis, Rich. "Exclusive: Nick Meyer Says He Hopes Discovery 'Helps People See Themselves.'" TrekMovie.com, 21 Feb. 2017, http://trekmovie.com/2017/02/21/exclusive-nick-meyer-says-he-hopes-discovery-helps-people-see-themselves/.
Shatner, William. Narrator. *How William Shatner Changed the World*. Allumination Filmworks. 2005. Film.
Shatner, William. *Star Trek Memories*. HarperCollins: 1993. Print.
Shaw, Bernard. *As Far as Thought Can Reach*. Dodd, Mead & Company, 1963. Print.
Shedroff, Nathan, and Christopher Noessel. *Make It So: Interaction Design Lessons from Science Fiction*. Rosenfeld Media, 2012. Print.
Solow, Herbert F., and Robert H. Justman. *Inside Star Trek: The Real Story*. Pocket Books, 1996. Print.
Stableford, Brian. *Science Fact and Science Fiction: An Encyclopedia*. Routledge, 2006. Print.
Sterling, Bruce. "Homo Sapiens Declared Extinct." *Supermen: Tales of the Posthuman Future*, edited by Gardner Dozois, St. Martin's Griffin, 2002. Print.
"A Symmetry of Imperfection." *Gene Roddenberry's Andromeda*, season 4, episode 19, directed by Allan Harmon, 26 Apr. 2004.
Takei, George. *To the Stars*. Pocket Books, 1994. Print.
Ulster, Laurie. "Hello, Computer! Amazon Echo Now Takes a Cue from 'Star Trek IV: The Voyage Home.'" TrekMovie.com, 25 Jan. 2017, http://trekmovie.com/2017/01/25/hello-computer-amazon-echo-now-takes-a-cue-from-star-trek-iv-the-voyage-home/.
Van Hise, James. *The Unauthorized History of Trek*. HarperPrism, 1995. Print.
Van Luling, Todd. "J.J. Abrams on Why He Stopped Directing 'Star Trek.'" *Huffington Post*, 4 Oct. 2016, http://www.huffingtonpost.com/entry/J.J -abrams-star-trek_us_57f2d83ae 4b0703f759092fc.
Zoglin, Richard. "A Bold Vision." *Time Star Trek: Inside the Most Influential Science Fiction Series Ever*, Time, 2016. Amazon Kindle.

STAR TREK MEDIA CITED

"The City on the Edge of Forever." *Star Trek*, season 1, episode 28, written by Gene Roddenberry, directed by Joseph Pevney, 6 Apr. 1967.
"Gene Roddenberry's Vision." *Star Trek* (2009). Directed by J.J. Abrams, Paramount Pictures, 2009. Blu-ray.
Graf, L.A. *War Dragons. The Captain's Table: Books One Through Six (Star Trek)*. Pocket Books, 2000. Amazon Kindle.
"A Private Little War." *Star Trek*, season 2, episode 19, written by Gene Roddenberry, directed by Marc Daniels, 2 Feb. 1968.
Star Trek (2009). Directed by J.J. Abrams, Paramount Pictures, 2009.
Star Trek Beyond. Directed by Justin Lin, Paramount Pictures, 2016.
Star Trek IV: The Voyage Home. Directed by Leonard Nimoy, Paramount Pictures, 1986.
Star Trek into Darkness. Directed by J.J. Abrams, Paramount Pictures, 2013.
"Star Trek Magazine #17 Preview + Scott Chambliss Interview Extract." TrekMovie.com, 20 Mar. 2009, http://trekmovie.com/2009/03/20/star-trek-magazine-17-preview-scott-chambliss-interview-extract/.
Star Trek: The Motion Picture. Directed by Robert Wise, Paramount Pictures, 1979. Film.
"To Live Long and Prosper." *Star Trek Beyond*. Directed by Justin Lin, Paramount Pictures, 2016.
"Yorktown Base." *Star Trek Beyond*. Directed by Justin Lin, Paramount Pictures, 2016. Blu-ray.

Priming the Multiverse
Contextualizing the Kelvin Timeline Through Gene Roddenberry's Original Narrative

JESSICA SELLIN-BLANC

Within American history, the sixties remains a time of great social, political and cultural upheaval, as well as a rich moment of technological and artistic innovation. The Vietnam War dominated the decade, and with it brought social protests and a counterculture movement that would find its way into all aspects of American life. Likewise, the 1963 assassination of President John F. Kennedy marked an end to hopes for a more optimistic political future, and the Civil Rights Movement, gay rights activism, and second wave feminism became social answers for an ailing country. Culturally, the music industry saw a boom with the British Invasion, the maturing of Rock music, and Woodstock; the space race ran on toward the Apollo moon Landing of 1969; and the television continued to cement its imperative role within the domestic sphere with series such as *The Dick Van Dyle Show* (1961–1966), *The Twilight Zone* (1959–1964), and *Gilligan's Island* (1964–1967) finding success. With many middle and working class households first acquiring televisions in the late fifties, the medium was still in the process of negotiating its social function, and many programs featured formats such as the talk show, variety show, and wholesome sitcom content. Few shows pushed cultural boundaries with direct commentary on the events of the sixties, but of the series that came to fruition during this time, Gene Roddenberry's *Star Trek*, attempts to deal with relevant social and political issues in a unique and futuristic setting.

Premiering on NBC on September 6, 1966, *Star Trek: The Original Series* (1966–1969) would complete three seasons before its ultimate cancellation by the network in June of 1969. Within this time, the show would deal directly with issues of race, gender, personal identity, globalism, technological determinism, colonialism, and war. Despite its ultimate cancellation after seventy-nine episodes, Roddenberry's creation garnered a cult following that would continue to grow through its syndication during the late sixties, and throughout the Seventies. Aside from *Star Trek: The Animated Series* (1973–1975), the various television spin-offs that resulted from *The Original Series* (1966–1969), including: *Star Trek: Next Generation* (1987–1994), *Star Trek: Deep Space Nine* (1993–1999), *Star Trek: Voyager* (1995–2001), *Star Trek: Enterprise* (2001–2005), do not feature the characters from *The Original Series'* narrative. Instead, these shows feature new characters in different timelines, occupying the same universe as that inhabited by Captain Kirk, Spock and crew. However, between 1979 and 1991, *The Original Series* produced six films that follow Roddenberry's original crew after the timeframe seen within the series of the sixties. It would not be until 2009 that the diegetic world of *The Original Series* would be brought back to life in J.J. Abrams' 2009, *Star Trek*. Avoiding the traditional route that reboots have historically taken—where the same timeline, characters and narrative are recreated from the outset—2009's *Star Trek* featured the same characters and settings, but its timeline begins before *The Original Series* (ultimately converging with it in the next two films), while also taking place in an alternate reality.

Referred to as the Kelvin Timeline, *Star Trek* (2009), *Star Trek into Darkness* (2013) and *Star Trek Beyond* (2016) have been solidified as box office successes, but have not been without their own controversies and adaptations along the way. Through textual analyses of the Kelvin Timeline films, creative/production choices, placing them within a comparative lens with *The Original Series* can offer greater insight into the reception of the new films, in an attempt to create a mode of healthy/educated consumption. Likewise, a cultural analysis of our contemporary time can help offer intentionality behind divergences from Rodenberry's original diegesis, while simultaneously giving a causality for rebooting the original series in the early 2000's. Issues such as mode and medium specificity, character/actor bonding, nostalgia, current events, multiple writers, changing directors, and franchise loyalty will be explored to better understand the place that the Kelvin Timeline films hold within the historical *Star Trek* franchise, as well as the role they serve within our contemporary cultural moment. How these three films negotiate this space, as well as how their function has been received by fans, critics, and scholars is important in dissecting their contextualized reception. Similarly the paratexts and extratextual accumulations that coincide with these films are integral in informing their place within the larger franchise, along with the creative and narrative choices being made within the latest three films.

Defining the Reboot

J.J. Abrams, Roberto Orci and Alex Kurtzman's 2009 *Star Trek,* begins aboard the USS *Kelvin,* during the year 2233 (since date measurements have changed over time, for brevity's sake, we will replace stardates with year conversions). We last left the *Enterprise* under the helm of Jean-Luc Picard in Paramount's 2002 *Star Trek: Nemesis,* year 2379. Due to poor box office performance by *Nemesis,* the planned sequel never came to fruition, and Abrams' 2009 film serves as the first film in the franchise since 2002. The opening scene of *Star Trek* paints a slightly puzzling picture of the temporality at hand: The Romulan ship *Narada,* helmed by Captain Nero attacks the *Kelvin* in an attempt to reach a visibly aged Commander Spock (henceforth referred to as Spock Prime), in a role reprised by Leonard Nimoy. As the *Kelvin*'s captain, Robau, boards the *Narada,* Nero appears uncertain of the current stardate, which places our current narrative one hundred and forty-six years before the narrative of *Nemesis,* and thirty-two years before the beginning of *Star Trek: The Original Series*' narrative. On its own, the beginning of Abrams' reimagining reads as a prequel to the original series, as we witness the birth and brief upbringing of James T. Kirk, and his eventual admission to Starfleet Academy as a young man. The introduction of a young Spock, as well as a slightly less seasoned Leonard McCoy, again tells the audience that they are about to embark upon a fresh restart of *The Original Series*; however, there remains one incongruity: Spock Prime. Nimoy serves as a temporal foil, who will in fact determine the role that the three newest films play within the franchise at large.

From an industrial and economic standpoint, remakes, reboots and spinoffs have always been safer choices than creating new material, as the core values have already been audience tested, effectively reducing the risk associated with the production and distributive processes. Andrew Scahill posits that reboots have become a standardized way in which we "revisit familiar narratives with an altered origin story, narrative approach, or artistic aesthetic," while a remake is described as "an act of reverence towards the original" (Scahill 318). From this perspective, a reboot can be seen as an attempt to modernize a past narrative or franchise in a way that helps it resonate with contemporary audiences and current cinematic devices and styles. Scahill goes on to describe the role of the prequel within existing diegetic worlds and narratives that help aid in an overall coherence between the new origins, and the existing texts that came before them chronologically. While Scahill is studying televised horror texts, his hybrid term, "preboot," is helpful in explaining at least some of the various tactics being used within *Star Trek* and its subsequent sequels within the Kelvin Timeline.

A close analysis of the timeline presented in the new cycle suggests an all-encompassing, unique mode. The beginning of *Star Trek* does in fact begin thirty-two years before *The Original Series*, however, Spock Prime's journey back in time creates an alternate reality that transitions the three films from prequel status to something more akin to a reboot (with *Star Trek* [2009] falling under the "preboot" category), as the timelines link up in chronology. Since Spock Prime did not go back in time until after *The Original Series'* timeline, his narrative within the new films can also be seen as a figurative sequel to the series, with his storyline simultaneously coming before, after and alongside Rodenberry's serialized stories. With familiar narratives (such as the return of Khan), the new trilogy also suggests components of a remake. From this perspective, the new films take on a "Jack of All Trades," persona, where they are simultaneously conveying a multitude of perspectives, constantly negotiating their position within the existing universe, without ever invalidating any previous iterations. For these reasons, referring to the Kelvin Timeline films as mere reboots, or even preboots, does not do their narrative temporalities justice, and may perhaps suggest why the films have thus far evaded intense scholarly scrutiny.

Familiar Faces: Character/Actor Bonding

Maintaining the Kelvin Timeline films as simultaneous remakes/reboots/prequels/sequels to *The Original Series*, we are given familiar characters played by new actors and actresses. Chris Pine takes on the brash but ultimately selfless Captain James T. Kirk, Zoe Saldana maintains Uhura's strong, African intellectual female persona, Karl Urban gives Dr. Leonard McCoy (Bones) new life, Anton Yelchin resurrects the affable Checkov, John Cho fills the boots of Sulu, Simon Pegg maintains Scotty's original Aberdeen dialect, and Zachary Quinto takes on the pivotal role of Spock. Historically an ensemble based series, *The Original Series*, utilizes its serialized format to its full extent in terms of character development and focus. Due to the detail offered to each character during the original run, the actors who portrayed these individuals in Rodenberry's narrative became synonymous with the characters they played. In particular, the larger-than-life bravado of William Shatner became inextricably linked to that of James Kirk, and the soft-spoken intellect of Spock became indistinguishable from actor Leonard Nimoy. The inclusion of Nimoy only, suggests not only the importance of the character/actor bond, but also asks viewers and scholars to dig deeper into the role of this bond in the production and reception of the newest cycle.

When discussing the role of actor/character bonding, Murray Pomerance suggests that bonding strength, "leads viewers into a deeply embedded and continuing pattern of identification through which the actor and the character are rendered indistinguishable" (Pomerance 211). In the case of Spock, Nimoy played the character for nearly fifty years, from the start of *The Original Series* in 1969, until his death in 2015. Time alone cements Nimoy's conflation with Spock, and the choice of Abrams, Orci and Kurtzman to select Nimoy as the sole cameo role further solidifies a strong bond between the actor and character. Although Spock Prime plays a small role in the first two films of the Kelvin timeline, he serves as a determining factor in the Kelvin Timeline, and helps to place the films within the existing *Star Trek* universe. Nimoy's presence not only anchors the new films within the franchise, but also serves as a recognizable figure for returning fans, while also simultaneously allowing Quinto the possibility of making the role his own.

Desiring to step down after his appearance in the first film, Nimoy suggested that any further involvement would stand in the way of Quinto developing his own bond with his iteration of Spock. Nimoy's willingness to rejoin the Trek universe after his 1975 autobiography, *I Am Not Spock*, suggests a late-in-life coming to terms with his indelible association with the character, despite an initial desire to separate his identity from his onscreen persona. Perhaps his own personal acknowledgment of the actor-character bond was aided by the relationship he forged with J.J. Abrams (whose series *Fringe*, Nimoy regularly appeared on), as well as his connection to and mentorship of Zachary Quinto. The 2016 documentary *For the Love of Spock*, directed by Nimoy's son, Adam Nimoy, helps to commemorate not only the fiftieth anniversary of the *Star Trek* universe, but also fifty years of Spock, and ultimately, his now late father, further conflating the actor/character bond.

Within the documentary, Nimoy's relationship with Quinto is seen as father and son in nature, as both men lost their own fathers early in their lives, and the two remain ultimately bound by portraying the same meteoric science fiction character. This intense, yet complicated bond seems to parallel that of their onscreen personas, as Quinto's Spock looks toward Spock Prime as a wealth of lived knowledge, and someone to be trusted. After reprising his role within *Star Trek into Darkness* (2013), Nimoy's death in September of 2015 was felt not only in the real world, but also within the diegesis of the Kelvin Timeline films as well. Within the narrative of *Star Trek: Beyond* (2016), Quinto's Spock is deeply saddened by the news of the passing of Spock Prime, and his visible anguish at the news rivals the sadness seen when he witnessed the death of his mother in *Star Trek* (2009). Perhaps serving as one final rebuttal to Nimoy's *I Am Not Spock*, the actor's final role before his death was that of Spock, now eternally bonding actor and character.

The New Queer Frontier

While Leonard Nimoy's reprisal of his role as Spock is deterministic within the Kelvin Timeline narrative, and can easily be attributed to the actor-character bond cultivated over a fifty year period, there still remain echoes of past actors to be examined within the newest films. Surviving actors from *The Original Series*: William Shatner (James T. Kirk), George Takei (Hikaru Sulu), Nichelle Nichols (Uhura), and Walter Koenig (Pavel Checkov) have all offered their support via press outlets for their reincarnations through a new generation of actors and writers. Some actors have expressed not only their stamp of approval for a continuation of the universe, but also a desire to reprise an old role. In the case of Shatner and Captain James T. Kirk, the negation of the Kirk from *The Original Series* within the timeline is a narrative one, and fairly simplistic in nature: Kirk is dead. When asked why Shatner would not be allowed to appear in the new films, director J.J. Abrams offered a fairly straightforward answer in an interview with *IGN*:

> Obviously it's *Star Trek*, nearly anything is possible. There's the fairly simple notion that on the day Kirk was born another timeline began. But in the other timeline, Kirk died onscreen (in *Generations*). I don't know how he would come back unless we went into this other reality and we did a timeline and reality jump. In all the years we've been working on this, I've yet to hear a pitch that didn't sound too contorted and contrived for an audience to swallow. And I've talked to him (Shatner) about it. If Kirk had lived there'd be an answer. But there's something about his having died that makes it impossible" [O'Brien, "Abrams Doubts Shatner Will Ever Appear in New *Star Trek* Movies"].

Therefore, while Spock Prime's presence offers a deterministically controlled aspect to the new narrative that preserves the existing canon, bringing Kirk Prime back to life would essentially invalidate *The Original Series*. Likewise, an examination of the actor-character bond between Shatner and Kirk could prove to have an overwhelming amount of bravado that instead of aiding in the recognition of a new Kirk (Chris Pine), would overshadow the passing of the torch. While the exclusion of past actors from the Kelvin Timeline films is at times narratively necessary, that does not mean that the creators behind the new films do not seek the approval of past actors and actresses.

In the case of Nichelle Nichols, it was important that Uhura continue to be represented by a strong, African American woman, an achievement realized in the casting of Zoe Saldana, who also comes from Dominican, Haitian and Puerto Rican descent. Nichols' performance as Uhura during the sixties on a major network spoke to the Civil Rights movement and second wave feminism taking place during the decade (Aiken 11). Likewise, Saldana's maintenance of such a strong character comes at a time when Hollywood was not offering enough visibility to African American actors, writers and directors. George Takei possessed similar sentiments for John Cho's casting as Hikaru Sulu, citing a continuing absence of Asian American actors within Hollywood. However, Takei's blessing at the time now reads as premature, considering his very public reaction to the choice to make Sulu a homosexual character in the Kelvin Timeline's third installment, *Star Trek Beyond* (2013).

When *Beyond* writer, Simon Pegg (who also reprised his role as Scotty), and director, Justin Lin approached Takei in early 2016 to alert the actor that John Cho would be portraying a queer version of Sulu, Takei expressed his disappointment at the news in interviews leading up to the film's release. Within *The Original Series*, Sulu never had an onscreen romantic relationship, but a daughter, Demora, appeared in the 1994 film, *Star Trek: Generations*. Off camera, Takei came out as gay in 2005, in a *Frontiers* Magazine interview, where he also shared that he had been with his current partner for eighteen years, and the two would wed in 2008 (Vankin, "George Takei Is Giving 70 Years of His Belongings to a Museum"). Even before Takei's public declaration of his sexuality, he had a long history of being an LGBTQ advocate, a feat that continued in a more public fashion after 2005. According to interviews with Lin, Pegg and Cho leading up to *Beyond*'s release, the trio were hopeful that their portrayal of Sulu as a queer character would be a respectful homage to Takei, who had secured a strong bond with the character of Sulu over the last fifty years. In an interview in 2016, Takei was quoted as telling Cho: "Be imaginative and create a character who has a history of being gay, rather than Sulu, who had been straight all this time, suddenly being revealed as being closeted," and further expressing that he was "delighted that there's a gay character ... unfortunately, it's a twisting of Gene's creation, to which he put in so much thought. I think it's really unfortunate" (Lowder, "The Debate Over Sulu's Sexuality in *Star Trek Beyond* Should Set Off Your Red Alert"). This desire to nostalgically preserve Rodenberry's creation by Takei reads as problematic when a critical step back is taken to consider the Kelvin Timeline and its true place within the Trek universe.

In this instance of disavowal, Takei can be seen as a proxy for much of *Star Trek* fandom, whom have reacted in a historically similar manner when any liberties have been taken with Rodenberry's original narratives and diegesis. Such protests, however, can be seen as somewhat reactionary, failing to take into account the creative intentionality behind the newest films, and the specific role they serve within the larger universe (perhaps some of this blame can be placed on the Kelvin Timeline films' negation of any specific mode of prequel, reboot, remake, etc.). While John Cho's character of Sulu is certainly an homage to Takei's version within *The Original Series*, the show and the new films do not fit within the same chronological timeline that necessitates a linear coherence. Cho's Sulu exists in an alternate reality to that of Takei's, and, in fact, per the logic of the Kelvin Timeline, the two distinct iterations of Sulu exist simultaneously to one another but in completely different realities. This differentiation, as well as a desire to reflect contemporary culture, seem to have informed Simon Pegg's polite disagreement with Takei's response to the creative choices made for the third film.

Within interviews leading up to the film's premiere in the summer of 2016, Pegg shared Takei's sentiments that it is "unfortunate that the screen version of the most inclusive, tolerant universe in science fiction hasn't featured an LGBT character until now," certainly suggesting that continuing to ignore such inclusivity in contemporary society becomes a harder choice to defend (Shoard, "Simon Pegg: I Respectfully Disagree with George Takei Over Gay Sulu"). Pegg continues to answer Takei directly, by stating that the writers, "could have introduced a new gay character, but he or she would have been primarily defined by their sexuality, seen as the 'gay character,' rather than simply for who they are, and isn't that tokenism?" (Shoard, "Simon Pegg: I Respectfully Disagree with George Takei Over Gay Sulu"). To further justify the creative choice to make a familiar character have a queer aspect to his identity, Pegg suggests that he and Justin Lin, "loved the idea of it being someone we already knew because the audience have a pre-existing opinion of that character as a human being, unaffected by any prejudice. Their sexual orientation is just one of the many personal aspects, not the defining characteristic" (Shoard, "Simon Pegg: I Respectfully Disagree with George Takei Over Gay Sulu"). Within interviews, both Takei and Pegg have intimated that Roddenberry's own lack of inclusion of an LGBTQ character within the Prime timeline may have been more a sign of the times, than an intentional, creative decision. To seek out the limitations Roddenberry faced during the sixties, one need only refer to the backlash received from the televised interracial kiss between Uhura and Kirk in *The Original Series*' episode: "Plato's Stepchildren," which aired in November of 1968, during the height of the Civil Rights Movement. For Pegg and Lin, the Kelvin Timeline's notion of the multiverse seems the perfect setting to show just how minute a change is needed to transform a well known character, while still preserving the original version in totality.

Nostalgia: The Dark Turn and Finding the Light

In his 2015 text, *Mediated Nostalgia: Individual Memory and Contemporary Mass Media*, Ryan Lizardi discusses nostalgia in relation to how contemporary media constructs the individual: "The viewer of contemporary media culture has been placed in a similar position, lured by a recent narrative trend that is constructing us as past-focused subjects and has us fixing on a recent past" (Lizardi 4). Lizardi claims that this obsession with the past creates uncritical media consumers, especially when considering the recent proliferation of reboots, remakes and nostalgia themed texts. In place of this narcissistic, nostalgic desire, there exists the potential to use the past as a comparative and reflexive object that can be used as a learning tool, when placed in contrast with our contemporary situation. Hayden White suggests an adaptive historical discourse that calls for a continuum of history that is adapted and added to as time progresses, refusing to allow the past or the present to be separated from one another in a vacuum, unaffected by cultural, social and historical change. While both Lizardi and White discourage viewing nostalgia as inherently problematic, there is a clear distinction between healthy (adaptive) and unhealthy (narcissistic/melancholic) nostalgia, which can be applied to various reception practices surrounding the release of the Kelvin Timeline films.

Per Lizardi's definition, "narcissistic nostalgia is exploited by contemporary media to develop individualized pasts that are defined by idealized versions of beloved lost media texts," attempted breaks from such nostalgic practices are positioned as unwelcome in our current media landscape (Lizardi 2). Through Freudian definitions, melancholia suggests the inability to accept a new object of adoration due to one's inability to let go of a past object, and an intrinsic desire to see that object faithfully recreated. In large part, nostalgia is driven by the desire to revisit the past, and with current technologies and syndication, this desire can be easily achieved through *Star Trek* reruns on television, or through various streaming technologies, at the drop of a hat. With the original texts so easily accessible, a healthy, adaptive sense of nostalgia becomes more allusive, with a desired perpetual nostalgia more plausible, wherein the same source text is repeated again and again. With access to Roddenberry's version of the past constantly accessible, an unhealthy attachment to that vision becomes more easily perpetuated, as seen in George Takei's reaction to Simon Pegg's desire to adapt a healthy form of nostalgia in *Beyond*.

Takei's close connection to *The Original Series*, and firsthand experience of the show alongside Gene Roddenberry becomes further complicated when there is a refusal to see the contemporary films as anything other than a deviation from the original text. In this respect, Takei, and in-turn fans who claim loyalty to *The Original Series*, fall prey to Nietzsche's "malady of history," the inability to forget/unwillingness to relent any memories or attachments to the past. In contrast, through a selective mediation of the past, the writers and directors behind the three new films are fully recognizing the potential that lies in the past *Star Trek* universe, while also attempting to be affected by the current cultural moment. With this respectful view of the past, contemporary creators such as Pegg have managed to adapt the past canon for the contemporary mediascape without invalidating the narratives of the texts that came before them, effectively preserving Roddenberry's past vision while simultaneously adapting the franchise's overall narrative in a meaningful way for contemporary audiences. When re-examining Simon Pegg's rebuttal to George Takei's disappointment in creating a queer version of Sulu, the writer seems to be attempting to avoid Michael S. Roth's presumption that nostalgia has the means to position "an excess of remembrance as a smothering of creativity under the burden of history" (Lizardi 271). For Pegg, writing the script under the weight of Takei's personal nostalgic narrative would only be perpetuating the past historical conditions that did not allow Roddenberry to create a queer character within the inclusive utopia of the *Star Trek* universe.

Generational Nostalgia and Timelessness

In "Retro-Remaking: The 1980's Film Cycle in Contemporary Hollywood Cinema," Kathleen Loock examines a cycle of films released in 2010, a period deemed "the Year of the '80s Remake," a cycle that would continue on in the years that follow (Loock 175). Simon Reynolds refers to this tendency towards the retro (or "retro mood," as he terms it) as a welcome and historic move within the media, which "celebrates nostalgia and obsesses with the cultural artifacts of its own immediate past" (Loock 175). Michael Cieply refers to this Eighties revival as "part of a retro mood that has revved up the careers of baby-boom performers while providing comfort food for the audience" (Loock 175). Of the films analyzed, Loock has chosen those that, "directly rely on their cult status and presence in cultural memory and explicitly draw attention to the earlier texts" (Loock 176). This cycle of Eighties films is also chosen for their ability to evoke "sentimental attachments to its films and television series, and to associated childhood memories, and there is a general apprehension among audiences that cinematic remaking will destroy these personal ties to the past" (Loock 177). The acknowledgment of this fan based apprehension speaks to an unhealthy nostalgia with the past, one that desires to hold past texts in a state of arrested development, requesting that they not be adapted over time.

An emphasis on the "immediate past" within this Eighties boom suggests a need to capitalize on nostalgia while the given time period is still fresh in the childhood minds of the now grown fanbase. The choice to revive narrative elements from *The Original Series*, a show that ran during the sixties, simultaneously to the Eighties' cycles, creates a puzzling picture for contemporary nostalgia. The sense of generational belonging experienced by those attending Eighties films seems slightly less applicable when considering the more aged demographic of the generation associated with *The Original Series*. Aesthetically, the choice to film *Star Trek* (2009), *Into Darkness* (2013), and *Beyond* (2016) makes use of cinematographic technology, such as 3D, that offers a realness that has the potential to alienate the childhood memories associated with *The Original Series*. With nearly fifty years between the televised series and the newest filmic installments, the set-based, campy effects of the show appear virtually unrecognizable under the guise of CGI and other digital and audio based effects. Likewise, with a new director in J.J. Abrams (born in 1966), and new writers in Roberto Orci (born in 1973) and Alex Kurtzman (born in 1973), the newest installments are dependent upon the creative vision of men who were not old enough to watch the series during its original run. One large grievance fans and critics alike had for both *Star Trek* and *Into Darkness* was Abrams' overuse of lens flares, a visual style that had simultaneously become an authorial signature for the prolific director, while also offering the new films an aesthetic realness missing from older, more familiar *Star Trek* incarnations.

Given the nearly fifty years' time between the premiere of *The Original Series* and the premiere of *Star Trek*, the decision to revamp the original narrative seems largely dependent upon the show's presence on syndicated television, as well as the six films that premiered between 1979 and 1991. Contact with the *Star Trek* universe after the timeline of *The Original Series* occurred within Roddenberry's *Star Trek: The Next Generation* series between 1987 and 1994, as well as four films, which premiered between 1994 and 2002. The notion of cycles rebooting the "immediate past," would suggest that a reboot of narratives from *The Next Generation* would have made more sense in terms of timeliness, however, the failure of 2002's *Star Trek: Nemesis* at the box office (worldwide gross: $67.3 mil) may have made such a timely choice fiscally irresponsible for most production companies. Likewise, the choice to revive an older storyworld has the potential to yield less nostalgic resistance, especially for younger fans who have come to the series via streaming or syndication. While the nostalgia for the eighties spoke to childlike innocence, the sixties spoke to revolution and social upheaval, a history which seems to be repeating itself within the last decade. From this perspective, the themes of Roddenberry's original utopia appear timeless in their ability to be culturally and politically relevant some fifty years later, as evidenced by the continued box office success of all three films, and a fourth installment announced last summer.

The Timeless Nature of a Utopic Future Past

As noted in the introduction, the *Star Trek* universe, as created by Gene Roddenberry, dealt with the tumultuous issues of the sixties by pushing the boundaries of American television via a utopian and futuristic setting. From an interracial kiss that went against the concerns of network executives, to storylines that dealt with issues of war, colonization, sexuality, gender, and social identity, the show's social commentary was in stark juxtaposition with its dual emphasis on the progression of technology. Unlike other science fiction texts of the time, *Star Trek: The Original Series* chose to render the future in a positive, utopic light, instead of the dystopian future that seemed so fitting with the turmoil of the sixties. After the assassination of President John F. Kennedy, the United States was in need of a new replacement idealist, and that is what they got in Captain James T. Kirk.

In his essay, "The Kirk Doctrine: The Care and Repair of Archetypal Heroic Leadership in J.J. Abrams' *Star Trek*," Stephen McVeigh addresses the political climate surrounding 2009's *Star Trek*. According to an interview with Zachary Quinto, the catalyst for the timeliness of this new re-invention can be found in Barack Obama, a politician whose slogans of unity are extremely reflexive to those of the Star Trek franchise ("Zachary Quinto Says"). McVeigh goes on to quote director J.J. Abrams' desire to make "optimism cool again," as it was the universe's "unabashed idealism" that initially drew the director to the project in the first place (McVeigh 179). However, McVeigh argues that the first film actually follows the "cowboy diplomacy" logic of the Bush administration, positing that the paratextual reference to Obama may just be an idealistic marketing ploy on behalf of the film's director and actors. However, McVeigh very succinctly wraps up the ramifications of *Star Trek*'s (2009) timing amidst Bush's replacement by Obama in office:

> *Star Trek*'s response is more sophisticated though because it seeks not to dismiss or erase Bush, but to absorb him and the qualities he displayed as Commander-in-chief after 9/11, into the archetype of American heroic leadership. In this way, the James Kirk of 2009 can be read as an attempt to rehabilitate Bush and as such Kirk's narrative arc of rebellious youth to starship captain comes into focus as a version of Bush's own journey [McVeigh 180].

From this perspective, both Kirk and Bush are viewed as men who have had unwelcome situations thrust upon them (essentially both war-time leaders), whose essential identifiers act deterministically through their actions. McVeigh's essay leaves off by hinting at 9/11 as a re-opening of a cycle of turmoil and social upheaval that *The Original Series* dealt with, which places the first film of the new cycle in the precarious position of creating the foundation for not only narrative growth, but character growth as well.

Perhaps the newest Kirk's defining moment/catalyst for change comes at the beginning of the second installment's narrative, as a brash Captain Kirk is demoted after revealing his ship and crew to an indigenous people on the distant planet of Nibiru (a planet which then begins to worship the

USS *Enterprise*). Kirk's demotion to first officer, however, is short lived after Pike's untimely death at the hands of Starfleet agent John Harrison, a character all too familiar to fans of *The Original Series*. In the cryptic, and at times deliberately misleading, marketing for the film, audiences were largely torn between predicting Benedict Cumberbatch's antagonist as John Harrison or the infamous Khan. As the audience soon came to learn, Cumberbatch's character was the genetically modified/superhuman Khan masquerading as agent Harrison, hoping to infiltrate Starfleet in an attempt to regain the rest of his slumbering crew, in an attempt to finish their war on earth some three hundred years prior. Certainly these notions of infiltration and terrorism can be easily related to continuing global events, presenting an onslaught of moral and political agendas that often times seem at odds with one another. The 2010's were marked by global attacks masquerading as religious doctrine, and homegrown radicals committing acts of hateful intolerance within U.S. borders.

Again an unlikely hero thrust into the throes of battle and revenge, the Kirk from the first film has taken on a more tempered approach, seeming to learn the lesson that Pike had hoped would come to fruition after Kirk's error on Nibiru. In lieu of taking opportunities to kill Khan and his fellow crew members, both Kirk and Spock preserve their lives, with Kirk even trusting Khan enough to work with him upon learning of Admiral Marcus' betrayal. Kirk also offers himself for the lives of his crew multiple times, which ultimately results in Kirk's death due to radiation poisoning while realigning a key component of the *Enterprise*, saving his shipmates. This change in Kirk as a leader seems to come about most notably after the passing of his mentor, Captain Pike, officially cementing Kirk's new role as Captain, solidifying the transition. Politically, by the film's release in 2013, Obama had officially been president for three and a half years, with the Bush era officially in the immediate past. Likewise, with Kirk's revival at the hands of Spock (and Khan's blood), his rebirth as leader can be seen as fully realized, and upon waking, he makes it his first act to place Khan back into a cryogenic sleep with the rest of his crew, an act of maturity and mercy. With the brash, reactionary Kirk now seemingly in the past, 2016's *Into Darkness* finds "Kirk the diplomat," growing weary of his new role amidst the ship's latest five year mission.

At the point of the film's release, the Obama presidency was at its tail end, during a contentious campaign year with Bernie Sanders, Hillary Clinton and Donald Trump. Such events coincide with Kirk's ultimate decision to request a Vice Admiral position, asking that Spock be made the captain of the *Enterprise*. Earlier in the film, when conversing with Bones, Kirk is left unsure of his place in the world after so much time spent in his father's shadow, feeling the need to take a step back and reflect. In the face of new potential leadership, this film differs in tone slightly from the previous two films, as Kirk takes a slight backseat so that the film can focus on the crew as an ensemble cast (again, hinting at the current uncertainty of U.S. politics). This shift in focus allowed the film to take some contemporary liberties with characters, most notably through the troubled romance between Uhura and Spock (an "established" interracial relationship from the compelled kiss between Uhura and Kirk within *The Original Series*), and the choice to render Sulu as having a male partner and young daughter. As mentioned in an early section that discusses interviews with George Takei and Simon Pegg, the decision to portray Sulu as a queer character was received as extremely divisive, but nonetheless is a sign of the film's contemporary timeliness. While the scene lasts for a mere thirty seconds (or less), it manages to be profound, without being the defining moment of the character, and its brevity also suggests a point in time where such a scene is not out of place, or an act to be gawked at voyeuristically. Its inclusion within the diegesis, as well as the new franchise reads as a natural progression from Roddenberry's utopic vision, as opposed to a divergence from his ultimate narrative.

For Kirk, Krall represents the potentiality of a Captainship gone wrong, as a once great Starfleet graduate who was radicalized and changed while suspended in space. Again, referencing notions of home grown violence, and the potential to turn on one's native land, Krall's main goal is to destroy the base at Yorktown, killing thousands of innocent people, and taking out a Starfleet hub. Given the current political climate of 2017, marked by a Trump presidency and a recent immigrant ban, the fact that the *Enterprise* crew are helped by the strong and intelligent alien Jaylah, whose engineering know how and quick wit saves the crew on multiple occasions. Her later acceptance into the Starfleet Academy is extremely representative of the hopeful idealism that first drew J.J. Abrams to the franchise eight years ago, and the character of Jaylah was a huge motivation for newcomer Justin Lin behind the camera of *Beyond*. On a more somber note, the passing of Leonard Nimoy in February of 2015 marked the need to end Spock Prime's role within the Kelvin Timeline, officially handing the reins over to Zachary Quinto's own version of Spock, again perhaps reflexively foreshadowing the eventual end to the Obama administration some six months after the film's premiere.

Conclusion: For Leonard Nimoy and Anton Yelchin

With an idealistic, utopic diegesis and origins in the tumultuous sixties, Gene Roddenberry's *Star Trek: The Original Series* has revealed its timelessness through the box office success of the franchise's newest three film releases: *Star Trek* (2009; worldwide gross: $385 mil), *Star Trek into Darkness*

(2013; worldwide gross: $467 mil) and *Star Trek: Beyond* (2016; worldwide gross: $343 mil). However, while *The Original Series* helps to inform the new trio of films (and those to come in the future), the narratives and characterizations seen during the show's run in the sixties do not determine those of the contemporary reimagining. Likewise, various paratexts and extratextual pieces that surround the films help to not only inform the current run of films, but aim to offer solutions that can reconcile the franchise's past in a healthy way, that allows nostalgia for its past to be adapted for the present and future.

While Roddenberry's choice to place the franchise's diegetic world in the future opened its narratives up to infinite possibilities, and lent a contributory hand towards its timelessness, it remains crucial to still contextualize the film within the various timelines of existing texts. Despite past attempts to categorize the films as prequels or reboots, their place within the franchise is more complex, as the films (as discussed earlier) can simultaneously be read as prequels, reboots, revisions, and even sequels. Such definitions may seem erroneous, but they prove crucial when sifting through the many extratextual sources that surround the films, namely interviews and notions of nostalgia, as expressed through the differing viewpoints of Takei and the franchise's newest creative minds. Likewise, in order to begin to decipher the effects of contemporary cultural events, they must be viewed comparatively to those of the sixties, with fresh eyes that manage to avoid the potential pitfalls associated with a melancholic nostalgia towards the past.

After the July 18, 2016 announcement for a fourth installment, with Chris Pine and Zachary Quinto both signed on to reprise their roles as Kirk and Spock, the future of the film's narrative remains ever influenced by extratextual events, namely: the unfortunate passing of Leonard Nemoy (Spock Prime) and Anton Yelchin (Chekov). With Nimoy playing such a vital role in the determining factors that created the alternate reality of the Kelvin Timeline, as well as his guidance and mentorship towards Quinto's Spock, his absence from future films at once creates a void, while also officially passing the torch to Quinto to truly make the role his own. Similarly, Yelchin's Chekov had finally found his due screen time during *Beyond*, and his absence from the ensemble cast has been noted and mourned by fans and the franchise alike. With no plans to fill his role with a new actor, Abrams and his fellow producers are left with a narrative challenge that aptly preserves Yelchin's important role within the community, while also noting the significant loss the franchise endures without the presence of Chekov aboard the *Enterprise*. As the closing credits of *Star Trek: Beyond* say: "In loving memory of Leonard Nimoy," and "For Anton." (Lin *Star Trek Beyond*).

WORKS CITED

Aiken, Suzan E. "The Bad Boy and Feminism: Analyzing Captain Kirk." *To Boldly Go: Essays on Gender and Identity in the Star Trek Universe*, edited by Nadine Farghaly, McFarland, 2017.

Lizardi, Ryan. *Mediated Nostalgia: Individual Memory and Contemporary Mass Media*. Lexington Books, 2016.

Loock, Kathleen. "Retro-Remaking: The 1980's Film Cycle in Contemporary Hollywood Cinema." *Cycles, Sequels, Spin-Offs, Remakes, and Reboots: Multiplicities in Film and Television*, edited by Amanda Ann Klein and R. Barton Palmer, University of Texas Press, 2016.

Lowder, Bryan. "The Debate Over Sulu's Sexuality in Star Trek Beyond Should Set Off Your Red Alert." *Slate*, 8 Jul. 2016, http://www.slate.com/blogs/outward/2016/07/08/george_takei_ is_right_sulu_shouldn_t_be_gay_in_star_trek_beyond.html. Accessed 12 May 2017.

McVeigh, Stephen. "The Kirk Doctrine: The Care and Repair of Archetypal Heroic Leadership in J.J. Abrams' Star Trek." *Star Trek as Myth: Essays on Symbol and Archetype at the Final Frontier*, McFarland, 2010.

O'Brien, Lucy. "Abrams Doubts Shatner Will Ever Appear in New Star Trek Movies." *IGN*, 19 Jul. 2016, http://www.ign.com/articles/2016/07/20/abrams-doubts-shatner-will-ever-appear-in-new-star-trek-movies. Accessed 9 May 2017.

Pomerance, Murray. "Doing Dumbledore: Actor-Character Bonding and Accretionary Performance." *Cycles, Sequels, Spin-Offs, Remakes, and Reboots: Multiplicities in Film and Television*, edited by Amanda Ann Klein and R. Barton Palmer, University of Texas Press, 2016.

Shoard, Catherine. "Simon Pegg: I Respectfully Disagree with George Takei Over Gay Sulu." *The Guardian*, 8 Jul. 2016, https://www.theguardian.com/film/2016/jul/08/simon-pegg-defends-gay-sulu-after-george-takei-criticism. Accessed 9 May 2017.

Scahill, Andrew. "Serialized Killers: Prebooting Horror in Bates Motel and Hannibal." *Cycles, Sequels, Spin-Offs, Remakes, and Reboots: Multiplicities in Film and Television*, edited by Amanda Ann Klein and R. Barton Palmer, University of Texas Press, 2016.

Vankin, Deborah. "George Takei Is Giving 70 Years of His Belongings to a Museum." *The Los Angeles Times*, 30 Mar. 2016, http://www.latimes.com/entertainment/arts/la-ca-cm-george-takei-20161113-story.html. Accessed 9 May 2017.

"Zachary Quinto Says 'Star Trek' Will Be Big if Obama Is Elected." Starpulse.com, 17 Oct. 2008. http://www.starpulse.com/news/index.php/2008/10/17/zachary_quinto_says_star_trek_will_be_bi.

STAR TREK MEDIA CITED

For the Love of Spock. Directed by Adam Nimoy, 455 Films, 2016.

Star Trek (2009). Directed by J.J. Abrams, Paramount Pictures, 2009.

Star Trek Beyond. Directed by Justin Lin, Paramount Pictures, 2016.

Star Trek: Deep Space Nine. Berman, Rick, and Piller, Michael, creators. Paramount Television, 1993–1999.

Star Trek: Enterprise. Berman, Rick, and Braga, Brannon, creators. Paramount Television, 2001–2005.

Star Trek into Darkness. Directed by J.J. Abrams, Paramount Pictures, 2013.

Star Trek: The Animated Series. Roddenberry, Gene, creator. Paramount Television, 1973–1975.

Star Trek: The Next Generation. Roddenberry, Gene, creator. Paramount Television, 1987–1994.

Star Trek: The Original Series. Roddenberry, Gene, creator. NBC, 1966–1969.

Star Trek: Voyager. Berman, Rick, Piller, Michael, and Tayler, Jeri, creators. Paramount Television, 1995–2001.

Illegible and Unacceptable Representation
The Liminality of Spock in Star Trek *(2009)*

Natashia Lindsey

> Whatever our lives might have been, if the time continuum was disrupted, our destinies have changed.—Spock, *Star Trek*

In 2009, the Star *Trek: The Original Series* (*TOS*) characters were (re)imagined in director J.J. Abrams' *Star Trek*. Abrams attempted to create a *Star Trek* for the original fans, but one that would also introduce the beloved characters to a whole new generation. However, through the destruction of the USS *Kelvin*, this reboot (re)imagines character timelines and life experiences, creating new/different versions than presented on *TOS*. David Wittenberg would call this moment—the appearance of Nero and his ship, the destruction of the USS *Kelvin*, and the murder of George Kirk—a psychohistoriographical moment. According to Wittenberg, this is a single moment that has the "capacity to affect and define the broader historical record" (11). *TOS* fans are privy to the potentiality of this moment realizing that the James T. Kirk they know may very well become someone different in this timeline. And if this moment changes Kirk's timeline, it stands to reason that it can ripple out and affect the entire timeline; and so, it does.

Since this psychohistoriographical moment alters the timeline of *TOS*, and creates the potential for a multitude of possible futures, the space-time of the *Star Trek* reboot is a liminal phase. As Victor Turner describes, "liminality is full of potency and potentiality" ("Frame, Flow, and Reflection" 446) and it is a space where "people 'play' with the elements of the familiar and defamiliarize them" ("From Ritual to Theatre" 27). The Science Fiction trope of time travel works within the storyline to create this liminal phase without disrupting *TOS* timeline. Veteran fans see the familiar characters suspended between what they know them and their histories to be (the canon) and the changed histories that create potential for them to become something new/different. Viewers who are unaware of the *Star Trek* canon are not privy to the details of this liminal phase and potentiality.

While this liminal space exists for all the *TOS* characters, the combination of this liminal phase and the permanent liminality that Spock already occupies as mixed-race fosters a performance of mixed-race that exists between the stereotypes of the tragic mulatto and hybrid vigor.[1] This combination permits Spock the opportunity to resist these stereotypes and perform mixedness that cannot be read as either tragic or vigorous. Spock exists in a space that touches notions of being tragic and of being vigorous, but he cannot be viewed as one or the other. This essay contends that these two stereotypes—tragic mulatto and hybrid vigor—are the most acceptable and legible performances of mixed-race. For mainstream audiences, Spock ultimately represents an illegible and/or unacceptable performance of mixed-race due to the continuous white supremacist racialization of mixed-race characters. Hence, Spock's resistance to these stereotypes works two ways: to render his performance of mixed-race as unacceptable, if not illegible, to mainstream audiences and to solidify that he will not, in fact, become Spock Prime's tragic mulatto. It is because of his unacceptable performance—between these stereotypes—that the discursive power of race works to heap punishment upon him. These punishments, the destruction of Vulcan and the murder of his mother, act, but ultimately fail, to reinstate him into one of the legible stereotypes.

While Spock/Prime's parents both read phenotypically as white, his Vulcanness and humanness work as metaphors for real racialized bodies: Vulcanness stands in for whiteness and humanness stands in for the racialized other. Joe Kincheloe contends in his article "The Struggle to Define and Reinvent Whiteness: A Pedagogical Analysis," that whiteness is "shaped and confirmed" as "orderliness, rationality, and self-control ... by its close association with science" (163). Vulcans are a logical and stoic race that believe in nonviolence unless as a last resort. Their deep belief in logic is used to suppress any emotions they might feel. The ritual of Kolinahr rids the Vulcan of any residual emotions that a lifetime of suppression has missed ("Vulcans"). Vulcans make decisions based on logic and rationality and consider any emotional aspect that a human might feel unimportant. In fact, Spock Prime, in his attempted adherence to Vulcanness, has been described as "the representative of white rationality" (Golumbia 84).

It is through his humanness, however, that Spock/Prime must contend with the racialized other which Kincheloe maintains is shown "as chaos, irrationality, violence, and the breakdown of self-regulation" (Kincheloe 163). The humans in *Star Trek*, especially the *Enterprise's* doctor Leonard McCoy, are positioned as emotional creatures. McCoy often has emotional outbursts aimed at Spock/Prime and his stoicism. Captain James T. Kirk is presented as a balance between McCoy's hyper-emotional self and Spock/Prime's logical self: able to make rational and logical decisions while also relying on his emotions and gut feelings. However, as the child of "different and sharply contradictory worlds" (Williams-Leon 4), Spock/Prime is positioned as a liminal character. Being constantly positioned between the two worlds of his monoracial parents and their corresponding cultures creates an experience of "liminality, in-betweenness, and hybridity" (Brunsma and Delgado 339).

Bullies

The audience first meets Spock in *Star Trek* (2009) as a young child after his daily educational lessons. The camera sweeps over a large, dark room where Vulcan children stand in the center of bright concave computer displays in the floor. The children are vocally interacting with the computers as they respond to questions about geometry, ethics, and mathematics. The camera cuts to the dispersing children, focusing on three boys walking toward the camera. As another child comes into focus at the bottom of the screen, bent down facing the camera with his back to the other children, the middle boy calls his name: "Spock."

Without turning to look at the speaker, seemingly expecting the moment, young Spock responds, "I presume you've prepared new insults for today." The bully simply says, "affirmative." Without a single change in his blank facial expression, the young Spock stands and turns toward his bullies. He walks up to the three and matter-of-factly states, "This is your thirty-fifth attempt to elicit an emotional response from me." One of the bullies responds, "You're neither human nor Vulcan, and therefore have no place in this universe." Another chides, "Look. He has human eyes. They look sad, don't they?" The ringleader decides to try another tactic when he says, "Perhaps an emotional response requires physical stimuli." The bully shoves the much smaller young Spock. He continues to goad Spock, "He's a traitor, you know, your father, for marrying her, that human whore."

The taunt that Spock has "no place in the universe" is a textbook example of the ways in which white supremacy attempts to mark mixed-race people as tragic. The tragic mulatto stereotype positions mixed-race men as "the anguished victim of divided inheritance" (Brown 145). This situates the mulatto as possessing warring blood; the logical whiteness of the mixed-race person is constantly warring against the animalistic Blackness. As a biological belief, the war is thought to be never ending and it is never clear (for white people) which aspect will "win" in any given moment. Furthermore, "(t)he mulatto character has not escaped being cast as a pariah, a marginalized person. Seldom is the character permitted a choice or merger of identities" (Giles 78). Spock's classmates work as agents of hegemonic whiteness or, in this case, Vulcanness, and mark Spock as different and unwanted. They insinuate that he is not allowed to identify as either Vulcan or human because he is mixed; his mixedness thus renders him placeless in their eyes. It is significant that the line comes from the bullies and is not necessarily how Spock views himself or how he is presented. It is not the mixed child who presents as tragic but those around him that refuse to see him any other way.

Subsequently, the children pinpoint Spock's eyes as evidence of racial "truth." In her book *Racial Imperatives: Discipline, Performativity, and Struggles Against Subjection*, Nadine Ehlers argues that "(r)ace is performative because it is an act—or, more precisely a series of repeated acts—that brings into being what it means" (6). As a performative, race calls into question notions of racial 'truth' that are thought to show on the body, yet the reality is that racialized subjects perform racial signifiers that then position them as racialized subjects. Race, then, is about more than skin color or heredity, it includes such things as gestures, language, and actions. Furthermore, Ehlers declares that "(b)lood and color, as metaphoric markers of race consequently collapse into one another and together comprise the corpus of racial knowledges that generate racial "truths" (28). The concepts of blood (ancestry) and color have become ways in which the racial "truth" is thought to be seen "*in* and *on* the body" (27–8). The Vulcan children thus use what they read as sadness in Spock's eyes as corporeal proof that he is part human and not fully Vulcan since Vulcans strictly adhere to logic and the suppression of emotions. However, because the corporeal truth of race is a fallacy that requires constant recitation "in order to be maintained" (Ehlers 31), this marking of humanness via perceived emotions in Spock's eyes acts to discipline and racialize Spock's body. Yet again, the children are acting as agents of hegemonic Vulcanness/whiteness by asserting their power to read a racial "truth" on Spock's body. The fact that Spock's racial "truth" is read through sadness reiterates their attempts to mark him as tragic.

Moreover, because race is performative and holds no internal truth, Ehlers reworks racial passing to illustrate that everyone can be viewed as passing-*for* a racialized subject. It is not just those who are attempting to pass-*as* a racial identity "from which they are discursively prohibited" (7). "Through being read as 'belonging' to a particular racial category—that is visually appearing and conducting one's acts, manners, and behaviors in accordance to disciplinary racial demands—all subjects are passing-*for* a racial identity that they are said to be" (Ehlers 7). There are specific signifiers that everyone must perform in order to be viewed as the specific race they are attempting to pass-*for*. These signifiers are contextually and historically determined; the signifiers may shift and change based on location, cultural attitudes, and time.

In the reworking of racial passing that Ehlers postulates, it is possible to fail at this passing. Ehlers argues that to be considered "a viable racial subject, one must perpetually strive to inhabit the perceived discursive norms (or performative dictates) of the racial subject position one is assigned" (70). These norms, she claims, rely on constant "disciplinary surveillance" (8) that work to "coerce the individual into exercising self-discipline in the formation and enunciation of racial identity" (56). For instance, the final line from the lead bully, "He's a traitor, you know, your father, for marrying her, that human whore," is an example of the discipline that racialization requires. This single line positions the racialized and gendered other, via Amanda, as licentious for procreating outside of her species/race. This racialized and gendered slur harkens to the ever-present stereotypes of women of color, particularly Black and Latina women, as oversexualized. Simultaneously, this line calls into question Sarek's loyalty to Vulcanness. Ehler's contends that the "performative demands" of whiteness "require that the white individual maintain white purity by reproducing *within* the racial group" (74). Sarek's choice to marry and procreate with a human positions him as the "threat *from within* the very ranks of" Vulcanness (Ehlers 74). Sarek has stepped outside the performative demands of his race, and his choice pollutes the purity of Vulcanness via Spock. These comments work on the localized or microscopic level to regulate raced bodies.

This scene with the classroom bullies ends with Spock and the bully in a fist fight, one that the young Spock noticeably wins. This sequence gives us two examples of young Spock's resistance to their attempts to mark him as tragic. Firstly, he resists by refusing to be bothered by their first thirty-four days of bullying. The young Spock takes the "Vulcan way out" by remaining passive and logical in dealing with their constant assaults. However, his Vulcan-like resistance does not stop them from continuing to harass him. Secondly, he resists by literally fighting back on the thirty-fifth day. While the bullies may have gotten what they thought they wanted—an emotional response—the ringleader also receives quite the beating, perhaps something he did not consider. The bullies learn that the young Spock is more than capable of defending himself against their tactics. This scene calls into question why the young Vulcans are so focused on marking Spock as tragic. As discussed below, the Vulcan children learn their bigotry from their elders, much like human children.

In "The Journey to Babel" (Fontana), the tenth episode of the second season of *TOS*, the audience and *Enterprise* crew learn about Spock Prime's choice to join Starfleet over the Vulcan Science Academy (VAS). It is solely through Sarek, his Vulcan father, and Amanda, his human mother, that we learn of Spock Prime's decision to join Starfleet. Spock Prime never speaks on the issue; he is not even allowed a voice to speak on his own experiences. Amanda gives the only semblance of an explanation for his choice when she tells the Captain, "It hasn't been easy on Spock, neither human nor Vulcan, at home nowhere except Starfleet." It is insinuated that Spock Prime chose Starfleet because it is the only place he felt he could possibly fit in. This inability to "fit in" because one or both parent races cannot or will not accept the mixed-race child is a common characteristic of the tragic mulatto stereotype.

In *Star Trek* (2009) we are privy to the moment in which Spock chooses Starfleet over the VSA, unlike on *TOS*. Spock is shown standing with his back to the audience in front of the Vulcan High Council. The council is seated at a raised bench, twice Spock's height, similar to what an Earth judge uses in the courtroom. The massive room is full of harsh white lights shining through a ceiling constructed of metal and glass cross beams meeting at pristine angles, sterile, perfect, logical. The camera angle makes it seem as if the room is tilted to the right. It is silent until the Vulcan in the center—an older Vulcan with graying hair—asserts, "You have surpassed the expectations of your instructors." As he finishes his statement, the camera spins clockwise as if to mark time and zooms in on the back of Spock's head and the minister's face. He continues, "Your final record is flawless, with one exception," the camera comes around to focus on Spock's face, "I see that you have applied to Starfleet." With a small nod in affirmation Spock responds, "It was logical to cultivate multiple options." The focus shifts to show the podium. and it becomes apparent that the Vulcan to the minister's right is Sarek.

"Logical, but unnecessary. You are hereby accepted to the Vulcan Science Academy." As the focus tightens on the minister, he insists, "It is truly remarkable, Spock, that you have achieved so much despite your disadvantage." With a quick turn to Spock's face, we see him raise his head a mere few inches higher toward the minister as a nonverbal request at explanation. His left eye almost imperceptibly narrows, a small and silent confrontation. As the council rises at the minister's direction and bells begin to toll in the distance, Spock asks, "If you would clarify, Minister, to what disadvantage are you referring?" Without missing a beat, the focus now on his face, the minister replies "Your human mother."

The minister is no different than the classroom bullies that Spock must contend with as a child; he finds it remarkable that Spock is intelligent enough, with his humanness, to qualify for the VSA. It would only be deemed remarkable if the minister assumes that Spock's humanness lowers his potential. This assumption by the minister illustrates his acceptance of hybrid degeneracy, the belief that mixed-race people "lack physical, mental, and moral strength" (Squires 30), which undergirds the tragic mulatto stereotype. It is unclear in the minister's comment whether he is referring to the cultural or hereditary aspects that a human mother could pass on to her offspring. Nonetheless, his statement illustrates his belief that Spock should not be as intelligent or capable as full-blooded Vulcans. In fact, the minister's opening statement, "You have surpassed the expectations of your instructors," may seem like a benign comment to make to a student, yet when read against the minister's gibe, it takes on a new form. Spock's Vulcan instructors were also expecting less of him because he is part human. It is apparent that most of the Vulcans in Spock's life have held bigoted beliefs about his mixedness.

As soon as the minister finishes his sneer at Spock's mother, there is a refocus on Spock. The camera is positioned slightly below him, and it begins to slowly zoom upward and in, toward his face. The bells continue to toll in the distance and break the silence of the environment. As Spock ever so slightly tightens the muscles of his lips, stopping just before a purse, he cuts his eyes toward where his father is sitting and slightly draws the left side of his mouth toward his ear. A shift of focus to Sarek—who is seemingly meeting Spock's gaze—gives a slight nod. Spock speaks up, "Council, ministers, I must decline."

"No Vulcan has ever declined admission to this Academy," the minister seems to stiffen, speaks almost in surprise. Spock informs the minister, "Then, as I am half-human, your record remains untarnished." His mouth stays slightly open, at the ready, his lips pulled taut. While Spock's choice of Starfleet over the VSA is part of the *TOS* canon, witnessing his refusal to be viewed as "remarkable" because he "overcame" his humanness—and his simultaneous claim to that very humanness—emphasizes Spock's agency. There is no canonical record that Spock Prime applied for the Vulcan Science Academy.[2] We are only told about Spock Prime's defiance through Sarek and Amanda in "Journey to Babel." However, it is stated only that he chose Starfleet over the VSA. This public and emotional rejection of the minister's bigotry, the Vulcan Science Academy, and, thus, the tragic mulatto stereotype marks the moment Spock begins to become someone different from Spock Prime. The tolling bells act as an auditory marker of this shift in the timeline and in Spock's performance of mixedness.

There is a quick shift back to Sarek, who says, "Spock, you have made a commitment to honor the Vulcan way." We can now understand his nod to Spock as an affirmation of the minister's comment and not of Spock himself. Spock stares down his father with a stern face attempting to show no emotion. A small smirk to the left of his mouth marks his defiance. The minister asks, accuses, "Why did you come before this council today? Was it to satisfy your emotional need to rebel?"

While the camera is tightly focused on Spock's face he says, "The only emotion I wish to convey is gratitude." His eyes shift from his father to the minister, "Thank you," the camera shows Sarek's blank-face reaction, "ministers, for your consideration." Spock lowers his voice; it has an edge of a growl, as he says, "Live long and prosper." The same small smirk appears to the left of his mouth, he shifts his gaze to his father accusingly, and turns to leave. He walks off stage left. Spock Prime's most famous line, "Live Long and Prosper" as a sign of irritation or anger makes it possible to see this Spock as a revision (something slightly different but definitely changed), not just a remake (a new shiny version of the old).

It is a transgressive act and choice, when Spock identifies as mixed-race before the Vulcan Science Academy. Due to the belief that race has a corporeal truth, "identity is" often "determined by appearance" (Giles 78). However, because Spock can "pass-*as*" Vulcan there is no general need for him to acknowledge his human ancestry, no need to acknowledge the lesser parts of himself. His own father suggests that he should only identify as Vulcan, that which is emotionless, logical, and superior. Spock defiantly claims a mixed identity—despite a prior conversation with his mother that suggested he desires to identify as Vulcan—in front of his father and the most prestigious educational facility on Vulcan. He has now claimed a permanently liminal position, "a realm of pure possibility" (Turner, "Betwixt and Between" 236) by claiming his mixedness. This positionality means that Spock could become completely different from Spock Prime; he could become someone that fans do not even recognize.

Examining these two scenes—the schoolyard bullies and the VSA assembly—together raises the question: if Vulcans are logical beings, detached from useless emotions, how can they perpetuate racism and bullying? While Vulcan logic and deep suppression of emotion is a cultural aspect and not a biological one ("Vulcans"), Vulcans' insistence on their strict adherence to logic ignores the obvious bigotry that continues to be hurled at Spock and his mixedness. These scenes work to hide the emotional component of racism by blaming Spock for being emotional as a result of their obvious bigotry. For example, the minister insults Spock and his mother and insinuates he is being "emotional" for reacting negatively to it. These scenes also work to erase the ways in which Vulcans, positioned as the dominant race, erase and/or ignore their complicity in that racism by positioning their feelings—his eyes look sad because he's part human or Spock is disadvantaged by his humanness—as facts/logic. It should come as no shock that the Vulcan children spend so much time bullying young Spock if the adult Vulcans, who have suppressed their emotions, sitting on the highest scientific council on the planet cannot see past their own bigoted ideas.

Punishment

Spock's continued resistance of the tragic mulatto stereotype and his public and defiant claim to a mixed-race identity render his racial performance as unacceptable. His performance is not legible as mixed-race because he does not perform tragically or vigorously. These two stereotypes reflect the ways in which society, specifically people in the U.S., understand and recognize mixed-race characters. This diverges from Ehlers' theory in that she asserts that these un/acceptable performances are punished as a way to reinscribe the subject back into Black/white modes of racialization (77). For Ehlers, the liminal subject, or the mixed-race subject, must be "categorically reinserted back within the logic of binary understandings of race," or the mixed-race person must be deemed either white or Black (76). This reinsertion is a result of "the workings of *corrective* disciplinary punishment" (76) Unlike Ehlers, my articulation of the unacceptable performances of mixed-race is not about reinstating mixed-race characters into the binary racial system but, instead, about reinstating them into the stereotypes. Viewers cannot read a mixed-race character as mixed if he/she does not fall within tragic or vigorous stereotypes. Thus, aspects of the script function as "*corrective* disciplinary punishment" in a failed attempt to re-inscribe Spock into one of the mixed-race stereotypes (Ehlers 76).

Nero wants Spock Prime to feel the same pain that he felt when Romulus was destroyed. The angry Romulan waits twenty-five years just so he can destroy Vulcan and force Spock Prime to watch. The destruction of Vulcan works as punishment on several levels. First, it is a literal form of punishment within the context of the movie: Nero punishes Spock Prime for his failure to save the planet Romulus. Once Spock Prime comes through the black hole, Nero kidnaps him and leaves him stranded on Delta Vega, an ice planet. Delta Vega is close enough to Vulcan that Spock Prime watches as the planet implodes on itself, killing its billions of inhabitants. Since Starfleet is alerted to the "lightning storm in space" that threatens Vulcan, the *Enterprise* shows up right before the planet is destroyed. To Nero's delight, he realizes that Spock is on the *Enterprise* and tells him, "Spock, there is something I would like for you to see" right before he destroys Vulcan. Nero manages to punish Spock Prime for his failed attempt to save Romulus *and* the younger/different Spock for something he may never fail at in this timeline.

Second, and more important to my argument, the destruction of Vulcan illustrates how the discursive powers of race function through the script to punish Spock for his resistance to the mixed-race stereotypes. Even though Spock's character is a re-working of mixed-race representation, the punishment for his unacceptable performance is not a part of the storyline; instead, it is a symptom of the narrative confines of racialization that cannot imagine mixed-race characters outside of these stereotypes. This tragedy is shared by all Vulcans who survive the genocide but because Nero is specifically focused on Spock/Prime and because the audience sees its effects through Spock, the tragedy specifically marks him. Spock gives the voice over after the destruction of Vulcan:

> Acting Captain's Log Star date 2258.42: ... Nero who has destroyed my home planet and most of its six billion inhabitants.... While the essence of our culture has been saved in the elders who now reside upon this ship.... I estimate that no more than 10,000 have survived. I am now a member of an endangered species.

We can hear his voice waver as he logs that six billion Vulcans are now gone in an instant. He later confides in his father that he feels "anger at the one who took mother's life." Because it seems almost impossible to imagine a survivor of genocide as anything other than tragic, situating Spock thusly must be understood as an attempt to re-instate him into the tragic mulatto stereotype.

Third, as the destruction of Vulcan ends in the murder of Spock's mother, it also functions as a form of punishment for her racial and sexual transgression. Recall the ways in which the Vulcan children called her a whore in the bullying scene: since these words are placed in the child's mouth, insinuating that marriage to someone outside your race/species makes you licentious, the audience has already been prepared for her to reap the punishment for her actions. The intersection of her race and sexuality have been marked deviant, and she is forced to pay with her life.

Moreover, the destruction of Vulcan exemplifies how Spock balances between the stereotypes of the tragic mulatto and the hybrid vigor. Since Spock Prime has been positioned as the tragic mulatto for nearly 50 years that aspect of the analysis has required a lengthier examination. In Spock's failure to become Spock Prime, he also falls short of fulfilling the hybrid vigor stereotype or the belief that mixed-race people are "stronger, smarter, and more beautiful" than their monoracial counterparts (Nishime 296). Though the movie offers a few moments that exemplify Spock's vigorousness, moments when he accomplishes something his monoracial peers could not, Spock never solely exhibits vigorousness because those moments are quickly and swiftly undermined. The following example, for instance, not only undermines Spock's vigor but, again, attempts to re-inscribe him into the tragic stereotype.

As the Starfleet ships race to Vulcan to check out the distress call alerting them to a "lightning storm in space," it is James T. Kirk who realizes what is really happening. Dr. McCoy injected Kirk with a vaccine to produce physical symptoms so that Kirk could essentially sneak aboard the *Enterprise* under the guise of McCoy being his treating physician. Kirk experiences a horrible allergic reaction for which McCoy then gives him a sedative. As he awakens, groggy from the sedative and still experiencing an allergic reaction (swollen hands and a numb tongue), he races to Captain Pike and claims the distress call is actually an attack on Vulcan. He recalls the circumstances that occurred on the day of his birth, the same lightning storm in space, and relays to Captain Pike that Vulcan is being attacked, most likely by the Romulans. Spock confirms that all the pieces of Kirk's theory seem plausible and convinces Captain Pike to be ready for an attack when they get to Vulcan. With all of his logic and deductive skills, Spock was not the one to figure out the situation. He knew about the attack on the USS *Kelvin* because he had mentioned it mere hours before at Kirk's academic hearing. However, unbeknownst to the audience at this point, Spock is also dating Lt. Uhura. She confirmed for Kirk that she had heard Romulans in her sensor scans the night before. How can a drugged up human cadet gather all this information and see this correlation when Spock cannot? In this way, the film positions Kirk as more knowledgeable and capable of deductive reasoning than Spock, thereby undermining Spock's vigor.

Once the *Enterprise* drops out of warp, it is abundantly apparent that the lightning storm is, in fact, an attack on Vulcan. The entire fleet of starships—that arrived moments before the *Enterprise*—have been destroyed. As Nero works to destroy Vulcan, Spock beams down to the surface to save his parents. He finds them in the Katric Arc along with the rest of the Vulcan High Council (VHC). As the Arc begins to collapse, killing some of the council, Spock rushes them outside to the edge of a cliff so that they can be beamed aboard the *Enterprise*. As they are being beamed aboard, the cliff face gives way and his mother falls to her death mere inches from his hands.

Spock has vigorous moments but he is not presented as the super hybrid who can know and fix everything. By saving most of the Vulcan High Council, Spock has managed to save the culture and history bearers of Vulcan. While Vulcans are now an endangered species, their history and culture have not been completely erased by this destruction and genocide. This is unbelievably valuable in ensuring the continuation of Vulcan knowledge and it positions Spock as vigorous. He alone is able to seek out the elders and help preserve these aspects of Vulcan history and culture. No one else aboard the *Enterprise* knew where to find the VHC or were even considering how vital that could be to the future. Also, because Sarek is a member of the VHC, Spock knows where they will be located during this emergency. However, this moment cannot be praised too highly because as he saves the VHC, his mother falls to her death. His failure to save his mother, or even to save the planet, limits any vigor that he may have performed in this moment.

Is Love Logical?

As aspects of the script function as punishment to re-inscribe Spock into the tragic stereotype, he manages to resist this re-inscription. With the destruction of Vulcan and the murder of his mother, Spock does not pull away from his humanness or intimate connection. These horrific tragedies would be a perfect time to retreat into the serenity that logic offers Vulcans, shutting off the heartache and grief. Instead, Spock manages to express his grief, connect with his father, and sustain a romantic relationship with Lt. Uhura. He embraces the humanity within him by maintaining and fostering intimate connections with other people. This is vital in resisting the tragic mulatto stereotype because the tragic mulatto is often shown as failing at love and relationships (Carter, 155).

Immediately following the destruction of Vulcan, and Spock's log of the event, the audience gets the first confirmation that Spock and Uhura are romantically involved. As Spock steps into the lift to leave the bridge, Uhura joins him. She faces him and leans to pause the lift so no one can interrupt them. Her body is intimately close to his. Her eyes begin to fill with tears as she softly speaks, "I'm sorry.... I'm sorry." She shakes her head as the weight of Spock's loss seems unspeakable. She raises her hands and places them on his face as she says, "I am so sorry." With her hands still on his face, she leans up and kisses his lips. He doesn't seem to respond as he stands rigid with his hands to his sides. She starts to wrap her arms around his neck as she kisses his face several times. Spock's arms finally wrap around her as his fingers dig into her back and he buries his face in the crook of her neck: a moment of softness and intimacy amidst an unfathomable tragedy. As he begins to pull away, she places her hands on his face and asks, "What do you need? Tell me." Spock leans for the lift buttons and resumes the ride. He simply, but in a wavering voice, responds, "I need everyone to continue performing admirably." She nods her head and tells him, "Okay." She leans up one more time to kiss him. This time he obviously kisses her back.

This is a powerful moment on several levels; first, the audience now knows for certain that they are romantically involved. This is diametrically opposed to Spock Prime's prominent asexuality. It was only under circumstances such as alien plant spores—which affected the crew's access to emotions—that Spock Prime ever expressed romantic interest (Butler and Fontana). Spock Prime was never fully permitted to explore these aspects of his humanness, and so this relationship with Uhura alerts us to the fact that Spock is not Spock Prime. More importantly, this intimate moment between Spock and Uhura illustrates Spock's acceptance of his humanness. He has chosen and maintained a romantic relationship with a human woman. Unlike his father, who claimed that as an ambassador to Earth it was logical to marry

Amanda, Spock cannot claim that their relationship is logical. In fact, as her superior officer, it would seem illogical for them to pursue a relationship. This can be seen in their attempts to keep the relationship hidden from their fellow officers. On a deeper level, however, this moment exemplifies the grief that Spock is experiencing. Initially, I read his response to her, "I need everyone to continue performing admirably," as a way for him to distance himself from his own emotions, his humanness, and from her. However, after losing my own father, I realized that this line means so much more in the depths of grief. This simple response and their kiss are his way of saying that he needs *something* to be normal and functional because his world has literally ended; *something* must feel or work the same as before. Spock uses the cold logical language of a Vulcan to express a deeply human need: when everything has changed in an instant, the bereaved search for some form of normalcy.

Spock's grief later manifests in rage and anger, but it allows him to connect with his father. Following orders from Spock Prime, Kirk tries to prove that Spock is emotionally compromised by the tragic events so that Kirk can take command of the *Enterprise*. Like the bullies from Spock's childhood, Kirk hurls verbal abuse at him, abuse that yet again focuses on his (lack of) emotions. As he is in Spock's face, he says, "What is it like not to feel anger? Or heartbreak? Or the need to stop at nothing to avenge the death of the woman who gave birth to you?" Spock tight-lipped quietly tells Kirk, "Back away from me." Kirk starts yelling, "It must not even compute for you. You never loved her!" And much like with the schoolyard bullies, that is Spock's breaking point. He launches into a fist fight with Kirk—which he obviously wins. At this point, Spock admits he is emotionally compromised, relinquishes his post as acting Captain, and leaves the bridge. As Kirk announces to the ship that he is changing course, Spock can be seen making his way through the corridor; he is dazed. His usual upright stance with his head held high is gone. He looks at the floor as he walks, his mouth is partially open as if he has words to speak but none of them are speakable.

We soon find Spock in the transporter room, the place where his mother failed to appear when she died, speaking to his father. The movie makes it unclear if the two have spoken since Spock made his choice to join Starfleet, but this moment between father and son is healing for Spock. Sarek, having witnessed the fight on the bridge, asks Spock to speak his mind. Spock responds, "I am as conflicted as I once was as a child." Sarek tells him, "You will always be a child of two worlds. I am grateful for this. And for you." This is not the cold and logical Sarek of *TOS*. It seems the events of this timeline have also altered him and his ability to connect to the emotions he was taught to suppress. This statement illustrates that Sarek finds Spock's mixedness to be positive, perhaps revealing a veiled admission that hybridity makes him stronger. Spock opens up to him at this point, "I feel anger for the one who took mother's life. An anger I cannot control." Walking closer to his son, Sarek tells him, "I believe that she would say, 'do not try to.' You asked me once why I married your mother. I married her because I loved her." This is almost as if Sarek is giving Spock his blessing to be both Vulcan and human even though he was previously vocal about Spock choosing the Vulcan way. This interaction between father and son heals a divide between Spock Prime and his father, and it permits them a level of intimacy that is needed in this time of crisis. However, complicating this intimacy is the fact that for Sarek to heal the divide with his son, Amanda had to die.

Conclusion

After the crew of the *Enterprise* barely but successfully destroy Nero and the threat to the Federation of Planets, Spock gets the chance to meet and speak with Spock Prime. This scene is a visual representation and acknowledgment of the shift from Spock Prime, who spent much of *TOS* struggling with his mixed identity, to Spock, who defiantly claims his positionality. No longer the tragic mulatto, Spock is becoming something similar but different. This final moment between Spock Prime and Spock alerts the audience, both old fans and new ones, to the shifting images of the *Star Trek: The Original Series* characters and, specifically, to the shifting performance and representation of mixed-race. The possibilities for Spock are left limitless as he is finally situated as a new and different Spock: one without a Vulcan home world to return to, without a mother to connect with, and a romantic relationship that Spock Prime was never fully allowed.

Notes

1. For the remainder of the chapter Spock will refer to Zachary Quinto's character in the 2009 movie and Spock Prime will refer to Leonard Nimoy's character in all of its iterations. At some points, I refer to the child version of Spock as young Spock played by child actor Jacob Kogan. In some places, I use Spock/Prime to refer to the character in its totality.

2. Although this film set up the Kelvin timeline seen in this and later films, writer Roberto Orci stated that he felt that the actions were unaffected by the changes in this timeline and so would have occurred in the same manner prior to *The Original Series*. Roberto Orci, Alex Kurtzman, and J.J. Abrams. *Star Trek* (2009 Motion Picture). Directed by J.J. Abrams. Paramount Pictures, 2009. DVD.

Works Cited

Brown, Sterling. *Negro Poetry and Drama, and the Negro in American Fiction*. Atheneum, 1969.
Brunsma, David L., and Daniel J. Delgado. "Occupying the Third Space: Hybridity and Identity in the Multiracial Experience." *Hybrid Identities: Theoretical and Empirical Examinations*, edited by Keri E. Iyall Smith and Patricia Leavy, Brill Publishers, 2009, pp. 333–354.
Carter, Greg. *The United States of the United Races: A Utopian History of Racial Mixing*. NYU Press, 2013.

Ehlers, Nadine. *Racial Imperatives: Discipline, Performativity, and Struggles Against Subjection.* Indiana University Press, 2012.
Giles, Freda Scott. "From Melodrama to the Movies: The Tragic Mulatto as a Type Character." *American Mixed Race: The Culture of Microdiversity*, edited by Naomi Zack, Rowman & Littlefield, 1995, pp. 63–78.
Golumbia, David. "Black and White World: Race, Ideology, and Utopia in 'Triton' and 'Star Trek.'" *Cultural Critique*, no. 32, 1996, pp. 75–95.
Kincheloe, Joe L. "The Struggle to Define and Reinvent Whiteness: A Pedagogical Analysis." *College Literature*, vol. 26, no. 3, 1999, pp. 162–194.
Nishime, LeiLani. *Undercover Asian: Multiracial Asian Americans in Visual Culture.* University of Illinois Press, 2014.
Squires, Catherine. *Dispatches from the Color Line: The Press and Multiracial American.* SUNY Press, 2007.
Turner, Victor. "Betwixt and Between: The Liminal Period in *Rites De Passage*." *The Forest of Symbols: Aspects of Nnedmbu Ritual.* Cornell University Press, 1967, pp. 93–111.
Turner, Victor. "Frame, Flow, and Reflection: Ritual and Drama as Public Liminality." *Japanese Journal of Religious Studies*, vol. 6, no. 4, 1979, pp. 465–499.
Turner, Victor. *From Ritual to Theatre: The Human Seriousness of Play.* Performing Arts Journal Publications, 1982.
"Vulcans." *Memory Alpha*, Sept. 20, 2016. http://memory-alpha.wikia.com/wiki/Vulcan.
Williams-León, Teresa. "Reconfiguring Race, Rearticulating Ethnicity." *The Sum of Our Parts: Mixed Heritage Asian Americans*, edited by Teresa Williams-León and Cynthia L. Nakashima, Temple University Press, 2001, pp. 3–11.
Wittenberg, David. *Time Travel: The Popular Philosophy of Narrative.* Fordham University Press, 2013.

Star Trek Media Cited

"The Journey to Babel." *Star Trek*, season 2, episode 10, written by D.C. Fontana, directed by Joseph Pevney, 17 Nov. 1967.
Star Trek (2009). Directed by J.J. Abrams, Paramount Pictures, 2009.
"This Side of Paradise." *Star Trek*, season 1, episode 24, written by D.C. Fontana, directed by Ralph Senensky, 2 Mar. 1967.

James T. Kirk, Ideal Citizen
Shifting Rhetoric for a New Timeline

CAIT COKER

In their first meeting during the 2009 *Star Trek* film, Captain Pike tries to recruit Jim Kirk for Starfleet; he describes the Federation as "important ... a humanitarian and peacekeeping armada." This is notable because in (contemporary) Earth history there has only been one other well-known armada—the Spanish one that attempted to invade England in 1588. And indeed, the very word "armada" means a fleet of warships: a "humanitarian armada" is inherently ironic. In a single line Abrams transformed the new Kelvin Timeline into a world where the idealistic mission to seek out new life and new civilizations contrasted sharply with the implications of Starfleet as an ideologically weaponized force. Further, as witnessed by events throughout the film, after the Kelvin Disaster the Federation and Starfleet evolved from a primarily exploratory and diplomatic entity to one that is highly militarized: examples include Sulu's hobby of fencing from The Original Series (*TOS*) became, in Abrams's vision, a martial skill suitably useful for special ops missions, to the massive technological shifts that transformed the *TOS* Enterprise with its crew complement of 400 to a ship of over 1,100. At the conclusion of the film, the union of the classic crew aboard their ship seemed to imply something like epistemic closure, with everyone returned to their "rightful" place and Kirk's knowledge from Spock Prime acting as a positive influence for personal and larger change in the universe.

However, in 2013's *Star Trek into Darkness*, the formerly bright uniforms of classic Trek were largely replaced with dark uniforms that recalled the "Patterns of Force" *TOS* episode with Nazis as well as *Star Wars*' Imperial troops (and J.J. Abrams' open affection for and numerous nods to that franchise in this one should not be overlooked), and the plot revolved around xenophobia and political warmongering. Rather than things coming full circle to correction after all, yet more problems had opened up—including an even darker and more foreboding Starfleet caught between corruption within and enemies without. The decision to introduce a whitewashed Khan was not met favorably either; indeed, far from it. Both of these films also made heavy use of Othering; for the first time in *Star Trek*'s history, aliens were the funny-looking or frightening "Other," played for laughs or as threats, and in stark opposition to hero Jim Kirk's Aryan "perfect mind in a perfect body" that recalled more of the original Khan's outlook than the new Khan did.

The most recent film, *Star Trek Beyond* (2016), is a notable departure from Abrams's vision. Here the characters more than once have to reckon with what is and what should be, which culminate in the brief and moving memorial to Leonard Nimoy's passing. It also confronted Othering directly when Krall is revealed to be a human warped beyond recognition, both through the brutal circumstances of the world his ship crashed on and by his own hatred. *Star Trek Beyond* is about choosing the world you want to live in and who you want to be; at its conclusion the characters have directly chosen their role in the world rather than being pushed or manipulated into a predestined position. This essay would like to thus examine the film trilogy's evolution from a valorization of fascist ideals to grappling with and finally overcoming them, especially as read against the contemporary theater of global American politics, as now more than ever we are faced with recovering the possibility of utopia from a totalitarian regime.

"Sabotage" Part One: Rewriting Roddenberry

Star Trek begins with the attack on and subsequent destruction of the Starfleet ship the *Kelvin*, a scientific research vessel; the enemy ship is of unknown origin, and "the Kelvin Disaster" is a mysterious but well-documented anomaly—there is enough information available for Christopher Pike to write a dissertation on the topic as a student at the Academy, but not enough for meaningful conclusions to be drawn until Jim Kirk synthesizes the information at the Battle of Vulcan twenty-five years later. The Kelvin Disaster sets in motion not only the chain of events necessary to the reshaping of *TOS* characters and events but a symbolic shift within the make-up of Starfleet and the Federation, one with a higher emphasis on militarization and military action rather than on pure science and exploration. While *TOS* always used military-style parlance, customs, and legal forms (as in the episode "Court Martial"), the plots within the Kelvin Timeline have pushed those elements to the forefront of their storytelling, putting Gene Roddenberry's famous quote "The strength of a civilization is not measured by its ability to fight wars, but rather by its ability to prevent them" (which has been retold by actors in interviews and only "officially" appeared at the end of the "Scorched Earth" episode of *Earth: Final Conflict*) to the test of what is philosophically applicable in the transition of the franchise. Seemingly, in the Kelvin Timeline, wars and conflict *cannot* be prevented, and must therefore be won instead. Kirk is the incarnation of this philosophy.

Kirk's characterization throughout the Prime Timeline is that of a gifted military strategist with equal abilities in empathy and intellect. While his victory in the Kobayashi Maru test as told through *Wrath of Khan* remains legendary, it is his intellectual capability that allows him to best the scenario—to his instructors' apparent satisfaction. Though the full story of how Kirk won is never depicted or told, the mystique of the act itself remains powerful to Academy students well into his admiralty. In contrast, the Kirk of the Kelvin Timeline starts largely as a ne'er-do-well, getting by on a combination of his genius, charm, and as the official tie-in materials would have us believe, cheating. It is implied in both cut scenes and the novelization that Kirk's affair with the Orion Gaila was to inveigle programming secrets from her in order to defeat the Kobayashi Maru. Further, in the first issues of the tie-in comics, we see that Kirk is willing to cheat even when the odds aren't altogether unbeatable: Following closely the original storyline to "Where No Man Has Gone Before," the newly empowered Gary Mitchell sends Kirk down memory lane, saying "Remember this? Wasting your youth on farm girls and motorbikes while I was already training at the Academy? Or what about this? Sweating it out at exam time! Wishing your pal Gary was there to slip you the answers. You wouldn't have that Captain's chair without me" (Johnson, 14–15). While the comics' canonicity is ambiguous, and Mitchell himself is an untrustworthy narrator, the overall characterization of the new Kirk as intellectually fit but ethically dubious is worth exploring because of the ultimate message: The means justifies the ends in this universe, an authoritarian viewpoint that appears in marked contrast from the traditional *Star Trek* ethos of secular humanism.

The adult Kirk first appears in a bar where he flirts with Uhura in a sexually suggestive manner and then is beaten up in a bar flight with several male cadets. Afterwards, Captain Pike discusses the legacy of Kirk's heroic father, defining Starfleet as a "humanitarian and peacekeeping armada" and then daring Kirk "to do better" by following in his footsteps. Broken down into elements, this description reveals throughout its language that in the Kelvin Timeline, *humanity* is central to Starfleet, and to the Federation; this is visually reflected in multiple scenes of the Starfleet Academy body, which has only some aliens but many humans, and many of them white. While the Academy's emphasis has always been on being "the best," with these scenes "the best" is now inextricably bound up with human white male bodies. Daniel Whiting comments on this scene:

> Kirk *is* his father's son and it is inevitable that he would receive some input from his heritage, if only at the *biological level*. ... Pike's remark suggests that, to the extent that Kirk has inherited his past, Kirk should draw upon that heritage and its resources in a "better" fashion than has been done to date. ... [He] must be selective and draw upon only those aspects that are desirable in a superior fashion [195, emphasis added].

This selectivity might at first imply a connection to the 0 *TOS* ethos of being the best for the communal good, but as enacted in the first two films, it becomes part of the new timeline's established humanity-centered authoritarianism, with conceivable links to the Eugenics Wars that were previously held as the nadir of human culture, yet which, later, Admiral Marcus seems to admire.

This innate superiority also translates to problems of gender—and sexuality. While 0 *TOS* played upon changing sexual mores with revealing costumes, *Star Trek* takes this a step further into actual objectification in the scenes of Gaila and Uhura in their underwear; the the scene with Uhura is explicitly played as a voyeuristic scene for humor when she demands to know who "the mouthbreather under the bed" is. In Alan Dean Foster's novelization of the film, drawn from earlier versions of the script, the scene goes into further problematic territory when Uhura speaks to Gaila in Orion, and accuses Kirk not just of sexual looseness, but of functional miscegenation: "You know he's been through half the cadet corps since he got here?" she asks, "There are rumors that not all of them were humanoid" (64).

To her surprise, Kirk himself answers, also in Orion: "And hardly half. You're rounding up that number. Not that I'm not flattered, mind. [...] And," he added as he made his exit, "they were all humanoid—I think" (65). Though played for laughs, this scene reveals an anxiety about transgressive sexuality, one at odds not only with *TOS* but with the burgeoning romance between Spock and Uhura.[1] Further, the relationship between Spock and Uhura in all three films is largely portrayed as a source of tension and, after the destruction of Vulcan, a forthright point of racial anxiety. Though half–Vulcan, Spock frets about his duty towards his race and how his relationship with a human complicates that, especially given the prejudice he himself faced as a child. While these scenes do demonstrate that xenophobia cannot be easily overcome, it nonetheless paints a portrait of xenophobia as a fact of life in the Federation rather than as a singular aberration during contact with new species.

The end of *Star Trek* implied a return to the "rightful order" of the *TOS* timeline, with the crewmen taking their positions—Uhura at Communications, Chekov and Sulu at the helm, Scotty in Engineering, and Spock and McCoy at Kirk's side. *Star Trek into Darkness* retconned this return, or rather, explicated that what we had supposed to be true was, in fact, not; rather than embarking on a five-year mission at the end of the previous film, they were embarking on a one-year test-drive of sorts to test the newly minted crew. It is a test they, or at least Kirk, fail when he lies in a mission report. Furious, Admiral Pike berates Kirk for his failings and sets up the view of him that must change for him to become his best self for the Federation:

> You think you're infallible. You can't make a mistake. It's a pattern with you: that rules are for other people. And what's worse is you're using blind luck to justify you're playing God. … You don't comply with the rules. You don't take responsibility for anything, and *you don't respect the chair* [emphasis added].

This emphasis on authoritarian respect is twofold: it emphasizes both the literal government and the ideology behind it that becomes the core conflict of the film. Because of his actions, Kirk is demoted and placed under the command of Admiral Pike, who is shortly thereafter killed in a terrorist attack. The remainder of the film is a redemption arc for Kirk—and for the Federation itself, which has further degenerated into warmongering as Admiral Marcus creates an internal coup for power over Starfleet.

Marcus's plan sets up a terrorist attack: Harrison/Khan's bombing of the Kelvin Memorial Library which houses Section 31, Starfleet's intelligence and weapons-testing unit. That the dual library/site is named after the Kelvin Disaster reiterates the decades-long psychological scars that the *Kelvin*'s destruction left on Starfleet. Marcus himself believes that all-out war with the Klingon Empire is inevitable, stating that "[I]t's already begun. Since we first learned of their existence the Klingon Empire has conquered and occupied two planets that we know of, fired on our ships half a dozen times. They are coming our way." This is largely a political misdirect for a power-grab; in *Star Trek*, Uhura reports that the *Narada* destroys forty-seven Klingon ships when it escapes their prison planet; it should recall the similar redirect of American hostility from Afghanistan to Iraq. Stephen McVeigh's analysis puts this conflict fully into the context of Bush-era politics; it is worth remembering that *Star Trek into Darkness* is pointedly dedicated to post–9/11 veterans who were themselves used as tools in the real-world regime:

> Where the original Kirk was essentially reactive and operated within the Cold War paradigms of containment and deterrence, the new Kirk exists in a post-state context where containment is impossible and the enemies' motivations so fanatical that deterrence or negotiation are meaningless.… Kirk's actions are a twenty-third century enactment of the Bush doctrine, an essential component of the War on Terror [206].

Similarly, Norma Jones dissects the refocusing of threats from external to internal:

> In essence, we created our own "undefeatable" enemy. Additionally, while trying to defend against future versions of Nero, we created an even greater threat in Khan. ... In both instances, unlike other prime universe adversaries (like the Xindi, Borg, Klingons, and the Dominion), the two greatest threats (Nero and Khan) against the Federation are in fact created by the Federation. This might be thought of as reflective of our own realities, in that some of the greatest threats against the United States were made by those who were allegedly and previously supported by our own government [191–192].

As a duology, these first two films therefore set themselves up as analogs to contemporary American politics, with an emphasis on how a single act of terror by a foreign foe changes culture and diplomacy for years to come.

Intriguingly, it is Scotty the Engineer who is the voice of idealist, and even humanist, reason in this film. From the start, he is adamantly against the use of unexamined tech—and unexamined loyalties—when Admiral Marcus supplies the *Enterprise* with a series of new torpedoes and no information about them, which he rightly deems to be both a security risk and a safety hazard. When he points this out to Captain Kirk, Kirk angrily retorts, "We have our orders, Scotty!" Scotty replies, "That's what scares me. This is clearly a *military* operation. Is that what we are now? Because I thought we were *explorers*." These aspects to Starfleet are set up as a dichotomy: one can pursue knowledge or war, and Kirk must choose between them as well as the examples set before him through the Admiralty.

Functionally, Pike acts as Starfleet-as-peaceful-ideal with Marcus as Starfleet-as-military-ideal; that they both call Kirk "son" in their dialogues (Pike, after Kirk's demotion: "It's going to be okay, son." Marcus, several times: "Spit it out, son." "I'm going to ask you again, one last time, son. Lower your shields.") is not just paternalism but acknowledgment of how he has been shaped by these competing forces, and how it is up to him as the viewer's stand-in and film's hero to choose what direction to go in, war or peace. That Kirk chooses to die to save his ship (shades of Spock in *Wrath of Khan*) speaks to his choice, as does the seemingly light-hearted exchange with McCoy after his unexpected resurrection using Khan's "superblood." McCoy asks, "Tell me, are you feeling homicidal, power-mad, despotic?" Kirk answers, "No more than usual." Though amusing, the exchange hints at the deeper problems of power, both race and sex, discussed briefly above: a vision of the future at odds with Roddenberry's, in which utopia is problematized with the same old sins of race and sex that have long plagued the real world.

Again, this reactionary worldview of the "new" Starfleet reiterates the importance placed upon the white male body (and in contrast to the largely nude green, black, and white female bodies held up for audience delectation). Indeed, it is Kirk's own body that is used over and over again to save the day as he physically places himself between the threat and his crew/ship/culture.

Though we are never treated to a moment that savors the aesthetic of the violence on his body in the manner of St. Sebastian or Jesus Christ, we can still note that when he "dies" of radiation, Kirk's body remains immaculate to the end in contrast to that of Spock Prime's peeling flesh in *Wrath of Khan*. However, there is a visual hint in Kirk's bloodied features when he speaks to Marcus prior to the Admiral's attack: there is a bloody cut on Kirk's cheek that recalls the shape of the Starfleet chevron symbol. The damage to Kirk's body literalizes the conflict of what Starfleet is meant to be ideologically: an intellectual body of exploration and inquiry or a militarized body of enforced "peacekeeping"?

The question comes up again in the rechristening of the *Enterprise* at the end of the film. Kirk refers to the words of "the Captain's oath," the famous refrain to "boldly go where no one has gone before." Kirk sees them not just as a directive for idealistic action, but also "as a call for us to remember who we once were, and who we must be again." This is the crux of the Reboot universe, the theme that carries on throughout all three films. The first two films are about remembering, and it's the third, *Star Trek Beyond* (2016), that is most completely about that restoration.

"Sabotage" Part Two: Rewriting Abrams

In the post–Trump world, *Star Trek Beyond* is an incredible political parable that was not adequately appreciated when it came out the summer before the 2016 U.S. Presidential election. But consider the plot: A reactionary, xenophobic man with unnaturally long life hates the new world he lives in and wants to destroy it. He is opposed by a diverse group of young people whose lives were forever changed because of terrorist acts—and who, rather than succumbing to fear, say things like "Unity is our strength," and "It's better to die saving lives than live with taking them." Oh, and who also call Beastie Boys "classical music."

Much like *Star Trek into Darkness*, *Beyond* revolves around a seemingly external threat that has in fact emerged from within. The alien Krall, who speaks Standard with difficulty through sharp teeth, is, in fact, human: Captain Balthazar M. Edison, formerly of the USS *Franklin* and a former soldier rendered obsolete by the conclusion of the Xindi and Romulan Wars and the foundation of the Federation itself. Erroneously believing that the Federation purposefully abandoned him, Krall embarks on a century-long plan for revenge, building a drone army and capturing other starships' crews to drain their life-force. One of the only surviving former captives, Jaylah, describes the camps in language that recalls the Holocaust: "When we were in that place, Krall would come and take someone. There were screams, I can still hear them. Then we would not see that person again. We did not know who would be the next." The idea of recovering from the Holocaust was one of the recurring themes of *TOS*, from Kirk's survival of a eugenics-based genocide as a child (in "The Conscience of the King") to the (mis)usage of Nazi ideology to save a failing society (in "Patterns of Force"). Nazi ideology is also what shaped the Eugenics Wars and Khan's own rise to power (and his retreat—as a war criminal along with his "crew"). If Khan and Krall/Edison stand for Earth's misspent past, Kirk and his crew are meant to stand for enlightened progress. And indeed, the notions of progress and "being better" are consistent themes in the film.

Appearing on the cusp of the franchise's fiftieth anniversary, *Star Trek Beyond* has Kirk taking stock of his life—and his ship's mission. "The more time we spend out here, the harder it is to tell where one day ends and the next one begins. It can be a challenge to feel grounded when even gravity is artificial. [...] The farther out we go, the more I find myself wondering what it is we're trying to accomplish. If the universe is truly endless, then are we not striving for something forever out of reach?" Kirk's fatigue echoes that of the audience that quietly allowed the last franchise television show (*Enterprise*, 2001–2005) to evaporate into the cultural ether; the reception to *Beyond* was, sadly, similarly muted. Nonetheless, its in-film tribute to the passing of Leonard Nimoy as Spock Prime was both a moving acknowledgment and a plot device. The Kelvin Timeline Spock is *not* Spock Prime, and while he can continue his predecessor's work, he will do it in other, alternative ways.

The film is also a return to the ideological roots of *TOS*, particularly in terms of reinforcing the communal good. There are two key scenes that demonstrate this, both revolving around Scotty. In *Into Darkness*, Scotty was the voice of idealist reason, but here he is idealist reason in action, even recruiting a new member to the team and possibly Starfleet, through his "adoption" of Jaylah. While restoring the broken USS *Franklin* to functionality, he asks Kirk for permission to use the transporter to rescue Spock and McCoy. "Why would you need my permission?" Kirk asks—asking itself being a significant change from his authoritarian belligerence from the previous film—to which Scotty responds, "Because if I screw it up, I don't want it to be just my fault." Responsibility lies not just with a Captain but with a crew here; it is this strength in numbers that is the theme of the film. Later, Scotty examines a video record of the *Franklin*'s previous crew, noting that the time period they are from, just at the creation of Starfleet ("*We* happened."), was also an ideological crux between the military and exploration. Scotty elaborates on his "we": "The Federation, sir, Starfleet. We are not a military agency," he states, echoing his stance from the previous film.

Indeed, we find out that Krall/Edison was a loyal soldier who was pressed into service as a Starfleet captain, a role he was not prepared for. When Kirk confronts him directly in the film's climax, their exchange is loaded with the burden of what, for Edison, *was* versus what he *could be*, as he physically shifts between mutated "alien" and his human self: "I've missed being me. We lost ourselves but gained a purpose! A means to bring the galaxy back to the struggle that made humanity strong," Krall says, shortly before being swallowed by the weapon of his own making. Kirk responds, "We change. We have to. Or we spend the rest of our lives fighting the same battles." This battle of ideological identities is at the heart of the trilogy, and why here *Beyond* brings the story to full close here using the *Kelvin* itself: If the *Kelvin* was a terrorist Disaster in the first film and a site of military operation in the second, in the third it becomes an act of salvation through the Kelvin pods by the bridge. George Kirk died because he couldn't abandon manual controls or reach an escape pod in the first film, and so he died a hero. While there are escape pods on the *Enterprise*, escape pods on the bridge were added during the refit, acknowledging the dangers that Starfleet must accept as part of their mission, but emphasizing preservation rather than destruction. As Kirk says to Krall, "It's better to die saving lives than live with taking them. That's what I was born into." This line doubly acknowledges his debt to his father as well as to the idealism of the *Star Trek* franchise itself.

Another pivotal scene reinforces these aspects, when the captured Starfleet officers are being herded into Krall's camps. "You don't know who we are, but you'll soon find out," Sulu declares in a line that again harkens back to the core conflicts in place. Further, in trailers for the film, Uhura promises Krall that their Captain will come for them, and that "He will show you no mercy." This line is no longer present in the theatrical release, nor in the release available for private purchase. (One wonders if the audience's perception of the film's unused quote negatively affected its box-office.) Therefore, the film-as-text itself denies this lack of compassion, and indeed, it is compassion that saves the day: When the crew takes in Jaylah, they have information and a ship that are both key to saving the day. And afterwards, Kirk "pulls some strings at the Academy," granting Jaylah admission to Starfleet Academy if she wants it, in emulation of Chris Pike. It is inclusion rather than exclusion that is rewarding; peace rather than war; love rather than hate. The final moment of the film is given over once again to "the Captain's oath," making use of an audio collage of the ensemble's voices; it is no mistake that at the very end, it is Uhura saying that they will "boldly go where no one has gone before" to show how completely the narrative had changed from Kirk's monologue.

Conclusions

The Reboot films are a problematic favorite, revealing ideological schisms of hope and fear both inside and outside of the text. It is perhaps meaningful that in the friendly rivalry between *Star Trek* and *Star Wars* the latter has become the more progressive franchise in recent years, especially given the difference in protagonists—minorities versus a blonde-haired blue-eyed white man. Nonetheless, both franchises push forward the idea that resistance to Imperialism, whether through warmongering à la Marcus or through an actual Empire, is the key to a better world for all. In years past we may have taken such a pop culture imperative for granted, but given the contemporary world's increasingly nationalistic tendencies, we should rethink their meanings and our readings more closely. The Kelvin Timeline is conspicuously about how acts of terror reshape ideology, politics, and actions on a mass scale for generations—and how it can take the better part of a generation to put the world right again. *Star Trek* has always been about hope, and perhaps now more than ever we in the audience need these messages of optimism and hope in the face of real world warmongering and xenophobia. If Kirk, an arrogant white man from the American heartland, can learn to "be better" and see through the oppressive system that seeks to manipulate him even as it conspicuously rewards him, and so live out the true idealism that he wishes to espouse, then we have a true parable of hope for the times.

If we read all three films of the Kelvin Timeline—*Star Trek, Star Trek into Darkness*, and *Star Trek Beyond*—as a unified text, the narrative changes from an episodic trilogy to a singular story about the search for personal and ideological identity: Who is James T. Kirk and how does he change?

What is Starfleet and how does it change? Above all, it shows that institutional change *is* possible, both for the worse and for the better; it shows that a system that seems to be broken can, in fact, be fixed. Utopia is possible, but it must be protected and it must even be fought for, even in cheesy hand-to-hand combat in zero gravity. James T. Kirk as an ideal citizen, in the truest sense of the word, is someone who is ultimately willing to question the morality and ideology of his superiors in order to save people, and is also willing to save other people at the expense of his own life, whether or not they are members of his crew.

Note

1. It would be irresponsible to avoid discussion of the Uhura Racefail during summer 2009. Racefail was an extended fracas in SFF fandom generally that year, focused on the problematic portrayal and reception of POC in the genre generally, pitted against the backlash of POC SFF fans. Christine Scodari's article "Nyota Uhura Is Not a White Girl" sums up many of the intersectional issues on this topic, and examines numerous fan responses to Uhura in depth.

Works Cited

Foster, Alan Dean. *Star Trek* [Film novelization]. Pocket Books, 2010.
Johnson, Mike. "Where No Man Has Gone Before, Parts One and Two." *Star Trek Ongoing* No. 1-2. IDW Publishing, 2011.
Jones, Norma. "Rebooting Utopia: Reimagining *Star Trek* in Post-9/11 America." *The Star Trek Universe: Franchising the Final Frontier*, edited by Douglas Brode and Shea T. Brode, Rowman & Littlefield, 2015, pp. 185-195.
McVeigh, Stephen. "The Kirk Doctrine: The Care and Repair of Archetypal Heroic Leadership in J.J. Abrams' *Star Trek*." *Star Trek as Myth: Essays on Symbol and Archetype at the Final Frontier*, edited by Matthew Wilhelm Kapell, McFarland, 2010, pp. 197-212.
"Patterns of Force." *Star Trek*, season 2, episode 1, written by John Meredyth Lucas, directed by Vincent McEveety, 16 Feb. 1968.
Scodari, Christine. "'Nyota Uhura Is Not a White Girl': Gender, Intersectionality, and *Star Trek* 2009's Alternate Romantic Universes." *Feminist Media Studies*, vol. 12, no. 3, 2011, pp. 335-351.
"Scorched Earth." *Earth: Final Conflict*, season 3, episode 14, written by Howard Chaykin, directed by J. Miles Dale, 7 Feb. 2000.
Whiting, Daniel. "Is Abrams's *Star Trek* a *Star Trek* Film?" *The Philosophy of J.J. Abrams*, edited by Patricia Brace and Robert Arp, University Press of Kentucky, 2014, pp. 189-203.

Star Trek Media Cited

"The Conscience of the King." *Star Trek*, season 1, episode 13, written by Barry Trivers, directed by Gerd Oswald, 8 Dec. 1966.
"Court Martial." *Star Trek*, season 1, episode 20, written by Don M. Mankiewicz and Steven W. Carabatsos, directed by Marc Daniels, 2 Feb. 1967.
Foster, Alan Dean. *Star Trek* [Film novelization]. New York: Pocket Books, 2010.
Johnson, Mike. "Where No Man Has Gone Before, Parts One and Two." *Star Trek Ongoing* No. 1-2. IDW Comics, 2011.
"Patterns of Force." *Star Trek*, season 2, episode 1, written by John Meredyth Lucas, directed by Vincent McEveety, 16 Feb. 1968.
Star Trek (2009). Directed by J.J. Abrams, Paramount Pictures, 2009.
Star Trek Beyond. Directed by Justin Lin, Paramount Pictures, 2016.
Star Trek into Darkness. Directed by J.J. Abrams, Paramount Pictures, 2013.
Star Trek II: The Wrath of Khan. Directed Nicholas Meyer, Paramount Pictures, 1982.

Conclusion

Is There a Future for Star Trek?

ACE G. PILKINGTON *and*
MATTHEW WILHELM KAPELL

Franchises don't last forever. At least there was a time when that was true, but now it seems as though anything that grows big enough, can survive in some form. James Bond, Harry Potter, *Star Wars*, and Marvel have all had their problems, but they are with us yet, mostly owned by Disney. Can *Trek* also survive, and if so in what form or forms and for how long? Perhaps one of *Star Trek*'s problems is that it is a medium-sized dinosaur roaming the jungle of blockbuster movies with little chance of getting bigger.

Scott Mendelson argues that "*Star Trek* has never been an overseas player. The reboot earned a whopping $256 million domestic but just $127m overseas for a $385m worldwide total on a $150m budget. *Star Trek into Darkness* ... earned a series high of $238m overseas for a $467m worldwide total on a $190m budget. *Star Trek Beyond* earned $183m overseas, which coupled with its $158m domestic ... gave it a $340m gross on a $185m budget." Writing about *Star Trek 2009*, Anthony Pascale suggests, "As for why *Star Trek* underperformed in the non–English speaking world, there is no obvious single answer. One factor is clearly that *Star Trek* has never been a strong brand outside the English speaking countries (with the exception of Germany). In the past *Star Trek* films have been short on action and long on dialog, which has not worked well vs. other summer tentpoles" ("*Star Trek* Finishes").

There have clearly been attempts to change the ratio of action scenes to dialogue, especially in the first two films of the reset. However, there has not been a transformative change in *Trek* royalties for the rest of the world. Mendelson gives a comparative example with the James Bond film *Spectre*, a Bond movie that went back to its roots in somewhat the same way that *Star*

Trek Beyond did. *Spectre* was the 25th James Bond film, which was treated as a chance to pay homage to the Roger Moore films. Mendelson says, "*Spectre* made $880 million worldwide, which is one of the very biggest 'non-fantasy' action movies ever.... *Spectre* made so much overseas ($680m) that it would have been the second-biggest 007 film ever even if it had never played in U.S. theaters."

Mendolson argues that *Star Trek Beyond* was caught between an audience that wanted a more traditional *Trek* film and a blockbuster budget that needed higher power marketing (and a hook to make that possible) to increase the audience beyond the current fans. One indication of the kinds of problems that blockbuster films can cause was the announcement in August of 2018 that contract talks for the fourth film in the reset had stalled. Chris Hemsley, who had played George Kirk (James T.'s father) very briefly in the first film of the reset and Chris Pine, who had played James T. Kirk in all three, "balked at Paramount's attempt to renegotiate previous deals in an attempt to cut the budget for the film" (Pascale "Report"). Because of *Star Trek Beyond*'s lower revenues, Paramount has "a concern that the *Trek* films have a ceiling and the studio can't budget them at the same levels as other tent poles." Or to put it a bit differently, *Star Trek* is a medium-sized dinosaur.

Both Hemsley and Pine have experience with more lucrative franchises. "Pine is currently in production on the sequel to 2017's *Wonder Woman*, which brought in over $821 million worldwide. In that same year, Hemsworth starred in *Thor: Ragnarok*, which brought in $854 million" (Pascale "Report"). Paramount, meanwhile, has expressed a willingness to recast the roles in order to get on with the production of the movie, which is tentatively scheduled for 2019. After all, Hemsworth's time on screen in *Star Trek 2009* was so brief that there were probably many viewers who could not identify the actor with the role. And while Chris Pine has been successful as Captain Kirk, it would not be like replacing William Shatner. We've all grown accustomed to the changing faces, costumes, and rubber suits for James Bond, Spider-Man, Superman, Wonder Woman, and Batman. Fans frequently debate which of many actors has performed best in a role.

What is more interesting here is the landscape of the blockbuster films jungle and Paramount's reaction to it. We have to admit that it seems odd to us that there are a number of people expressing the opinion that *Star Trek* cannot hope to compete with something like *Guardians of the Galaxy*. While we have nothing against sentient raccoons and talking trees, we would not have expected them to achieve permanent fame and wild financial success. Major blockbusters at the moment (with the exception of James Bond) seem to be largely based on comic books, to have far more action than dialogue in their scripts, and to include fairly straightforward (sometimes verging on primitive) humor. The James Bond series, which premiered in 1962 with *Dr.*

No and is the oldest of the major franchises, is based on the novels of Ian Fleming. It has gradually evolved to a format of very little dialogue with more and more (and more fantastic) violence. It is obviously building on its history and its strengths. For instance, Bond has always been popular in Russia (and many other places) perhaps in part because the Bond villains have almost always been international businessmen with no clear connection to any national group. The Soviets were often presented in the films more as partners for British intelligence than enemies (in part, of course, this was to make the British seem more important on the world stage). At the end of *A View to a Kill* (1985), the head of the KGB gives James Bond the Order of Lenin for saving Silicon Valley!

Paramount believes it has found a way for *Star Trek* to survive in this rather strange and very competitive world: reduce the budgets, assume *Trek* films have a ceiling, and let them do what they have always done. And perhaps this is the best option. The studio certainly seems committed to the franchise. Viacom [Paramount's parent company] CEO Robert Bakish "has previously cited *Star Trek* as one of the key franchises for the company" (Pascale "Report"). We see no easy path to increasing *Star Trek*'s international sales without essentially remaking the franchise. And even then there would be a period of time while this newest of all *Star Trek*s convinced skeptical or merely indifferent audiences that it had indeed changed and had now become more like every other major franchise. But if we could take a step back for a moment, there is something disappointing in a world where, though nearly everything is labeled scifi, there is only one science fiction franchise. (*Star Wars* is fantasy with elements of science fiction but no more.) Admittedly, James Bond often wanders into technothriller territory. "A technothriller is a story set in the very near future (or even the present) with technological elements that may or may not be science fiction; it is often difficult (and often deliberately made to be difficult) to tell" (Pilkington 190). *The Jurassic Park* franchise is another example, so there are a couple of borderline science fiction franchises and *Star Trek*.

But standalone science fiction films have done better than this might suggest. Three films in three consecutive years make the point. *Gravity* (2013) made $723,192,705; *Interstellar* (2014) brought in $677,463,813; and *The Martian* (2015) had a total of $630,161,890. Each film made over $400 million in international sales. None of them is like *Star Trek*, and none of them is like the others. *Interstellar* is the most "science fictiony" of the three, with extended space travel and time travel. *The Martian* is an excellent example of Hard Science fiction, that is "Science fiction that extrapolates from science and provides rational (and often detailed) technical explanations for its wonders" (Pilkington 170). Perhaps there is a path then for a high-earning science fiction version of *Star Trek*.

We put it that way deliberately because in all the talk of a return to *TOS* or a film that seemed like a combination of episodes (said most often about *Star Trek Beyond*), there was an essential failure to recognize that many episodes of *TOS* were science fiction only by courtesy (and the great hunger of the audience for a genre that had never truly been on television before.) Some episodes like "The Man Trap," "The Squire of Gothos," "Catspaw," and "Wolf in the Fold" were horror. A few such as "Assignment Earth" were fantasy, and one ("Spectre of the Gun") was even a Western. That doesn't count the episodes such as "Bread and Circuses," a "Piece of the Action," and "Patterns of Force" which seemed to have more to do with available sets and costumes than SF motifs. That's not to say that *TOS* and the other series were not, by and large, science fiction even when they also fit into other genres. It's only to point out that there were other elements, other texts, as well.

Nevertheless, as Ace pointed out in his essay, *Star Trek* has a long legacy with science fiction and science. Many members of the various casts have helped to recruit for NASA, and as Ace's essay makes clear, *Star Trek* is responsible for inspiring ideas and inventions and even for recruiting people into the sciences in the first place. If there is one place where the franchise is truly powerful and greatly appreciated it is in this juxtaposition of science and science fiction, present reality and future possibilities. The impact of that history seems to have touched almost all of the people who have worked on the new films, even J.J. Abrams, who certainly did not start out as a fan and admirer of the franchise.

So where can *Star Trek* go with all this experience and good will? Why not make a real science fiction film that could do what some of the *TOS* and later episodes did—confront scientific issues that are changing our lives around us and even take a position or make a prediction or two. Ace has already discussed in some detail the possibilities of biological changes and genetic manipulations for a future film. *TOS* raised the issue but did not pursue it beyond the bogeyman of genetically modified supermen. But there are two other transformations that science is making in our lives that *TOS* looked at and that could be activated easily by the reset series. The first was the issue of AI or Artificial Intelligence, and the second was nanotechnology.

The *Oxford English Dictionary* defines AI as "The capacity of computers or other machines to exhibit or simulate intelligent behaviour...." Their first example is from 1955, but the concept goes back as far as Homer's *Iliad*. In Hephaestus' workshop, "There were golden handmaids also who worked for him, and were like real young women, with sense and reason, voice also and strength, and all the learning of the immortals" (Homer 293). The term is almost frustratingly general and may mean anything from the routine functioning of an expert system to a superintelligent and newly sentient being, though the latter is—so far—limited to the speculations of futurists and SF authors. An additional frustration, not only in defining terms but in developing technology is that the meaning of the word "intelligence" seems, like the horizon, to move ever further away as the explorer advances. Thus, playing chess clearly required intelligence, but once it had been accomplished by a program and the method explained, it just as clearly did not. The same was true for defeating the world's best chess player, for driving a car, and for writing sports stories for the Associated Press. In the words of Alex Armstrong, "Whenever you make something work, you know how it works and it no longer seems intelligent."

There are, however, many other terms swirling around Artificial Intelligence, modifying it, expanding it, and sometimes even helping to explain it. Two older terms divide up AI into broad categories. Weak AI is any system, no matter how simple or complex, that does work which would otherwise require a human, but does not seek to replicate a thinking being. Strong AI, on the other hand, means to do just that. To quote Alex Armstrong again, "At its most extreme strong AI aims to create an artificial consciousness." Exactly what a consciousness would be and whether a machine consciousness would differ, of necessity, from our own, are vital questions. Two more recent terms (and abbreviations) help to clarify the possible goals of Strong AI. Artificial General Intelligence (AGI) is, roughly speaking, the achievement of human-level intelligence [Pilkington 27].

Isaac Asimov's robots fit into this category, and Data is an excellent example of the type. "Artificial Super Intelligence (ASI) is mental power greater than that of humans, perhaps far greater" (Pilkington 27–28).

TOS treated AI with almost the same disdain that it had applied to genetic engineering, but there were far more explorations. While genetic engineering is confined to the "Space Seed" episode, AI appears most clearly in "What Are Little Girls Made Of," "The Changeling," "The Apple," "I, Mudd," and "The Ultimate Computer." In each case, Captain Kirk and company destroy the computer mind in question by subjecting it to some species of logical or moral paradox. Also in each case, the AI in question is assumed to be malign or at least enormously inconvenient for humans. Spock expresses brief regret for the society they have destroyed in "The Apple," and a reprogrammed version of the androids still survives to torment Harry Mudd in the comic episode "I, Mudd," but AIs are uniformly treated as threats. After the nearly disastrous attempt to turn over the command of starships to AIs in "The Ultimate Computer," the whole subject of AIs and intelligent robots and androids seems to have been banned from the Federation. This is, to put it mildly, an unrealistic situation.

Roddenberry clearly foresaw the advent of computers as information storage devices, and much of what he casually put into *TOS* was groundbreaking. However, he (and other showrunners) failed to explore the issues of AI in any coherent way. "The Measure of a Man" episode in *Star Trek: The Next Generation* clearly indicates support for the "human" rights of robots and androids, but Data is treated as an aberration, the creation of a rogue scientist in secret. There is a similarly contained and limited exploration of the rights of sentient holograms in *Star Trek: Voyager*, but again, there is no attempt to look beyond a very specialized situation.

Currently, we face automation on a truly massive scale, with threats to jobs ranging from fast-food workers to drivers to surgeons. Whole industries have been transformed; some have been created; others have been eliminated. Tech billionaires have begun to talk consistently about the need for a minimum guaranteed income to cushion the transition that is coming, and some political parties have begun to advocate it as well. Large groups of scientists have banded together to condemn the development of AIs, especially for use in the military, but some of the condemnations have been for the very idea of creating a computer mind that is massively smarter than its human equivalents. Surely, in all the turmoil and opportunity of this moment there is a science fiction story that *Star Trek* can tell, compelling, immediately relevant, perhaps terrifying, perhaps reassuring but nevertheless authentic science fiction with an extraordinary narrative and possibilities for the characters but without conspiracy theories and galaxy-threatening villains.

The question of a minimum guaranteed income is a nice stepping stone from AI to our discussion of nanotechnology. *Star Trek* is sometimes criticized as old fashioned or outmoded because of its clear utopian elements. Not only are we presented with a human society that has united and eliminated war and disease, but also with a human and Federation society that has essentially guaranteed the material welfare of its citizens, without work or struggle, without wealth or power. Some critics have seen this as a form of socialism, but that is a serious misunderstanding of the technology at work here, and make no mistake, it is the technology that is transformative and that will soon be transforming our society as well.

Nanotechnology is "The manipulation of matter at the atomic level (or 1 to 100 nanometers), most commonly visualized as truly tiny machines (or alternatively chemical, biological, or other processes) maneuvering individual atoms into predetermined patterns" (Pilkington 105). It is, of course, already happening in a variety of ways, and it is becoming part of the overall web of automation that is ever more rapidly enfolding our planet. Though *Star Trek* doesn't use the term very often, the concept is alive and well in its various technologies.

"Imagine a world, not of scarcity as ours has always been but of plenty, where everyone could have almost everything. Imagine a world where even the poorest human would live better than American millionaires do now. In a limited number of ways, such a thing has already happened as technologies advanced. Most inhabitants of industrialized countries have transportation, entertainment, and information available to them which would be the envy of kings and emperors from earlier times. Few millionaires in the 1940s had film libraries to match those in or immediately available to most middle-class homes today. Nanotech (if it turns out to be technically feasible but not prohibitively high in energy cost) would similarly transform the lives of almost all humans. Anything (including art masterpieces and DNA-specific human organs) could be manufactured from the atoms up. Raw materials could be mined from the sea, from garbage dumps, or from asteroids. Space explorations and space colonies would finally be cheap.... Nearly unlimited goods and services (most manufactured or performed by robots and programmable machines of various sizes) would become part of life for nearly everyone....

Desktop 3D printers, primitive harbingers of the machines to come, are already for sale on Amazon and at Staples. The capabilities of the comparatively new technology are increasing with surprising speed. To give a single example, "GE engineers working on the future of aircraft manufacturing recently ... made a simple 3D-printed mini jet engine that roared at 33,000 rotations per minute" (Keller). And to get back to nanotech itself, the 2016 Nobel Prize in Chemistry went to Jean-Pierre Sauvage, Sir J. Fraser Stoddart, and Bernard L. Feringa "for their design and production of molecular machines...."

One of the many end results of the coming of nanotech will be that money (as people keep saying in *Star Trek: The Next Generation*) will cease to have meaning, and working for a living, as we presently understand it, will no longer be necessary—or possible. However, as many episodes in every series in the *Star Trek* franchise make clear, it is tremendously difficult for writers to create stories that do not involve the scarcity of property as a given. One of the better attempts to come to terms with this enormous disparity in mindsets (and one of the better *STNG* episodes) is "The Neutral Zone," where the crew of the *Enterprise* has to explain the shape of the future to some twentieth-century humans whom Beverly Crusher, the ship's chief medical officer, has revived from cryogenic sleep. Captain Picard says, speaking to a millionaire whose money has vanished over time, "This is the 24th century. Material needs no longer exist." And the former millionaire replies, "Then what's the challenge?" Picard's answer is, "The challenge, Mr. Offenhouse, is to improve yourself, to enrich yourself. Enjoy it" (most of this is taken from *Science Fiction and Futurism: Their Terms and Ideas,* Pilkington 106–108).

This is a truly startling idea. It is no wonder that many critics have misunderstood it. It is not, however, as much a social change as it is a technological one. The goal of the digital revolution was not to make millions of free books available to almost every human on the planet, but that has been one end result. The goal of nanotechnology is not to produce a society of plenty where merely being human brings with it a kind of wealth that was previously unimaginable, but that is in all probability (as *Star Trek* suggests) what will happen. The science fiction possibilities for this technology are not as immediately obvious to us as is AI. Nevertheless, what will happen to a new society where such a technology is introduced? Is there a case to be made that the *Trek* utopia, the unity and universal peace are no more than the reflection of nanotechnology? At the very least there is a possibility to examine Federation society with a thoroughness and from an angle that has never been done before. Along the way, we may very well be looking at ourselves not very many years from now, which is, after all, one of the most important things science fiction does.

Ultimately, the survival of *Star Trek* will be the work of many people, including the audiences, without whom actors, directors, and studios can't survive. There is, though, something interesting in asking if there is a future for *Star Trek* because *Star Trek* has been for so many people for so long a part of the hope that there will be a better future for all of us. Perhaps that is the real answer to our question: as long as *Star Trek* remains true to its core values, as long as it continues to provide that bridge between science and science fiction and between possibility and what we can actually make of the future, it will survive. In those circumstances, we hope at least this one franchise will live long and prosper.

Works Cited

Armstrong, Alex. "Artificial Intelligence—Strong and Weak." *I Programmer*, 10 Oct. 2016, http://www.i-programmer.info/babbages-bag/297-artificial-intelligence.html.

Homer. *The Illiad*. Translated by Samuel Butler. Walter J. Black, Inc., 1944.

Keller, Mike. "These Engineers 3d Printed a Mini Jet Engine, Then Took It to 33,000 RPM." GE.com, 5 Sep. 2016. https://www.ge.com/reports/post/118394013625/these-engineers-3d-printed-a-mini-jet-engine-then/.

Mendelson, Scott. "Box Office: 'Star Trek Beyond' Was Caught Between Its Fans and Its Budget." *Forbes*, 1 Nov. 2016, https://www.forbes.com/sites/scottmendelson/2016/11/01/box-office-star-trek-beyond-was-caught-between-its-fans-and-its-budget/#43744cde5e07.

Pascale, Anthony. "Report: 'Star Trek 4' Deals for Chris Pine and Chris Hemsworth Have Stalled." Trek Movie.com, 10 Aug. 2018, https://trekmovie.com/2018/08/10/report-star-trek-4-deals-for-chris-pine-and-chris-hemsworth-have-stalled/.

Pascale, Anthony. "*Star Trek* Finishes Theatrical Run with $385m—Full Box Office Analysis." TrekMovie.com. 5 Oct. 2009. https://trekmovie.com/2009/10/05/star-trek-finishes-theatrical-run-with-385m-full-box-office-analysis/.

Pilkington, Ace G. *Science Fiction and Futurism: Their Terms and Ideas*. McFarland, 2017.

About the Contributors

Bart **Bishop** teaches writing at Cincinnati State Technical and Community. He has a master's degree in English from Xavier University. He has been writing books and essays on movies for over a decade now. He has previously contributed to *What's Eating You?: Food and Horror on Screen* and also *Divine Horror: Essays on the Cinematic Battle Between the Sacred and the Diabolical*. More of his writing on movies and literature can be found at www.birthmoviesdeath.com and www.litreactor.com.

Cait **Coker** is a doctoral candidate at Texas A&M University, a genre historian, and *Trek* fan. Her articles and essays have appeared in *Transformative Works and Cultures* and *The Journal of Fan Studies*, among others. She is also an associate editor for *Foundation: The International Review of Science Fiction*.

Teresa **Cutler-Broyles** has an MA in cultural studies and a PDCERT in architectural historic preservation. During the academic year, she teaches film, architectural, and cultural theory at the University of New Mexico. In summers, she teaches creative writing at the Umbra Institute in Perugia, Italy. Her publications include chapters in *Children of Afghanistan, To Boldly Go: Essays on Gender and Identity in Star Trek, Belly Dance Around the World*, and *Monstrosity from the Inside Out*.

Penelope **Ingram** is a Distinguished Teaching Professor of English at the University of Texas at Arlington. Her research areas include feminist theory, postcolonial and race theory, and film studies. She is the author of *The Signifying Body: Toward an Ethics of Sexual and Racial Difference* (SUNY 2008). She has published articles in *New Literary History, Cultural Critique, feminist review, Philosophy and Literature, Jump Cut*, and elsewhere. She is working on a book that examines the relationship between politics and popular culture.

Matthew Wilhelm **Kapell** has graduate degrees in biological anthropology and history and a doctorate in American studies from Swansea University in Wales. He has written or edited numerous books in film and television studies and the cultural history of the late 1960s including *The Fantastic Made Visible* (with Ace G. Pilkington). He is the series editor for McFarland's Studies in Gaming and teaches at San Jose State University.

About the Contributors

Sarah Beth **Kiliman** is a graduate of University of Wisconsin–Milwaukee and holds an MA in English with a focus in literature and cultural theory. She received her BA from Northern Illinois University, during which time she completed two internships with the Pick Museum of Anthropology. She teaches classes at Northwest Mississippi Community College. Though much of her work focuses on contemporary Irish literature, she has also written about media and technology.

Natashia **Lindsey** is an assistant professor in the Department of Theatre at Central Washington University. Her research broadly focuses on the intersections of race and performance. More specifically, her work examines how diverse texts within the Obama era present mixed-race performances that call into question white supremacist racialization. She finished her Ph.D. in performance as public practice at the University of Texas at Austin and has BS and MA degrees in Pan-African studies from the University of Louisville.

Ace G. **Pilkington** died in February 2019 just as this book was headed to the printer. He was a professor at Dixie State University and had a D.Phil. from Oxford. He is the author of *Science Fiction and Futurism: Their Terms and Ideas*, *Our Lady Guenevere*, and *Screening Shakespeare from Richard II to Henry V*, and the coeditor of *The Fantastic Made Visible*, *Fairy Tales of the Russians and Other Slavs*, and *Lab Lit: Exploring Literary Fictions About Science*.

Olga A. **Pilkington** has a Ph.D. in applied linguistics from the University of Birmingham, UK. She is an assistant professor of English at Dixie State University, author of *Presented Discourse in Popular Science: Professional Voices in Books for Lay Audiences*, and coeditor of *Lab Lit: Exploring Literary Fictions About Science*.

Lynnette **Porter** is a professor in the humanities and communication department at Embry-Riddle Aeronautical University in Daytona Beach, Florida. Among her many publications are books or chapters about science fiction series (e.g., *LOST*, *Doctor Who*). She has also written three performance biographies of Benedict Cumberbatch. She is a member of the Popular Culture Association, a board member of the Popular Culture Association in the South, and the editor of the journal *Studies in Popular Culture*.

Jessica **Sellin-Blanc** is finishing her Ph.D. at the University of Wisconsin–Milwaukee, where she also works as an instructor in the department of English, teaching rhetoric and composition, film and television courses. Her research interests include contemporary television, television history, aesthetics, and technology and production studies.

Andrea **Whitacre** teaches courses on science fiction and medievalism at Indiana University. She is the author of two articles: "The Translation of Transformation: A Comparison of *Bisclavret* and *Yonec* with the Old Norse *Bisclaret* and *Jonet*," and "The Body That Is Not One: Overclothing as Bodily Transformation in *Topographia Hibernica*." Her article "Looking in the Mirror: The Negotiation of Franchise Identity in *Star Trek: Discovery*" is forthcoming in the edited collection *Context Is for Kings*.

Index

Abrams, J.J. 1, 4, 7, 8, 13, 21, 25, 28, 30, 31, 35, 36, 39, 40, 44, 45, 49, 58, 59, 66, 69, 84, 85, 89, 90, 92, 97, 100–102, 107–109, 111, 115–117, 120, 123, 125–127, 129, 130, 132, 136, 137, 139, 140, 145, 146, 148, 149, 151, 166, 167, 172, 180
Abramsverse 6, 115, 124, 125, 132
Afghanistan 63, 67, 170,
Aldrin, Neil 87
Amanda (Spock's mother) 155–157, 163, 164
America 1, 2, 6, 7, 40, 41, 42, 44, 46, 51, 54, 58, 60, 66–68, 73, 76, 80, 86–89, 96, 97, 135, 146, 167, 170, 171, 175, 182
Armstrong, Neil 87, 124
artificial intelligence (AI) 80, 180–181
Asimov, Isaac 74, 118–121, 181
authoritarianism 169

Beastie Boys 52, 132, 172
Bernardi, Daniel 85, 87, 88, 105, 110, 111
Bezos, Jeff 123
Bond, James 177–179
bonding, actor/character 136, 138, 139
Burnham, Michael 113
Bush, George W. 46, 48, 64, 66, 68, 69–70, 146, 147
Bush, George H.W. 59
the Bush doctrine 170

Chapel, Christine 102, 104, 108, 112
Chekov, Pavel 6, 27, 34, 74, 75, 90, 93, 108, 109, 111, 112, 149, 170
Cold War 58, 59, 64, 65, 67, 87, 170
communications officer 77, 78, 86, 87, 89, 91
Cumberbatch, Benedict 8, 25, 26, 29, 31–36, 40, 41, 44, 45, 51, 58, 59, 62, 147, 186

data 121, 181
DNA 128–129, 180; *see also* Singh, Khan Noonien
de Camp, L. Sprague 73
del Toro, Benecio 29, 69

Earth: Final Conflict 168
Edison, Captain Balthazar M. 49, 50, 51–55, 172–174; *see also* Krall
English (language) 73–76, 78, 80, 81, 95, 177, 180
USS *Enterprise* 1, 2, 7, 9, 13, 14, 18, 19, 20–23, 26, 32, 34, 45, 46, 49, 50, 52, 60–64, 67, 68, 72, 74–78, 85, 89, 90, 91, 93, 95–97, 110, 118, 120–123, 126, 127, 130, 131, 132, 137, 147–149, 153, 156, 159, 160, 161, 163, 164, 166, 171–174, 183
Eugenics Wars 25, 45, 46, 169, 173

feminism 108, 135, 140
Forbidden Planet 117
Foster, Alan Dean 17, 23, 31, 124, 169
USS *Franklin* 52, 74, 172, 173

Goldberg, Whoopi 96

hard SF 6, 120, 123
Harrison, John 25, 32, 33, 45, 47, 48, 53, 59, 63, 147; *see also* Cumberbatch, Benedict; Montalbán, Ricardo; Singh, Khan Noonien
Holocaust 125, 172, 173
humanism 50, 107–112, 168

Infinite Diversity in Infinite Combinations (IDIC) 27, 34
Iraq 63, 67, 170

Jaylah 50, 52, 74, 90, 112, 131, 148, 172–174
Jemison, Mae 96
Johnson, Mike 16, 34, 168
Jones, Norma 170
Jung, Doug 132

USS *Kelvin* 66, 84, 126, 137, 151, 161
Kelvin timeline/universe 2, 3, 6–8, 13–19, 20–23, 59, 73, 78, 87, 93–97, 99, 115, 129, 130, 136, 138–143, 148, 149, 166–168, 173, 175
Khan *see* Singh, Khan Noonien

187

188   Index

King, Martin Luther 86
Kirk, George 19, 59, 85, 92, 151, 174, 178
Kirk, James Tiberius 2, 4, 5, 9, 10, 13, 19–21, 23, 26, 27, 32, 34, 35, 45, 46, 48–55, 58–62, 64–70, 72, 74, 75, 77, 78, 85, 87–90, 92–97, 99, 100, 103–109, 111, 112, 116, 119, 120–122, 124, 125, 127, 129–132, 136–138, 140, 142, 146–149, 151, 153, 160, 161, 163, 166–175, 178, 181
kiss, interracial 26, 88, 142, 146, 148
Klingon: ethnicity 2, 48, 59, 63–67, 77, 94, 111, 127, 170, 171; language 80–81, 97
Koenig, Walter 6, 27, 140
Krall 40, 148, 167; *see also* Edison, Captain Balthazar M.
Kuleshov Effect 91
Kurtzman, Alex 60, 92, 116, 137, 139, 145

language, gendered 80; artificial 80–81; *see also* English; Klingon; linguistics; phonation; phonetics; Russian
liminality 20, 151–164
Lin, Justin 40, 78, 90, 129, 132, 141, 142, 148
linguistics 6, 8, 72–82; *see also* xenolinguistics
Lizardi, Ryan 142–143, 144
Loock, Kathleen 144

Marcus, Admiral Alexander 32–34, 45, 48, 59, 147, 169–171
Marcus, Carol 104
masculinity 103–105, 107, 108, 112, 113
McCoy, Leonard 6, 23, 61, 88, 91–93, 95–97, 104, 116, 118, 122, 126, 129, 131, 132, 137, 138, 153, 160, 161, 170, 171, 173
McVeigh, Stephen 2, 66, 67, 146, 170
Meyer, Nicholas 115, 120
minority, model 58, 60, 68–70
Mitchell, Gary 168
Montalbán, Ricardo 25–27, 29, 31, 34, 40, 45, 47, 62
Morrison, Toni 96
mulatto, tragic 8, 152–154, 156, 157, 159, 160, 162, 164

nanotechnology 180, 182–184
NASA 66, 81, 87, 123, 124, 180
Nero 6, 13–23, 61, 90, 126, 137, 151, 159, 160, 161, 164, 171
Nichols, Nichelle 5, 26, 27, 60, 72, 77, 86, 88, 124, 140
Nimoy, Leonard 1, 5, 27, 60, 69, 116, 118, 119, 137–140, 148, 149, 167, 173
nostalgia 136, 142–145, 149
Nyota *see* Uhura

Orci, Roberto 7, 31, 47, 58, 60, 63, 64, 68, 69, 92, 116, 139
the Other 58, 59, 60, 62, 110, 111, 167

Paramount 40, 84, 101, 102, 115, 137, 178, 179

Pegg, Simon 34, 131, 132, 138, 141–144, 148
phonation 77
phonetics 81
Pike, Captain Christopher 13, 16, 17, 19, 66, 67, 75, 93, 100, 111, 121, 124, 147, 161, 166–171, 174
Pine, Chris 34, 138, 140, 149, 178
Pomerance, Murray 138–139
Prime Directive 45, 59, 67, 124
Prime timeline 18, 19, 21, 22, 23, 92, 168
pronoun, gender neutral 73
Proust, Marcel 3

Quinto, Zachary 34, 61, 69, 131, 138, 139, 146, 148, 149

race 4, 6, 8, 27–29, 33, 35, 39–55, 58, 59, 61, 64, 68, 76, 87, 95, 97, 105, 109, 124, 125, 136, 152–160, 164, 169, 171
Robau, Captain Richard 85, 137
Roddenberry, Gene 2, 5, 6, 7, 13, 15, 22, 26–28, 30, 34, 36, 44, 49, 51, 60, 63, 85–88, 97, 100–103, 105, 107–109, 112, 116–124, 127, 128, 130–132, 135–149, 167–172, 181
Roddenberry, Eugene "Rod" 2
Romulan: ethnicity 6, 13, 16–18, 54, 61, 64–67, 76, 90, 137, 159, 161, 172; language 75–77
Romulus 15–18, 21, 75, 76, 124, 159,
Rony, Fatimah 96
Russia 34, 65, 66, 87, 179
Russian: ethnicity 6, 27, 108; language 74–76

Saldana, Zoe 34, 61, 72, 106, 108, 109, 111, 138, 140
Sarek 155–158, 161, 163, 164
Scahill, Andrew 137
science fiction 3, 6, 7, 40, 41, 43, 51, 53, 72–75, 88, 115–132, 139, 142, 146, 152, 179, 180, 182–184
Scodari, Christine 89, 105
Scott, Montgomery (Scotty) 6, 8, 14, 20, 22, 23, 34, 50, 61, 74, 87–90, 92, 95 97, 122, 126,, 131, 138, 141, 170, 171, 173
Section 31 63, 117, 170
September 11, 2001 29, 48, 54, 58, 59, 63, 64, 66, 146, 170
sexualization 35, 99–113
Shatner, William 5, 26, 27, 60, 116, 118, 119, 121, 122, 131, 138, 140, 178
Shelley, Mary 72–73
Singh, Khan Noonien 8, 13, 14, 25–36, 40, 41, 44–48, 53, 58–60, 62–70, 92, 109, 129, 138, 147, 167, 168, 170–173
Snead, James 96
Spock 4, 5, 8, 13, 18–21, 23, 26, 32–34, 46, 48, 50, 54, 58–61, 64–70, 75–77, 85, 86, 87, 89–97, 100, 102, 104, 105, 108, 109, 111, 112, 116, 118–121, 124, 126, 127, 131, 132, 136–140, 147–149, 151–164, 166, 169–173, 181
Star-TAC 122

Starfleet 7, 9, 13, 19, 22, 32, 33, 45, 48, 50, 51, 54, 58, 59, 63, 64, 66, 74, 92, 93, 99, 100, 104, 111, 113, 123–125, 127, 131, 137, 147, 148, 156, 157, 159, 160, 163, 166, 167, 168, 170–174, 175
Sulu, Hikaru 5, 7, 20, 28, 34, 50, 51, 60, 69, 74, 88, 93, 108, 112, 132, 138, 140–142, 144, 148, 166, 170, 174

Takei, George 6, 27, 28, 60, 119, 140, 141–144, 148, 149
Tricorder 78, 121–123,

Uhura, Nyota 4–6, 8, 20, 26, 34, 49–52, 54, 60, 61, 65, 66, 69, 72–82, 86–93, 96, 97, 99, 100, 104–109, 111, 112, 124, 126, 132, 138, 140, 142, 148, 161, 162, 168–170, 174
Universal Grammar 76, 79, 81
universal translator 77–80
Urban, Karl 132, 138
utopia 10, 44, 60, 96, 100, 101, 103, 108, 113, 116, 144–146, 148, 167, 171, 175, 182, 184

vigor, hybrid 8, 152, 160, 161
voyeurism 104
Vulcan: ethnicity 2, 8, 9, 26, 58, 60, 61, 68, 74, 75, 87–89, 124, 127, 152–158, 160, 161, 164; language 76, 81; planet 152, 159–162, 167, 169

war on terror 49, 170
Weller, Peter 32, 59
whitewashing 8, 25–36, 40, 41, 44, 45, 47, 58, 62
Whiting, Daniel 169

X Prize 122–123
xenolinguistics 92, 99, 100, 107

Yelchin, Anton 34, 138, 148, 149; *see also* Chekov, Pavel

www.ingramcontent.com/pod-product-compliance
Ingram Content Group UK Ltd.
Pitfield, Milton Keynes, MK11 3LW, UK
UKHW042012140426
5217IPUK00015B/1131